Sports Journalism

Telep

Sports Journalism

Context and Issues

Raymond Boyle

SAGE Publications
London • Thousand Oaks • New Delhi

First published 2006

SAGE Publications Ltd
1 Oliver's Yard
55 City Road
London EC1Y 1SP

SAGE Publications Inc.
2455 Teller Road
Thousand Oaks, California 91320

SAGE Publications India Pvt Ltd
B-42, Panchsheel Enclave
Post Box 4109
New Delhi 110 017

British Library Cataloguing in Publication data

A catalogue record for this book is available
from the British Library

ISBN-10 1-4129-0797-7   ISBN-13 978-1-4129-0797-2
ISBN-10 1-4129-0798-5 (pbk)   ISBN-13 978-1-4129-0798-9

Library of Congress Control Number: 2005936364

Typeset by C&M Digitals (P) Ltd, Chennai, India
Printed and bound in Great Britain by TJ International, Padstow, Cornwall
Printed on paper from sustainable resources

To Noelle and Lauren

CONTENTS

Sometimes I think that I'm happiest in an empty stadium in the hours before the action begins, when the place is filled with a sense of what might be about to happen. Or when the contest is all over and the stadium has emptied, leaving only the memory of what took place. Sport exists in the anticipation and the recollection as well as in the moment, which is what makes it so rich and incremental a pleasure.

Richard Williams, Sportswriter, *The Guardian*, 2003

No wonder people burn out more quickly. No wonder you see old guys with gin bottles inside brown paper bags stashed inside their desk drawers. Queuing outside dressing-room doors, being pushed around by stewards, extracting quotes from nineteen-year-olds. It's no job for serious people.

Nobody ever told me I was a serious person though. I try not to be. There are a few things that keep you going in this game. The mortgage. The knowledge that you failed at everything else in life. The odd good quote. The rare moment of genius from a D.J. Carey or Sonia O'Sullivan.

And the anticipation. Just waiting to see how it all turns out, next weekend, next season, next year. Waiting. Watching. Wondering if you have the words left in you to fill the space that the occasion wants.

Tom Humphries, Sportswriter, *The Irish Times*, 2003.

ACKNOWLEDGEMENTS

I would like to thank all the people who agreed to speak with me during the researching of the book. They include David Chappell, David Conn, Paul Cooney, Eamon Dunphy, Roy Greenslade, Amy Lawrence, Annie Maguire, Mark Magee, Brian Oliver, Ashling O'Connor, Matt Tench, Craig Tregurtha, Jon Ryan, Graham Spiers, Andrew Thompson, Donald Walker, Stewart Weir, Richard Williams and Natasha Woods.

Also a range of informal conversations with (in no particular order) John Corner, Alan Tomlinson, John Sugden, Richard Haynes, Maggie Magor, Peter Martin, Philip Schlesinger, Simon Frith, Neil Blain, Kris Kjositits, Claudia Monterio, Matthew Hibberd, David Rowe, Garry Whannel and Kevin Williams all helped add to the mix of ideas that are part of putting any book length project together.

The study leave granted by the University of Stirling was vital in allowing me to complete the book.

This is a book that has been rattling around in my head for a while, so it is a relief of sorts to have it finished. Thanks to Jamilah Ahmed at Sage for encouraging me to get on with it. While on the home front, a massive thanks to both Noelle and Lauren, without whom nothing would get done and who are I suspect even more delighted than I am that it's now finished.

Raymond Boyle
January 2006

INTRODUCTION: SPORTS JOURNALISM AND JOURNALISM ABOUT SPORTS

I'm a sportswriter. I watch all sorts of sports in all sorts of countries, then write reports and feature articles about them which are published in a newspaper. This is a fine and privileged occupation, and one to be disclosed with tact. People who do respectable, important jobs don't like to hear about it. They get grumpy, or vindictive. Sports writing is categorised alongside beer-tasting and aphrodisiac-evaluation. People say: 'More of a hobby than a job, isn't it?'

Andrew Baker, Sportswriter, *The Daily Telegraph* **(2004: ix)** *Where Am I & Who's Winning?* **London: Yellow Jersey Press.**

OPENING UP

Sports journalism in many ways remains a paradox. In the hierarchy of professional journalism it has been traditionally viewed disparagingly as the 'toy department', a bastion of easy living, sloppy journalism and 'soft' news. Within the British context sports journalism, until recently, has been largely absent from journalism education and practice and similarly invisible among the growing critical literature from within media and communication studies which examines issues in and around journalism.

However, commercially, sports journalism has always mattered to newspapers and the popular press specifically. What has changed in the last decade in the British newspaper market has been the explosion in the volume and range of sports journalism that one now finds across the media. For some, the fact that newspapers such as *The Times* and *The Daily Telegraph* now regularly can devote up to a third of editorial space to coverage of sports is another example of the 'dumbing down of society', with journalism heavily implicated in this process.

This book argues that this expansion in sports journalism actually says something more complex about the evolving relationship between journalism, the media and popular culture, and offers challenges to both critics and educators involved not only in teaching about journalism but in critically evaluating its wider cultural, social and political impact.

Sports journalism has also been implicated in the construction of various sporting discourses that often connect with wider issues of gender, race, ethnicity and national identity formation. Within media and communication studies a body of work concerned with the role of the media, and in part sports journalism, in this process of identity formation is now well established (Whannel, 1992; Blain et al., 1993; O'Donnell, 1994; Wenner, 1998; Rowe, 1999; Garland and Rowe, 1999; Boyle and Haynes, 2000; Brookes, 2002; Crolley and Hand, 2002; Crolley and Hand, 2005). Much of this work has focused on the various texts produced by forms of sports journalism and broadcasting and these debates about the role of sporting representation and society have been well addressed by such work. As a result, concerns about representation are not the main focus of this book, although reference is made to this issue where appropriate.

This book is also not a practical guide on how to become a sports journalist. Neither is it overly concerned with outlining the specific aspects of the job that inform the day-to-day working practice of those engaged in sports journalism although, of course, reference to these issues is made where directly relevant. These issues are admirably addressed by Andrews (2005) in his book on sports journalism, in which he examines in detail the challenges and skills involved in the craft of sportswriting across the print, broadcast and online media environments.

Rather, this book is about identifying sports journalism's wider place within the broader field of journalism and journalism studies. The book attempts to offer a historically informed snapshot of some of the issues, debates and challenges that are reshaping the boundaries of contemporary sports journalism, specifically, but not exclusively, within the UK media context.

There are three implicit strands that run through the book, and while they may not always be addressed directly in every chapter, they are important factors in shaping the environment within which contemporary sports journalism operates. These forces are reconfiguring both the sports and the media industries from within which sports journalism emerges. Their varying impact on journalism may be disputed, but globalisation, digitisation and marketisation are key underlying aspects of any analysis of contemporary journalism.

GLOBALISATION

There is no doubt that sports have become increasingly global in the contemporary mediated age. The fusion of sports and the media, and television in particular, has helped propel and transform major events such as the FIFA World Cup and the Olympic Games. This is also a process in which sports journalism is deeply implicated.

The American political journalist Franklin Foer (2004) argued that the global nature of sport offered the possibility of the construction of some form of global identity. However, the reality that he found on his travels around the world was a global cultural form that acted as a vehicle for the expression of conflict, tension and a range of deeply rooted local identities. This tension between the global aspect of sport as a cultural form and its intrinsic national or local dimension has also been noted by Rowe (2003). These processes are informed by economic, cultural and ethnic factors, and often reinforced by sports journalism.

Sports journalism offers a fascinating case study in how global and local media interact in contemporary societies. Sport can at times appear global and outward-looking, and can also be local in focus and intensely domestic in its concerns. While this book is primarily centred on the UK experience, it will also be noticeable the extent to which the development of sports journalism in, say, the United States has helped influence British sports writing. Echoing the earlier point about the local and the global, the book will, however, reinforce the extent to which sports journalism is heavily shaped by the particular patterns of social, cultural and political evolution that shape both the sports and the media industries in the UK.

DIGITISATION

Related to globalisation is digitisation. Digitisation has clearly impacted on journalism in various forms. Within the arena of sports journalism, it has seen the emergence of an increasingly sophisticated battle for control of sports and how they are delivered, reported and made sense of for readers, listeners and viewers.

Previous research (Boyle and Haynes, 2004) has examined the ways in which sports clubs and organisations are attempting to use the new media platforms of the Internet, digital TV and mobile telephony to deliver exclusive content and journalism to spectators. In so doing, many are seeking to bypass the traditional journalistic communication structures and speak directly to their audience. In the digital age, the sports industry increasingly attempts to police its image through the control of its intellectual property (IP) and the growing use of public relations and other aspects of media management.

For sports journalists, the issue of access to players and information has become more difficult as the commercial stakeholders in the game attempt to use the digital landscape to usurp and bypass traditional sports journalism.

There seems little doubt that over the next few years the battle lines will continue to be redrawn as sports seek to extract commercial value from all their assets, while media institutions (in particular those not holding specific coverage rights) will argue for the importance of continuing to journalistically report on all aspects of the sports industry.

MARKETISATION

Marketisation has impacted on both the sports and the media industries. The reporting of the political and economic dimension of sports has become more important in recent years as the commercialisation of the industry across the globe has developed. The sports industry now regularly involves major media and financial institutions as well as government intervention. This process has helped blur the boundaries between traditional notions of sports journalism and journalism about sports-related activity. The increased centrality of the market in the media industries has helped propel the expansion of a celebrity culture, into which sports stars increasingly find themselves drawn. This development has also shaped aspects of sports journalism where there has been an increase in the number of journalists both freelance and staffers reporting and commenting on this aspect of sports.

Sports journalism and writing is now also seen as a key element of the wider branding of most newspapers as they reposition their appeals in attempts to attract new readers. The general dismantling of a more paternal media system in the UK, and its replacement with a more commercially driven demand-led entity, has both benefited and constrained sports journalism. However, without the introduction of increased competition in the UK television market, and the corresponding explosion in the coverage of sport, there is little doubt that the expansion in sports journalism that is so evident in the UK media market would simply not have happened to the same degree.

A combination of the global expansion of sport, the new opportunities offered by digital media and sport's growing commercial value have helped to extend the range of opportunities for those graduates seeking to break into sports journalism.

And of course, the expansion of the sports industry and the range of commercial and political stakeholders involved also mean that rigorous, uncomplicit journalism is required in this area as never before. This represents a major ethical challenge for contemporary sports journalism.

The book is also concerned with the professional context within which sports journalism is positioned. Is the often used analogy of the 'toy department' still valid? Are sports journalists simply 'fans with a typewriter' or laptops as it would be these days? Or, as the range of sports journalism has expanded is it more accurate to talk about journalism about sports, in its wider context, rather than simply a narrowly defined and niche form of journalism, labelled, sports journalism.

THE BOOK

Before visiting China in late 2004 I was struck by the fact that the most perceptive and insightful journalism about the wider political, economic and cultural context of the inaugural Chinese Formula One Grand Prix, which was taking place in Shanghai, was to be found not in the political comment section but, rather, in the sports pages of the London-based *Independent* newspaper. Such a perceptive political and economic analysis of a sporting event would probably not have found a home in the sports pages even ten years ago.

Clearly sports journalism in Britain is changing and this book attempts to map out the organisational, technological and cultural factors driving this process. While the book looks at sports journalism, inevitably a large element is devoted to football-related journalism. In part, this is because in the UK the expansion in sports journalism has been driven by expanded football coverage, and also it is football that overpowers other sports in terms of resources and coverage. However, the book examines sportswriters, who by their very nature are writing across a range of sports, of which football will often be only one, albeit important, part of their portfolio and profile.

Chapters 1–3 place the growth of print and broadcast sports journalism in some historical and academic context. This is not a social history of sports journalism but, rather, an attempt to highlight the key moments that have shaped the trajectory of sports journalism in the UK. Chapter 1 also looks at the extent to which this aspect of journalism history remains chronically underdeveloped despite the growth of journalism studies research over the last decade.

Chapters 4–6 focus on the issues and challenges faced by contemporary sports journalists as they deal with major changes in both the sports and the media industries. Areas looked at include the shifting boundaries of sports news, the rise in public relations and issues of access and the impact that the digital media environment is having on modern sports journalism.

The last two chapters before the Conclusion focus on the changing professional image of the sports journalist and examine whether in the UK it remains an area of journalism characterised by a significant gender imbalance.

The range of sports journalism that exists across broadcast, print and online media platforms is now considerable. This book attempts to get to grips and make sense of the changing milieu within which this contemporary journalism is produced and consumed.

1

ENGAGING WITH SPORTS JOURNALISM: CONTEXT AND ISSUES

'What a wonderful life you enjoy', sports journalists are often told by people in the pub.

Michael Henderson 'Why I dread a summer of sport', *The Observer Sports Monthly,* **May (2004), No. 51**

This reluctance to take sports journalism seriously produces the paradoxical outcome that sports newspaper writers are much read but little admired.

David Rowe (1999: 36) *Sport, Culture and the Media.*

Sports journalism is largely absent from histories of journalism in the UK. This chapter examines previous writing on sports journalism and looks at how this area of journalism has been positioned within the hierarchy of journalistic practice. It is also interested in identifying the wider discourses associated with how we think about, and value, sports journalism.

While focusing primarily on the UK, material is also drawn from elsewhere, for example the USA; however, the book argues that the distinctive economic and cultural contexts of UK journalism have shaped the broader trajectory and culture of sports journalism in this country. This chapter is also interested in mapping out ways in which sports journalism has altered and changed in response to changes in the media's influence on the sports economy. This particular theme is then developed in more detail throughout the rest of the book.

SPORTS JOURNALISM WITHIN JOURNALISM STUDIES

Despite agreeing on its commercial importance, research into sports journalism is largely absent from the growing body of work that might be called 'journalism studies'. From within the arena of media and communication studies, journalism and its relationship to politics and democracy has been a central concern for as long as communication research has been carried out; however, the rise in the UK of a more specific focus on journalism as a distinct teaching discipline at university level over the last decade has helped define a more distinctive terrain within which more journalism research is being focused. The arrival of a number of journalism-specific academic journals such as *Journalism: Theory, Culture and Practice* also signifies a distinctive stage in the evolution of a particular teaching and research arena within the UK academy.

It could be argued that given the massive range of content across media platforms that calls itself sports journalism in some shape or form, the research trajectory within journalism studies has been relatively narrow and heavily informed by particular political and economic concerns. To this end it has often drawn heavily from social science and political sociology.

Within this particular research tradition there appears to be a general consensus that journalism is in some form of crisis (Franklin, 1997; Sparks and Tulloch, 2000; Hargreaves, 2003; Campbell, 2004; Kettle, 2004; Lloyd, 2004a; Marr, 2004; Allan, 2005). The extent and depth of the crisis is vigorously debated between those who see an increasingly commercial and market-driven media economy as having a detrimental impact on the quality of journalism and its ability to fulfil its key role in democratic societies and others who view the breaking down of traditional journalistic hierarchies and the advent of new communication networks, such as the Internet, as offering as many opportunities as challenges to extend the democratic function of journalistic practice in information-saturated societies (Langer, 1998; McNair, 1999). Often this debate is framed within a wider concern about the impact of journalistic standards on the democratic process.

In the wake of the sacking in May 2004 of Piers Morgan, editor of the tabloid *Daily Mirror* newspaper, following the revelation that pictures showing British soldiers supposedly abusing Iraqi prisoners carried by that paper were false, fellow journalist Martin Kettle argued that:

> The *Mirror*'s faked tale was not some one-off event. It was merely the latest manifestation of a widespread and in some ways peculiarly British disease. This holds that, within increasingly elastic limits, a journalist is entitled to say pretty much what he or she likes, whether or not it is precisely true, without being subject to any sanctions or professional penalties for doing so. (Kettle, 2004)

Indeed, this debate about journalistic standards extends beyond more overt political concerns and focuses on the wider cultural impact of what some have termed the 'dumbing down' of culture (Sampson, 1996; Bromley, 1998). While this concern about cultural and moral standards embraces a range of areas of civil society beyond the media, it is the latter which is centrally implicated in this process of decline. Both television and journalism are viewed as two of the key areas of cultural production that most clearly illustrate the concerns of lowering public standards. As Hargreaves (2003: 12–13) points out: 'Journalism stands accused of sacrificing accuracy for speed, purposeful investigation for cheap intrusion and reliability for entertainment. "Dumbed down" news media are charged with privileging sensation over significance and celebrity over achievement.' It might even be suggested that what Hargreaves outlines could also be a caricature of what is perceived to be the practice associated with sports journalism at the popular end of the newspaper market.

However, you do not have to subscribe fully to the 'dumbing down' thesis to be concerned about the current state of the journalism profession. As journalist, economist and writer Will Hutton has argued:

> Journalism and the entertainment culture in which we now live are uneasy bedfellows. Facts are not always clear-cut, easy to understand and dramatic; good and bad rarely lend themselves to the demands of soundbites. Yet for those who can deliver dramatic, clear-cut stories, the entertainment culture delivers celebrity status with salaries and standing to match. The temptation to over dramatise grows by the month; to cut corners for some is irresistible. (Hutton, 2004)

Ostensibly these debates are about the impact of commercialisation on the provision of impartial and uncomplict news, something viewed as fundamental if people are to make informed choices in a democratic society, and at their core is a concern about the quality and range of political and economic information being made available. Why then should these concerns impact on a study of sports journalism?

SPORTS JOURNALISM AND 'TABLOIDISATION'

The rise of the preoccupation of journalism with celebrity-driven news, part of a wider 'tabloidization' thesis (Sparks, 2000), has seen the increasing profile allocated to sports become implicated in a wider debate about 'dumbing down'. In other words, the rise in quantity of sports coverage and its supposed attendant fixation with celebrity sports stars, particularly in the broadsheet press since the 1990s, as well as its increasing profile with mainstream television news, is seen as an example of 'dumbing down'. If, as Franklin (1997: 5) argues, news organisations and journalism in general is now fixatcd with entertainment-driven news and 'the task of journalism has become merely to deliver and serve up whatever the customer wants', then it appears increasingly what they want is sports-related news.

There remains a certain irony in this situation. The key claims now levelled at journalism in general about a decline in the standard and rigour that journalists bring to their craft have been a common criticism aimed at sections of sports journalism for decades. When the then President of Baseball's National League in the USA addressed the American Society of Newspaper editors in the 1980s, he lambasted the quality of sports journalism and its internal policing by newspaper editors. He argued that editors ignored the sports section:

> They ignore it in the sense, and it is an important one, that the same set of editorial standards for accuracy, competence, distinguishing fact from opinion, rewriting, and editing are simply not applied consistently or rigorously to sports sections as they are applied to other sections of the newspaper. (Giamatti, 1988: 204)

The paradox being that at a time when similar accusations are being made about the wider culture of political and economic journalism, and the growth of sports journalism, certainly in the UK, is seen as a symbolic example of declining standards, sports journalism is probably better policed than at any time in its history. While the tabloid market undoubtedly retains many aspects outlined by Giamatti, the expanded range and coverage in the broadsheet/compact market means there has never been more systematic, insightful and rigorous sports journalism of what Rowe (1992) calls the 'reflexive analysis' type available in the UK newspaper market. Thus sports journalism interfaces with the wider 'tabloidisation' of the press thesis in an interesting manner.

Sparks (2000), in his excellent overview of the supposed 'tabloidisation' of journalism is keen to stress the historical dimension to this process and its attendant debate. He also argues that the current concerns should be seen as part of this longer process that is 'reformulating' the news media, as 'serious' newspapers in particular seek to address a changing 'readership'. This is a readership dramatically altered through a rise in educational levels and changes in the labour market and family structures. When this is combined with a more commercially aggressive news marketplace he argues that what we are experiencing is a specific staging post in the evolution of the relationship between journalism, society and democracy.

Some newspaper editors view this shifting terrain as less of a threat and agree with Sparks (2000) that what has changed is society's expectations of what it requires from its media. To this end they argue that newspapers to a greater extent accurately reflect the breaking down of more traditional class-based barriers related to cultural taste: the public and the private and the centrality of popular culture in our everyday lives. Alan Rusbridger, editor of the then broadsheet *Guardian* newspaper[1], argued in November 2000 that changes in the broadsheet press simply reflected wider cultural shifts in taste and the breaking down of areas of supposedly high and low culture. He asks incredulously that:

> You can't possibly care about debt relief and *The Simpsons*. If you listen to Ligeti and James Macmillan then why would you want to know who won the United game last night or which Cabernet Sauvignon to drink with your meal tonight? Get back into your box.
> Something else missing from *The Times* of 1968 was anything to do with the home or emotional life. There is nothing about marriage, divorce, children, schools, au pairs, depression, drinking, health, drugs, teenagers, affairs, fashion, sex, successful relationships, failing relationships, interior decor, cancer, infertility, faith, grandparents – or any of the other things that make up the texture of our non-working lives. (Rusbridger, 2000)

This ties in with what Sparks (2000: 32) suggests is the need to view such broadsheet newspapers as 'bundles of serious and less serious materials'; the challenge for newspapers is getting that mix or balance correct in terms of attracting and retaining their target readership. Hence the rise in the space and resource allocated to the coverage of sports in the 'serious' broadsheet press in the UK over the last decade or so is in part explained by placing it within this wider context of the 'reformulation' of a more market-driven journalism.

However, an interesting wider theoretical position implicitly underpins much of the debate around the 'tabloidisation' and 'dumbing down' of journalism. This suggests that ultimately sports journalism (and other forms of entertainment-focused journalism) is actually the antithesis of what journalism should be really about. Sparks (2000: 14), for example, places scandal, sports and entertainment on one end of an axis of 'different press fields' in contrast to politics, economics and society. It appears that sports journalism does appear still to lie beyond the boundary of 'serious journalism'. Sparks (2000: 16), however, does recognise that when a broadsheet newspaper such as *The Financial Times* carries analysis of the relationship between football and 'the business strategies of global broadcasting companies', this represents a different form of journalism. He argues that:

> The true tabloid story is about the sexual antics of a footballer (any kind of football), and an operational definition of tabloidization is the process by which the press pays more and more attention to that kind of material at the expense of the coverage of public affairs. (Sparks, 2000: 16)

This position is helpful in explaining the traditional lowly status of the sports journalist within the profession, something that is picked up and developed in the work of Rowe (1992, 1995, 1999, 2004, 2005), discussed later. However, what is argued throughout the book is that the boundaries associated with sports journalism, and say business news, have now become so stretched that categorising sports journalism has become more difficult. While certain types of tabloid stories remain an important element of sports journalism, they are not necessarily representative of an overall field that is becoming more diverse.

Political journalist Andrew Marr's account (2004) of the history of British journalism makes little reference to sports journalism. Marr admits this is an area of the print media that he does not know well, or indeed for that matter have a great deal of interest in. However, his critique of the problems facing contemporary journalism, indicates that sports journalism faces similar issues to that being experienced in other areas of the trade. Indeed, in one area, the rise of the influence of public relations on journalism (which is examined in Chapter 5), Marr argues that rather than being overly concerned with the prevalence of celebrity-driven news:

> The more worrying trends in British news values are related instead to the growth of an office-based, editorial culture, rather than a reporters' journalism . ... The trouble is office-bound journalists from modern newspapers become dependent on fixers: the PR men manipulating celebrity careers; the university-trained media experts; the polling companies with a story to sell. (2004: 115)

In this area, sports journalists tend to buck the trend. They spend less time office-bound than other journalists, either being out at actual sporting events, or attending press conferences or chasing interviews. This is not to suggest that the tendency to be drip-fed information from other media sources, such as rolling sports news broadcasts and television coverage of sport, means that sports journalists are completely exempt from this general drift to stay wedded to the office, simply that it is interesting to note how sports reporting still offers opportunities to move beyond the increasingly prevalent office culture of the contemporary journalist.

What becomes increasingly evident from the research carried out on the print media, particularly in the UK, is that for many scholars sports coverage and sports journalism are not really viewed as part of what journalism (and certainly *serious* journalism) is really about. It is also worth noting that many within the profession itself also share these doubts as to the veracity of sports journalism being a legitimate part of the wider journalistic landscape. In 2002, the *Columbia Journalism Review* special issue on American sports journalism notably began its series of articles by asking whether sports journalism was indeed journalism.

Campbell (2004: 203) also notes how sports have often been grouped together with entertainment and lifestyle journalism, categories that have sat uneasily within more traditional definitions of journalism. Rooney identifies showbiz and sports as two of the key areas of content in his study of the tabloid newspapers the *Sun* and the *Mirror*. He argues: 'We should consider the *Mirror* and the *Sun* as completely separate cultural artefacts from newspapers proper. They do not offer public-affairs material, preferring instead nonserious entertainment' (Rooney, 2000: 103), He concludes his study by noting that: 'The *Mirror* and the *Sun* can no longer be regarded as "newspapers" and we must find new ways to explain their importance within working-class culture' (Rooney, 2000: 107).

While debate over the role, importance and social value of sports journalism, both within and outside the journalism profession is very much an ongoing issue, its dismissal as a form of 'nonserious entertainment' is simply to underestimate the range of material now to be found under the heading of sports journalism.

In the first instance, this approach unproblematically lumps all sports journalism together, making no distinction between the modes of address used by journalists or indeed the type of story being covered. For example, one can make a case that a report of a football match may have little impact on issues relating to public affairs (unless as some would argue it is an international perhaps between England and Germany); however, sports news coverage of London's 2012 Olympic bid or England's hosting of the 1996 European Football Championships is directly related to a range of political, economic and public policy issues, which in various guises are addressed by such tabloid coverage. At the core here is an argument about what journalism is about. If journalism is about disseminating information and facilitating discussion on a range of social, political, economic and cultural issues pertinent to a society, then sports, however much some academics may dislike it, is part of that mix. At times sport can be trivial and unimportant, at others a symbolically significant cultural form that is an indicator of wider social and cultural forces in society.

Sparks (2000) has advocated a more nuanced categorisation of a newspaper's market position driven by content and readership (into about five interrelated areas) rather than the cruder dichotomy of broadsheet and tabloid. However, these two categories remain important in shaping the mindset of journalists and readers alike, in much the same way as 'Fleet Street' remains the phrase to describe the heart of the British national press, despite the fact that it hasn't been the home of the newspaper industry for over a decade.

Thus, within journalism studies research, sports journalism has largely been under-researched. As Campbell (2004: 213) has convincingly argued: 'In Britain sports journalism is both literally and figuratively on the back pages in discussions on journalism.' Rather, as we have noted above, the field has been concerned with a range of key themes around the defining of journalism in the 21st century: political journalism and communication and democracy; ethics and the impact of a growing commercialisation of the media on journalistic practice.

Campbell himself suggests that, on the one hand, while the rhythms of the sports calendar lend themselves to many of the requirements of news organisations in terms of regular predictable events with a clear resolution, 'on the other hand, this very routine nature of sports, the repetition of events, and the relative simplicity of those events (in comparison to say, a war or election), has left sports writing with a less important status than other forms of journalism' (2004: 214).

From within the Academy, then, we have to look elsewhere before we find sports journalism being investigated with any sustained degree of rigour or enthusiasm.

SPORTS JOURNALISM WITHIN MEDIA AND COMMUNICATIONS RESEARCH

Significantly, much of the most interesting writing about the culture of sports journalism has not come from journalism studies research but, rather, from those scholars engaged in the broader field of media sport research (Rowe, 1992, 1995, 1999, 2004, 2005; Whannel, 1992, 2002; Blain and O'Donnell, 1998; Wenner, 1998; Boyle and Haynes, 2000, 2004; Brookes, 2002; Blain and Beirnstein, 2003). Often located within the media and communication studies research tradition, when media sport has been discussed, and the print media in particular, aspects of sports journalism and writing have been examined.

More often than not this research has been concerned with issues of representation and how sporting discourses connect with wider social, political and economic structures and discourses. Much of this work has focused on the print media and specifically the role it plays in constituting and reconstituting aspects of cultural and national identities in its coverage of sports and major sporting events (Blain et al., 1993; O'Donnell, 1994; Garland and Rowe, 1999; Alabarces et al., 2001; Crolley and Hand, 2002; Boyle and Monteiro, 2005; Hand and Crolley, 2005). This research has been largely concerned with the sports text, either print or, to a lesser extent, televisual, and the placing of it within a broader frame of reference that extends beyond the parameters of sports discourse and often connects it to wider discourses associated with gender, race and ethnicity and national and cultural identity-formation.

Central to this body of work is the extent to which a study of sport's relationship with the media and society illuminates wider social, political and economic factors at play in the culturally politicised arena of popular culture. In their major study of sports journalism texts across Europe in the early 1990s, Blain et al. also identified the implicit ideological conservatism of much sports journalism. They concluded that when it came to international sporting events that:

> sports journalism, albeit very unevenly, is as likely to produce a turning inward toward national concerns, and a buttressing of a sense of difference, as it is to operate ideologically on behalf of a harmonious world, even, as we have seen, at that mythic habitat of the familial, the Olympics. (Blain et al., 1993: 196)

While reference in this current book has been made to the production context of sports journalism, the issue of its ideological impact is not the main focus of this particular project; yet the analysis from the early 1990s would appear to remain valid over a decade later.

Some of the most astute academic writing on sports journalism has come from Rowe (1992, 1995, 1999, 2004, 2005). While the main drive of his work has focused on the more general issues of debates about the relationship between the media, sport and culture, within this work has been a concern about the key role that sports journalists play as cultural producers of media sports texts. This work has tended to focus on Australian sports journalism, but research has also been focused on the UK situation.

To this end Rowe (1999, 2004) has argued that an understanding of the wider cultural and occupational position of sports journalists is vital to any process that is interested in understanding media sports texts. He suggests that:

> Sports journalists, furthermore, are caught in a particularly difficult bind because of the different, sometimes contradictory professional demands made on them; they are expected, often at the same time, to be objective reporters, critical investigators, apologists for sports and teams, representatives of fans, and, not unusually, to have performed in sport at elite levels. (Rowe, 1999: 37)

The general perception that emerges from the research carried out by Rowe is one in which sports journalists appear to lead a relatively protected, insular and comfortable existence. Indeed we might argue that this description could be equally applicable to the culture of the elite sportspeople who are often the focus of attention for these journalists.

Another issue raised by Rowe (1999) is what he calls the lack of 'sceptical enquiry' among sports journalists. The *Irish Times* sportswriter Tom Humphries (2003: 118) has identified the danger for journalists of 'travelling too close to the circus' or the intrinsic complicity of sports journalism with its over-reliance on access to sources among elite sports organisations and individuals (Boyle et al., 2002; Brookes, 2002: 37–8; Bower, 2003; Campbell, 2004: 215–6). This particular aspect of the contemporary culture of sports journalism is examined in some detail in Chapter 5.

Related to this concern is the extent to which the ever-growing commercialisation of elite sports, and their interplay with media institutions and interests, impacts on or helps distort news values and reporting priorities. Thus the holding of exclusive live coverage of a major sporting event by a particular television channel will certainly mean that it is more likely to carry sports-related news stories on that channel's mainstream news broadcasts or across associated media platforms. For example, when BBC TV successfully recaptured the terrestrial highlights for English Premiership football in 2004 from their rival ITV, there was clearly a greater prominence given to Premiership-related news stories than there had been when exclusivity to the television rights lay elsewhere. To the same extent, one can also see extensive cross-promotion of sporting events between newspapers that are part of the News International stable and Sky Sports, part of the same corporation (see Chapters 2 and 5 for a more detailed discussion of this issue).

Brookes (2002: 32–3) suggests that central in any attempt to map out the terrain of sports journalism is the issue of news values. In his discussion of the print media, he suggests that sports journalism is a mixture of the spectacular and routine. He argues that often when sports stories connect with wider sets of news values, such as those around '*sports scandal, public policy issues* and *business news involving sport*' (Brookes, 2002: 34–5), this can lead to conflict when 'traditional' sports journalists find their terrain impinged upon by other news journalists in ways that can put a strain on relationships of trust with sports sources which may have been developed over time.

However, one of the key elements this book wants to look at is the ways in which news values associated with sports journalism are in fact altering and evolving, driven by changes not only in media organisations, but also in the wider political economy of the sports industries. In other words, to what extent have the three key areas – sports scandal, public policy issues and business news involving sport – identified by Brookes above become increasingly routinised areas of inquiry for mainstream sports journalism in a manner unimaginable even a decade ago? Or given the issues raised by Brookes about the importance of sources, do they still remain largely off limits for sports journalists and are covered by news and business reporters instead (Boyle et al., 2002)?

Sports journalism is, of course, a far from homogeneous culture. There are tensions between print and broadcast journalists, evidenced by Salwen and Garrison's work (1998: 99), which focused on US sports journalists and indicated some considerable hostility from print sports journalists towards their broadcast media colleagues. The newspaper sports journalists argued that they felt that the rise of broadcast sports journalism had helped to diminish their professional status. From within the print sector itself, of course, tensions exist, most notably within the UK context between tabloid journalists and those working in the broadsheet/compact sector. As Rowe (1995: 159) argued:

> Within the print media, a distinction is made between the 'tabloids' and the 'qualities', a split that I replicated in the typology of 'sports reporters' and 'sports writers'. The 'writer-driven' style of the quality papers is routinely contrasted with the assumed opposite, the reader-driven tabloid paper seen as cynically exploitative of sport and its personnel according to the demands of market based profit maximization.

However, to what extent is this distinction still the case today? One of the areas discussed in the book is the extent to which the blurring between the traditional boundaries of the broadsheet and the popular press, which some critics (Franklin, 1997) have argued has been one of the characteristics of print journalism in the UK over the last decade or so, has impacted on the arena of sports journalism.

PROFESSIONAL IMAGE

In his research, Rowe also examines the key issues of both professional image and the position of sports journalism within the wider journalism hierarchy. For Rowe: 'This assertion of the "quality" writing function over and against that of "hack" journalism is constantly made by those who wish to elevate media sports texts, especially of the print variety, almost to the status of art' (1999: 58). There is clearly an issue here with regard to the status of those journalists who cover aspects of popular culture. The assertion that has been made by previous writing on this area is that sports editors, for example, never become editors of newspapers. Yet the 1990s saw the elevation of Piers Morgan from a journalist covering showbusiness/celebrity issues to editor of the *Daily Mirror*, one of the major tabloid newspapers in the UK. Simon Kelner went on to become editor of *The Independent*, having once been sports editor on the *Independent on Sunday,* while the *Daily Telegraph*'s columnist Jeff Randall also edited *The Sunday Business* newspaper and worked for the BBC, having served his time as sports editor with *The Sunday Times.*

It is a concern with mapping this shifting in the values and status associated with sports journalism as the field itself mutates under a range of commercial and cultural pressures that runs through this book and is addressed in more detail in Chapter 8.

While Haynes (1999) has carried out interesting research on the historical evolution of a particular aspect of broadcast sports: the sports commentary, the writing from within media sociology on aspects of radio and television forms of sports journalism remains underdeveloped. While there is clearly a relationship between what Rowe (1999) calls sports journalism, sports commentary and sports presentation, it is also true, as we note in Chapter 3, that clear distinctions exist between these categories.

There is a distinct lack of studies of UK sports journalists from within the Academy. It could be argued that Tunstall's study (1971) into specialist correspondents, which was carried out in the 1960s and included looking at football specialist correspondents as part of its range of journalists, remains one of the main studies in this field. It certainly provided some interesting historical material on the broader production process within which the football journalist operated. This study focused on print journalists, and studies examining the professional ideologies and practices of broadcast sports journalists have also been largely absent from the sociology of journalism research agenda. Tunstall's concern (1971) with understanding the constraints, professional ideologies and particular work practices that shape journalism are all elements which, in varying degrees, inform this research project.

SPORTS JOURNALISM AND JOURNALISM VALUES

Concerned with similar themes, but with a more textual orientation, Whannel's study of sport and television (1992) remains one of the few that embraces aspects of broadcast sports journalism. This research highlighted the tension between journalistic modes of address and a more entertainment-driven focus in television sport. He notes that while at first glance sport on television appears to rely heavily on aspects of the reportage journalistic traditions, in reality this is a more complex interrelationship. He suggests that: 'in the structure of its programmes, its modes of representation and modes of addressing its audiences, in its place in relation to scheduling and in the type of audiences it attempts to win and hold, it is also shaped by the conventions of entertainment' (Whannel, 1992: 92).

Significantly, he also argues that the traditional concerns of television journalism regarding neutrality and impartiality are extended to broadcast sports journalism. It is not clear whether domestic sports coverage is primarily being discussed here; certainly, within television coverage of international sports events, it could be argued that contemporary broadcast sports journalism – Whannel's research is based on the situation in the 1980s – appears to increasingly pay scant regard to issues of impartiality and neutrality. What this highlights is the extent that broadcast sports reporters/journalists appear exempt from the normal codes of professional practice. On the more commercially driven broadcast outlets, such as Sky Sports television or TalkSport radio, this type of partial journalism appears increasingly to be accepted as standard practice among sports reporting.

Rudin and Ibbotson (2002: 72) seem to suggest that impartiality is not part of the lexicon of sports journalism when they argue:

> In many ways, sports reporting of actual events are very similar to hard news as regards attention to detail, accuracy and meeting deadlines. The main difference is that some form of comment or opinion is allowed and may involve partisanship, interviews with players, coaches and managers, comparisons with earlier encounters, fans reactions. It is worth noting that sports stories can also include personal profiles, investigative features, humorous pieces and commentary.

What is of interest here is that while Rudin and Ibbotson are primarily discussing print sports journalism, to what extent should differences exist between the traditionally more partisan print media and commercial and public service sports broadcasting? Or is more partisan journalism simply an example of how sports reporting and journalism has evolved to reflect both a changing sporting environment and differing audience expectations? These are just some of the issues that are explored in the rest of the book.

SPORTS JOURNALISM: THE INSIDE TRACK?

There have also been more discursive engagements with the culture and milieu within which the sports journalist operates. In some instances these involve reflection on the practice from those within the industry, although these remain rare within the growing library of journalistic memoirs, partly no doubt as a result of the lowly position that sports journalism has historically occupied within the industry.

Most are gentle reminiscences of the trials and tribulations associated with working in sports broadcasting, which has been viewed as a form of journalism that requires particular skills related to commentary and television presenting. The Irish sports broadcaster/journalist Michael O'Hehir, for example, has occupied such a long and central location in the evolution of that country's broadcasting psyche that any social history of Irish broadcasting or indeed Irish sport would be incomplete without reference to his cultural influence and professional flexibility that spans various sports and both radio and television (see Chapter 2).

Beverley Turner's *The Pits: The Real World of Formula One* (2004), however, remains a rarity among books written about sport by sports broadcasters, in that it is candid, honest and ultimately damning about the sport. She attacks both the impact that rampant commercialisation has had on Formula One motor sport, and the entrenched sexism that is deeply embedded in its sports culture and which makes it a deeply unpleasant environment for female commentators or journalists to work within (see Chapter 7).

As noted above, there has been, of course, a hierarchy of sorts within the field of sports journalism itself. In the UK, broadsheet sports writers have been positioned towards the 'serious' and 'literary' end of the market, juxtaposed with the 'sports hacks' at the lower end of the tabloid market, a dichotomy that has both enraged and dismayed sports journalists such as Brian Glanville who throughout his long career has moved with ease across this supposed divide. He has argued:

> for so many years I had insisted that sports journalism should be one seamless garment. In the magazine *Encounter* in 1965 I had published an article called 'Looking for the Idiom', emphasising the difference between British sport writing, with its quality–popular dichotomy, and American, whose chief sportswriters wrote for everybody … My thesis was that both the 'quality' and the 'popular' writer were in some senses failures. The first because although he could largely write as he pleased, about mass-interest sports, he reached only a fraction of the public. The second, because although he reached the public at large, he was rigidly confined to a highly stylised, ultimately patronising, form of journalism, which treated the readership with implicit contempt. (Glanville, 1999: 257)

Other sports journalists, such as Richard Williams and Hugh McIlvanney, see an intrinsic truth in sporting performance. McIlvanney, still the only sports journalist to have been voted Journalist of the Year in the UK, could reflect in 1991 that:

> After more than thirty years of writing on sport it is still possible to be assailed by doubts about whether it really is a proper job for a grown person. But I console myself with the thought that it is easier to find a kind of truth in sport than it is, for example, in the activities covered by political or economic journalists. Sports truth may be simplistic but it is not negligible. (BBC, 1991)

While Williams, a former music journalist, draws a comparison between sports and music journalism that is linked to notions of truth and performance. He suggests that:

> To put it bluntly, the sweetest music is sometimes made by the most obnoxious people, and vice versa … in sport, by contrast, the way people play the game is generally also the way they are as human beings, which makes it legitimate to discuss how someone's performance is affected by his or her character. (Williams, 2003: 3–4)

For Williams the opportunity that covering sport allows for connecting with wider social debates about moral issues is also something that is both appealing and 'frequently uncomfortable'. Williams acknowledges that much has changed for the contemporary sportswriter and for some, sports journalism's golden age is well and truly over. In his reflections on a year in the life of a sportswriter, Tom Humphries, working for the Dublin based *Irish Times*, begins his book by announcing: 'We sportswriters are a breed in decline. We aren't endangered, there are more of us then ever before – we are just withering. We are further and further from the action and we are shouting louder and louder just to make ourselves heard' (Humphries, 2003: 3).

Humphries paints a picture of a profession in crisis, as the commercialisation of sport, its ubiquitous televisual nature and the intense competition in media markets all distort a form of journalism that was once more dignified. Crucially, sportswriters such as Humphries and the *Daily Telegraph's* Andrew Baker (2004) are no longer on the inside of modern sport, but are themselves outsiders, deluding themselves that they have the inside track on information. Humphries continues:

> We know only what sportswriting shouldn't be. We shouldn't be purveyors of sports entertainment. We shouldn't be the running dogs of prawn-sandwich corporatism. Then again, we shouldn't be sour drunks, heckling all the way through the show. Sport is a form of entertainment. Sportswriting is a form of journalism. In the fog in between the ideals of sport and journalism, we have to make a living, we have to entertain. We have to do it in 900 words or less. And quickly. (2003: 6–7)

While written in a self-deprecating style, what Humphries does is shed light on the contemporary production context within which sports journalists operate. The pressures are partly institutional; the financial difficulties being experienced by *The Irish Times* threatening to lead to more cut-backs in staff, and to affect the often strained relationship the paper's sports journalists have with their sports editor. He captures the relentlessness of the modern all-year-round sports calendar, driven as it is by the demands of television and corporate sponsorship. He also notes how television and technology are altering the role of the sports journalist, by making it possible to cover a major international sports tournament without ever leaving the media centre.

His concerns are echoed in further reflections on the trade from other sportswriters. Both Leonard Koppett (2003) and Jerry Eskenazi (2003) lament the passing of an era and while nostalgia often forms a core part of any memoirs, there is a clear indication that the rules of the game for sportswriters have changed in recent years. In his insightful account of his career as a sportswriter, which spanned the pre-television age through to the advent of new media such as the Internet in his later years, Koppett notes how the key aspect of the press box in the pre-television age was its ability to allow you as a sportswriter to become an 'insider'. He argues that it:

> flourished in a world that existed before television, before universal access to 'up close and personal' depictions of any and all celebrities, before we assumed that everyone could and would enjoy (or endure) 15 minutes of fame. A respect for privacy and propriety, more widely felt in 'decent' society then than now, helped maintain the distance between the unapproachably famous and 'ordinary' folk, even the ones who had considerable status within their own circles. (Koppett, 2003: 4)

It will be aspects of this changing journalistic sports culture and its attendant pressures that are examined in later chapters of this book.

THE VIEW FROM PROFESSIONAL SPORTSPEOPLE

Eamon Dunphy's seminal book *Only a Game?,* first published in the mid-1970s when he was a professional player in the English game, gives a clear insight into the ambiguous relationship that existed at that time between professional footballers and sports journalists. Dunphy (1987) argued that players had double standards towards journalists. He suggests: 'On the one hand they despise them, thinking they know nothing about the game. … On the other hand, players are flattered by their attention. Flattered by the idea that this guy has come along especially to write about them' (Dunphy, 1987: 132–3). In this sense, despite the perceptions among sportswriters about the breakdown of trust being a contemporary issue, for Dunphy there has always been an element of mistrust between the people that play and the journalists who write about the game. His criticism of football journalists is implicitly related to levels of insight, knowledge and understanding. As he argues: 'Whereas theatre critics and film critics do know what the mechanics of a production are, most football writers don't. So players tend to despise journalists. … They don't go into a story to discover but to substantiate preconceived ideas' (Dunphy, 1987: 133–4).

Dunphy's critique is interesting and raises issues about the extent to which he offers a snapshot of a relationship that has long changed, or has simply been updated to facilitate the drives of the contemporary media.

As a journalist, broadcaster and author Dunphy has been writing about sport for over 30 years. He is a former professional footballer who has successfully reinvented himself as a journalist, an author and a broadcaster working across newspapers, radio and television on a wide range of subjects from sport to politics. Dunphy has had trenchant views on the role and function of a sports journalist and has never shied away from expressing opinions in print or on air that have cut against the dominant journalistic consensus. One such occasion was during the Republic of Ireland's campaign at the 1990 FIFA World Cup finals in Italy, when his public criticism of the team's style of play, at a time when the team was enjoying its most successful run in its history, provoked a storm of protest raged against him. In particular, the then Irish football manager Jack Charlton refused to take questions from Dunphy at press conferences. Recalling that period, journalist and author Colm Toibin noted that as a colleague he had been requested by his newspaper editor back in Dublin to look after Dunphy when he was in Italy: 'Ireland had fallen in love with Charlton. No journalist dared say anything against him. Only one did, and I was now his bodyguard' (Toibin, 1995: 140). The most telling line in Toibin's account of the vilification experienced by Dunphy in the months and years after the tournament is when he notes that for all the hassle, Dunphy realised: 'It's what happens, he understood, when you speak your mind in a small country which has invented a new set of heroes' (Toibin, 1995: 143).

In many ways this characterises some of the core tensions at the centre of sports journalism and writing. On the one hand, as a journalist you face the challenge of telling the story as you find it and often have to resist the temptation to simply run with the 'media pack'. While on the other, you must recognise that at the cultural and commercial core of the sports industry is the process of myth-making, with sports journalists a central element in that process.

Sports journalism and journalists have also enjoyed cameo roles in non-fiction sports books written by novelists and journalists. Davies's account (1990) of the 1990 FIFA World Cup in Italy presents a less than flattering picture of the English football press pack abroad as they cover England's campaign. The level of disdain between players and press is clearly evident from the categorising of the press as 'the rotters', with particular contempt being reserved for those 'news journalists' sent to Italy by their papers to cover and/or seek out scandal or hooliganism stories involving players and fans.

As noted above, the relationship between football player and the press is a highly ambiguous one. Davies (1990) captures this relationship on the cusp of change, as the 1990s would see massive amounts of money flow into the game from television and related sponsorship, making millionaires out of the elite players in the sport. This process has clearly altered the labour dynamics within the sport as well as the relationships players have with the media. No longer does media appearance money nor the lure of a ghosted column in a national newspaper (once the staple diet of additional income for relatively poorly paid players) hold much appeal for players earning up to £100,000 a week.

Humphries (2003) brilliantly captures the impact of this new level of financial independence on the player–journalist relationship when he recalls his attempt to get an interview with the then Tottenham Hotspur and

Republic of Ireland player Stephen Carr in the run-up to the 2002 FIFA World Cup. He writes:

> As individuals, if you can separate a player from the herd, there are some fine people among them … A couple of the older guys, in particular are capable of holding real grown-up conversations. In the main, though, when the players get together they radiate the surliness of supermodels who have just woken up to find acne all over their faces.
>
> I once asked Steve Carr, the Spurs fullback, if he had a few minutes to spare in order to do a short piece with me. He turned around with almost theatrical slowness, looked me up and down and laughed, 'No way pal'. Off he walked, shaking his head. I'd never met him or written about him before, but I came away and bought a bell for around my neck and for weeks thereafter walked through the streets shouting 'unclean, unclean, unclean'. (Humphries, 2003: 27)

From this exchange, one can perhaps assume that unlike many of his more cash-strapped professional predecessors, Carr does not plan a career in sports journalism when his playing days are over.

Lest we think it is only footballers who have this cynical relationship with journalists, Burns's examination (1986) of the increasingly global television-driven professional snooker circuit saw the sports journalists who covered the sport and the 'stars' associated with it, being nicknamed 'the reptiles' by the players. The strained relationship between the sport and sections of the media intensified as the tabloid press attempted to run stories of scandal and sexual intrigue involving players who enjoyed a celebrity status bestowed on them through a combination of television coverage and tabloid interest. These more aggressive forms of tabloid intrusion, which began to intensify in the 1980s, increasingly saw news journalists view sports and sportspeople as part of their natural beat and within their orbit of influence.

At the core of much of the discursive writing about sports journalism tend to be a number of assumptions. Perhaps, not surprisingly, given that these accounts are likely to come from the print media, there is a perception that it is the written word and newspapers specifically that remain the true home of sports journalism, rather than the journalism found in sports broadcasting. When sports journalism is being discussed, the overarching frame of reference remains the sportswriter, with broadcasting and its historical connotations of impartiality being more associated with sports commentary and presentation.

CONCLUSION: SPORTS JOURNALISM IN THE 21ST CENTURY

In her foreword to *Tabloid Tales: Global Debates Over Media Standards*, Barbie Zelizer (2000: ix) noted that: 'The thrust to identify certain forms of

journalistic practice as "good" journalism and the prevailing counter-thrust –
excommunicating certain practices from the elevated journalistic standard –
have remained a consensual way of encountering the journalistic world.' We
have seen how this process is clearly evident in many academic encounters
with sports journalism and in the role, status and position of the sports journalist within the profession.

Differing attitudes towards the status of sports journalism in specific countries tell us much about the differing status of sport in particular national cultures and societies. The ability of countries such as Spain, Italy and France to
support long-term sports journalism publications and the particular status
given to the sportswriter within US journalism all indicate the centrality of
sport as a cultural form in helping to both shape and reflect wider national
myths. In the UK, more so than these countries, class has been an important
marker in shaping the wider social and cultural parameters within which
sports culture and its attendant sports media have evolved and developed. As
Coleman and Hornby writing in the mid-1990s have argued:

> Yet those who write about sport still create a whole set of problems for themselves in
> Britain, many of them relating, predictably, to the subject of class. Sport in Britain has
> all sorts of class associations apparently absent elsewhere in the world. Cricket and
> (English, rather than Welsh) rugby union are 'posh' sports, played and watched by
> 'posh' people, and it is therefore acceptable to write in a 'posh' way about them; but
> anyone who dares to write about the more traditional working-class sports – football
> or rugby league, say – in a way which recognises the existence of polysyllabic words,
> or metaphors, or even ideas, is asking for trouble, or at the very least a great deal of
> suspicion. (1996: 1)

Indeed, as Glanville (1999: 269) has suggested, football has 'enraptured'
the middle classes elsewhere in both Europe and South America for
decades. Broadly speaking, this argument could be extended more generally
to sports reporting and writing. Put simply, the class-based support for sports
has been reflected in the way they have been covered, reported and made
sense of by sports journalists and has also dictated this broader dichotomy
between 'quality' and 'popular' journalism. Thus sports such as cricket have
a long literary tradition associated with both its print and its broadcast media
coverage, with writers such as Neville Cardus embedding the sport in
mythological images of England and Englishness.

Previous research by Boyle and Haynes (2000: 176–86) has commented
on the explosion in both the volume and the range of sports writing within
the traditional 'broadsheet' print media market that became evident in
the 1990s. They identify how a combination of the changing print media
marketplace, increased newspaper competition, broader cultural shifts in the
social position of sport (and specifically football) and new technology

helped facilitate the expansion in the sports sections of all the national broadsheets.

Rowe's research (1999) highlighted one of the key contradictions evident from any examination of the sports journalism culture. He noted: 'it is also often the case that the economic power of the sports department (in terms of the large number and handsome remuneration of personnel; importance for circulation, ratings, advertising revenue and so on) is at variance with its cultural power (low professional reputation and esteem)' (Rowe, 1999: 62). Rowe also suggested that this was beginning to change in the late 1990s as the popularity and profile of sport across a range of media platforms increased. One of the key issues this book examines is whether the broader economic and cultural shifts in sports journalism culture, driven by media interest, has fundamentally altered the situation outlined from the research carried out by Rowe in the 1990s.

There is also a need to examine the extent to which the wider social, economic and indeed political factors that are reformulating journalistic practice (Sparks, 2000: 36) are being played out across the field of sports journalism. If one agrees with Harcup (2004: 9) that at its basic core 'Journalism is not simply fact-gathering. It involves dealing with sources, selecting information and opinion, and telling stories – all within the framework of ... constraints, routines, principles and practices', then to what extent do the wider cultural codes of journalism apply to sports journalism?

Rowe (1999: 38) has argued that it was the print rather than the broadcasting form of sports journalism that dominated this sector of the journalistic terrain, both in profile and in prominence. To what extent has the explosion in broadcast media coverage of sport over the last decade or so altered this ecology? Or is much that passes for broadcast sports journalism more accurately labelled presentation, analysis and commentary? One of the interesting areas of growth both on television and on radio is the rise of the sports news correspondent, a clear recognition of the wider shift in the news values associated with sport and its growing hinterland.

A key factor, often ignored by those academic critics of sports journalism, is the impact that the changing position of sports within society has had on the range of reporting of sports-related news. For example, the economic and political profile that was given to the successful campaign by London in securing the 2012 Olympic Games was covered across the business, news and features pages of broadsheet/compact newspapers through to the back and front pages of the popular press. Issues relating to the governance of sport and the politics associated with aspects of the industry have also become more prominent in recent years. In other words, the ongoing commercialisation and internationalisation of the business of sport, its relationship with corporate capital and national and international media companies has resulted in those journalists who write about sport finding their traditional beat being encroached upon by business and political journalists or the broadcast 'sports news' correspondent. As sportswriter Richard Williams (2003: 4) has noted: 'The last few years in sport have been full of examples of philosophical questions overshadowing the business of straightforward games-playing.'

Closely linked with this process are the wider structural and cultural shifts that have seen elite sport increasingly located within the entertainment industries as money from television in particular has flowed into some sports, and the athletes in these areas have become stars. While the concept of sports stardom and the extent to which the print media specifically are implicated in this process is not a new phenomenon within the sporting arena (Andrews and Jackson, 2001; Whannel, 2002; Smart, 2005), what is changed is its scale and the increasingly ubiquitous nature of the process; what Whannel (2002) has called the 'vortextuality' of media sports stardom.

To this end the rise of sport public relations and the formalising of access and relationships between sports stars, clubs and various media outlets have become a significant aspect of the landscape of sports journalism in the 21st century. Informed and underpinned by the seemingly relentless commercialisation of popular cultural activity, sport has found itself at the intersection of new media technologies allowing greater exploitation of image rights and a massively expanded, highly competitive print and broadcast media sector keen to secure differing forms of sports content as they chase readers, viewers and listeners in a complex media marketplace. As we see throughout this book, at the centre of this maelstrom, being buffeted by a range of forces, is sports journalism and sports journalists, some of whom feel they no longer recognise the games they have made a living reporting on, or indeed the profession they originally fell in love with.

So, what are the processes at work that are reformulating what sports journalism is, and who sports journalists are? In this respect the book aims to identify and map out the combination of internal pressures that are occurring within media organisations as journalism adapts to both the changing patterns and expectations among media consumers and the wider structural economic and cultural shifts in what now can be called the sports economy. Other concerns also addressed include asking to what extent has the growth of the online sector impacted on the traditional sports print media?

What is also clear is that any book about sports journalism must be at least as interested in the wider political economy of both the sports and the media industries that have shaped and reshaped the profession since its inception. It is these concerns, allied with a desire to understand the contemporary professional ideologies and production constraints that shape sports journalism, that are at the core of this book.

In previous work, Boyle and Haynes (2000: 174–6) have examined Rowe's typology of modes of sports writing (1992), which he categorised as *hard news*, *soft news*, *orthodox rhetoric* and *reflexive analysis*. These ways of thinking about the modes of address found within print media sports journalism are important in helping to make sense of the vast outpouring of sports copy (see Chapter 2 for a more detailed discussion).

What is of particular interest in this book is the extent to which the volume of material within these categories is shifting or changing. In other words, at one end of the axis *hard news,* with its focus on a supposedly objective description of events and score lines, remains a staple part of the sports pages (although Blain and O'Donnell (1998) argue that the UK newspaper market is so saturated with politics that even this aspect of sports journalism is far from ideologically neutral), while soft news, with its fixation on speculation, comment and the centrality of stars and the star system in sports culture, continues to be the main staple diet of the tabloid sports section. At the other end of the axis is *reflexive analysis,* which places sport and the sports journalist at the centre of wider political, economic and cultural factors and influences, and is traditionally most likely to appear either outside of the sports pages or in small doses in the broadsheet press. Against the wider structural shifts in both the sports and the media industries has the balance of material within these categories altered or shifted in emphasis? Some of these issues are addressed in the latter part of Chapter 2.

Of course, historical context remains important. In their study of American sports journalists, Salwen and Garrison (1998) have argued that many sports journalists view their poor standing with their peers as being a legacy of poor past reputations. They suggest: 'That their shabby reputations cultivated over the years haunt them in this age of professional prestige and accountability. In this regard, we can see how the historical roots of sports journalism affect the field today' (Salwen and Garrison, 1998: 98). It is to these historical roots and 'shabby reputations' that we turn our attention to in the following chapter, as the broader cultural and historical frame of reference from within which contemporary print sports journalism has evolved is examined.

NOTE

1 The term broadsheet has become problematic with regard to the print media in the UK in the 21st century. By late 2005, a number of newspapers that had previously been broadsheets, such as *The Times*, *The Independent* and *The Scotsman,* were now tabloid, or compact (as they prefer to describe the change) in size, while the *Guardian* had relaunched in the *Berliner* form, which was larger

than a tabloid, but smaller than the traditional broadsheet. Throughout the book the term broadsheet or compact is used to refer to this section of the press that still differentiates itself in terms of content and news values from the tabloid and mid-market newspapers such as the *Daily Mail*. It is this broadsheet section of the market that has seen a considerable expansion in its sports journalism over the last decade or so. In turn, this has been symptomatic at times of a blurring of the journalistic divide between the broadsheet and the tabloid press.

SPORTS JOURNALISM
AND THE
PRINT MEDIA TRADITION

Once we were kings. A long time ago, in the stogie-fumed golden era of what is, essentially, a minor American art form, our predecessors illuminated the big papers in every town from New York to San Francisco. They had elegance. They had dignity. They had an audience.

Tom Humphries (2003: 3) *Laptop Dancing and the Nanny Goat Mambo: A Sportswriter's Year*, **Pocket Books/Townhouse: Dublin.**

The production of sports journalism is characterized by relatively fixed organizational structures and a professional culture similar to but distinct from journalism in general.

Rod Brookes (2002: 39) *Representing Sport*, **Arnold: London.**

When a sportswriter stops making heroes out of athletes, it's time to get out of the business.

Grantland Rice, Sportswriter, quoted in Ira Berkow (1986: 105) *Red: A Biography of Red Smith*, **Times Books, New York.**

Sports journalism has always been intrinsically associated with the print media, and while this chapter is not intended to provide a social history of the subject, it does offer a broader historical sense of the evolution of contemporary sports journalism. Thus, while this book is about modern sports journalism in an age when digital technology has helped to proliferate the range of media outlets concerned with covering sport in some shape or form, it would be incomplete without some historical context, as the Humphries quote at the start of the chapter reminds us, not least because the shadow cast by the historical traditions and legacy of previous forms of sports journalism and sportswriters is not insignificant.

What this part of the book and the next chapter attempt to offer is a snapshot of some of the wider social, cultural and economic processes that have helped shape the contemporary environment of the print and broadcast sports journalist. Throughout this process there has to be a recognition of the impact that wider changes in the media industries, themselves the subject of various political, social and economic shifts in society, have had on the particular terrain of sports journalism. Added to this is the significant impact that changes in the sports industry and its increasingly close relationship with the broadcast media in particular have had in reshaping sports journalism.

Any snapshot of the history of sports journalism will be as much about wider social attitudes towards both journalism and sport at any historical moment. This chapter maps some of the key moments from the origins of sports journalism in the print media. It is interested in how particular cultural and technological factors have shaped its evolution, practice and knowledge base and recognises the impact and influence of American sports writing on British journalism and the important relationship between the local and national press in the UK.

IN THE BEGINNING: THE AMERICAN EXPERIENCE

Sports journalism remains largely a footnote, albeit an important one, when set against the wider political and economic factors that shaped the newspaper industry, particularly in the 19th century (Williams, 1997; Curran and Seaton, 2003; Gorman and McLean, 2003). The earliest sustained interest in the reporting of sport in the print media is generally recognised to be associated with *Bell's Life* and the *Weekly Dispatch*, both popular London magazines of the early 1800s (Goldlust, 1987: 70). Indeed Betts (1953) has argued that other publications such as the *London Sporting Magazine* and the *English Sporting Magazine* pre-dated their American counterparts and were in fact used as models for US sporting publications. The sports that such journals were concerned with were the leisure pursuits of the landed classes.

However, it would be across the Atlantic that the development of particular forms of sports journalism would really advance, driven largely by a more commercially orientated sports and entertainment industry and newspapers keen to grow revenues from advertisers by capturing and holding onto readers. While Chandler (1996: 242) argues that as far back as 1733, newspapers such as the *Boston Gazette* were carrying 'sporadic reports on prizefighting, horse racing and cricket', it would not be until the 19th century and the development of the newspaper as an important part of a growing mass communication network that the interaction between sport and journalism would really flourish.

It is unsurprising when seen in its historical context that there has been a perennial struggle at the heart of sports journalism between notions of journalistic rigour and the more uncritical promotion of sports, teams and individuals by newspapers. By the end of the 19th century, newspapers in the UK were increasingly commercial, partisan and national commodities, and sports coverage was recognised as one of the elements that helped to drive sales. In turn, the fledgling sporting organisations, many keen to establish themselves as national bodies, recognised, to varying degrees, the importance and commercial value of the exposure and promotion of their sport that accrued from national newspaper coverage. As Goldlust has argued:

> The period of the latter part of the nineteenth and the early decades of the twentieth century was one of significant growth and expansion for both the commercial daily newspaper and entrepreneurially-based forms of popular entertainment. The newspaper served as an extremely effective vehicle for the marketing of the latter. (1987: 62)

This process took place not simply through any direct advertising, but through the promotion of sport with its integration as 'news' in the newspaper.

The print media were also heavily implicated in the creation of sports stars and the tangled relationships between players, agents, promoters and journalists that would come to characterise much of modern sports journalistic practice. Chandler (1996: 242) suggests that as far back as the mid-19th century: 'The first US sports star created by the press was John Carmel Heenan. His 1860 prizefight with the English champion Tom Sayers was treated as a matter of international prestige.'

While Henry Chadwick, hired by the *New York Herald* to cover baseball in 1862, is thought to be the first full-time newspaper sports reporter (Oriard, 1993: 58), it would be another 20 years or so before Joseph Pulitzer set up the first dedicated sports department within a newspaper when he bought the *New York Herald*. Pulitzer viewed sports journalism as an exemplar of the 'new journalism' of the time with its ready-made mass market appeal and human interest focus. Although the regular sports section as we would understand it today would not become standard in US newspapers until the 1920s and 1930s (Oriard, 2001: 27), the 1880s does mark the emergence of the sports journalist as a distinct figure in the growing professional journalism field.

From the outset, sportswriters in the US were differentiated from mere sports reporters or journalists by their ability, and licence, to place themselves at the centre of the story, rather than merely report the facts and figures associated with a sporting contest. The reader was under no illusion that what you were reading was an interpretation of an event through the eyes of the sportswriter.

Some of the more literary-inspired US sportswriters of the 1960s may have looked with disdain on some of the sportswriters who emerged around the turn of the century, but in their defence these early journalists were operating in a different sporting and media age. Writers such as Grantland Rice have since become synonymous with what has been viewed as a golden age of sport in America. This period is focused around the 1920s and the sport stars, such as Babe Ruth, made famous through newspaper reports. These sportswriters operated in an age when the printed word and later radio were the key cultural forms through which sport was mediated and made sense of for millions of readers and listeners.

Rice was among the most famous of this new generation of sporting myth-makers. Fountain (1993: 4) argues that while he was: 'Less celebrated than Ring Larder or Damon Runyon, Rice was nevertheless the first important American sportswriter. For, while Larder and Runyon used sportswriting to shape their own talents and careers, leaving their legacies in other areas, Rice used his talent and career to shape American sportswriting.' Rice helped secure his fame through his syndicated column *The Sportlight*, which began in 1913 and was carried in more than 250 papers across the US. Such was his influence across newspaper, magazine and radio coverage of sport during the 1920s that Inabinett (1994: 7) estimates that his income rose to over $100,000 during this decade. However, Inabinett (1994) also goes on to argue that the claim often made that Rice propagated a style of sentimentalised and clichéd sports journalism, overwrought with hyperbole, which made heroes out of sporting athletes and refused to address the darker side of the sport is largely misplaced. He suggests that while Rice's frame of sporting reference was to see sport as a mythical field of dreams and to look for what was noble in sport, his writing style, at its best, has more in common with the literary sports writing of later decades. He illustrates this point by quoting from Rice's report from the Paris Olympics of 1924 (Inabinett, 1994: 9).

It was an afternoon of blazing heat, heat blown northward from the Sahara in the wake of a sirocco, heat that was heat. The thermometer was at a hundred or more, and into this furnace the greatest runners of 30 nations were setting out upon a 10,000-meter cross country whirl. An almost endless parade started. Only a few finished. Along the route there were fine runners unconscious, completely out, with their faces upturned to the sun as the ambulances came by to rush them along to waiting trainers and physicians. There were others who were reeling and floundering – running a few yards, falling and then rising again as they fought their way. There was courage enough here to make up a war.

What is striking about this piece is how fresh it feels over 80 years later, and how it clearly stands comparison with some of the literary sports writing that would come to dominate the genre from the 1960s onwards.

From the turn of the 20th century, newspaper editors saw sports coverage as an established aspect of the newspaper that helped to drive sales, and sportswriters as a key part of that commercial contract between the paper and its readers. More so than British sports journalism, US sport and sports journalism has always been fixated with statistics, which then became the base for the writing. The rise of the syndicated sports column was a key element in this process and recognised that part of the pleasure and the extended commercial value of sport, was not simply the covering of the event itself but, rather, the anticipation of it, and the reliving and contextualising of it within a wider sporting history and tradition, when it had concluded. The newspaper was ideally suited for this task. The importance of syndicated newswire copy was also central to the building of a nationwide following that turned certain sportswriters in the US into celebrities. As Koppett (2003: 11) has argued: 'From the 1920s on, the sports writing community has developed a class system. Syndicated columnists and full-time baseball writers were the nobility; all others, commoners.' The chronicling of this sports history by these writers was, of course, one of the key roles that newspapers played in helping both to develop and to extend the popularity of sport while simultaneously creating overarching narratives that established traditions and histories associated with sport.

Oriard (2001: 29) has argued that: 'Because sport was not regarded as serious news, sportswriters on most newspapers had far greater license than other journalists.' He also notes that in a snapshot of US papers in the mid-1920s three-quarters of sports departments edited their own copy, free from the checking constraints being applied to other parts of the paper. These were important aspects of journalistic practices that were being laid down for generations to come, and in some cases helped contribute to the idea of the sports department and its journalists running largely unchecked fiefdoms within newspaper organisations. Leonard Koppett, a distinguished sportswriter for over 50 years, recalls the sense of liberation he enjoyed as a sports columnist when he joined the *New York Post* in the 1950s: 'We had total "artistic" freedom, encouraged to be amusing, allowed to be opinionated ... This was heaven for a writer. We could do anything we wanted, any way we wanted, as long as it was amusing or informative for the reader' (2003: 113).

Of course, in reality sports coverage in US newspapers continually shifted and changed as the papers themselves adapted to a changing media market and increased competition from initially radio and later television, and more recently, as we note later in the book, the arrival of the Internet.

THE POPULAR PRESS AND SPORTS CHATTER

In his study of the popular press, Conboy (2004: 54) argues that the ability of sporting narratives to be woven into a wider fabric of popular history was a key element in popularising newspapers with a growing readership. The newspapers that emerged from New York in the 1880s and 1890s were characterised by entertainment and information. As Oriard (1993: 60) has argued: 'As part of the entertainment function of the mass-circulation dailies, sport both benefited from and contributed to the newspaper revolution of the era; sports coverage attracted readers, who in turn looked to daily newspapers to satisfy their growing desire for more and more sport.' Thus newspapers quickly realised that the sports event, while crucial, was only part of the pleasure that this particular cultural form offered. The build-up to events could take weeks or even months in some cases and thus filled acres of newspaper space, both reflecting and creating the culture and language of sports talk among the fans/readers. This would be a process that radio and then television would attempt to reproduce in due course and it would be intensified with the advent of dedicated sports television channels with hours of airtime to fill and keen to engage in extensive amounts of what Eco (1986) would call 'sports chatter'.

The commercial value to a newspaper of sports journalism was well recognised by editors (many of whom had little interest in sport themselves), thus sporting empires were built within newspapers and sports journalists began to evolve their own particular codes and practices, often with little interaction with other journalists on the paper. Sports journalists were more likely to hang out with other sports journalists. However, as Goldlust notes:

> As with other specialist fields of journalism, there emerged a number of writers of considerable literary skill who brought to the genre of sports reporting a thoughtful, articulate and broadly philosophical approach, rooted both in the classical tradition and the nineteenth century ideals that saw sport as potentially ennobling to the human spirit and an expression of 'civilised progress'. (1987: 72)

As these well-educated US sportswriters drew from other areas of popular culture to illustrate their point or back up an argument, they reshaped the boundaries of sports journalism in a manner that was largely absent from the British experience. American sportswriters were often encouraged to extend their linguistic range ('to jazz it up a bit') on the sports pages, often in direct contrast to the rather staid prose of the rest of the paper. The British experience was different. As media commentator and former newspaper editor Roy Greenslade has suggested:

> We (in Britain) haven't approached anything like the freedom of expression that American sportswriters have where they can wander and they can indulge in whimsy. Even in the broadsheets that hasn't been so obvious. Also because in America sports are accepted as interchangeable, so you get the football, and baseball and the basketball and Americans watch all three of those sports. In Britain these are very separate areas. Also Americans have always had a lot of space in their newspapers and they've had a long tradition of lengthy writing on sport, going back to Damon Runyon, they allowed them that relaxed space. (Interview with author, 6 October 2004)

What was really significant in US sports writing was this mixing of popular idioms and wider cultural points of reference in the sports pages. However, it is also important to note how the commercial shape of the distinctive American and British print media markets shapes the wider contours of sports journalism. As sportswriter Richard Williams of the London-based *Guardian* notes:

> When you go to the Olympics or Wimbledon, where there are a lot of US sports journalists you really see how different the culture is. The British sports journalism culture is much more questioning, much more confrontational and that's driven by the nature of the newspaper industry. We are much more demanding of the journalist, they have to come up with stories. Indeed there is at times a mutual incomprehension between the US and British sports journalism cultures. (Interview with author, 10 March 2005)

In British sports journalism the class and market divisions between tabloid and broadsheet journalism were a significant feature, each with a marked and distinctive terrain and stylistic mode of address. As is discussed later in the book, it is the blurring of these once distinctive boundaries since the mid-1990s that is a major aspect of contemporary sports journalism.

Chandler (1996: 243) argues that at the core of much of the US style of sports writing was a concern with, 'the virtues of sportsmanship, teamwork, hard work, and coming back from adversity'. It was also a world characterised not by any class-based elitism but, rather, by a meritocratic ethos in which, if you had the talent and worked hard, anyone could be the champion and enjoy the financial rewards that the increasingly commercial professional world of US sport offered. There are also clearly shifts in the modes of address used by sportwriters to connect with their readerships at differing historical moments. Oriard (2001: 32) argues that: 'Sportswriters of the 1960s and beyond charged the generations of both Grantland Rice and Red Smith with taking sport both too seriously and too lightly; on the one hand, making heroes of athletes, on the other, pretending that sports were only games.' He argues that from the 1960s the contemporary sportswriter was interested in the wider social, cultural, economic position of sport, whereas since the 1920s, the predominant style of sports writing had an intimacy and visual flair that should not be underestimated in terms of its power and impact, that 'sportswriting before the age of television had to help readers see the games and players' (Oriard, 2001: 32). In this respect it is not difficult to understand how the ideological underpinning of much of this style of sports writing chimed with a readership imbued with the myths of the American dream and in this context helps explain the universality of both sport and sports writing in American popular cultural life (Fountain, 1993; Inabinett, 1994). Oriard (1993, 2001) convincingly argues that the popular press in America played a key role in helping to popularise sport across a disparate nation and helped to create a truly national sports culture.

By way of contrast, in Britain a more class-bound sporting and journalistic ethos existed and Holt has argued that:

> The progress of sport as a 'commodity' either to be sold to the media in its own right or to be used in order to sell other products was slower and more halting than might be imagined. ... The press reflected the living culture of the people; it could influence opinion and reinforce existing attitudes but it did not create new forms of entertainment and rarely attempted to alter the habits or loyalties of its readership. (1989: 306–7)

While this is true, it perhaps also underplays the role that the media had in transforming the cultural forms that it came into contact with. The newly emerging mass circulation press had covered sports such as football in the latter part of the 19th century; however, it remained relatively low key, with league games themselves not regularly attracting gates of more than 20,000 (Kelly, 1988: 7). Without the step change in newspaper coverage of the sport and the extensive national exposure given to the game, it is unlikely that football would have grown at the rate that it did.

THE BRITISH POPULAR PRESS AND SPORT

While the growing popular press in the UK at the turn of the 20th century certainly did not invent sport, their engagement with it, their ability to create and shape meaning around it, and the process of widespread dissemination of 'news' associated with sporting events all began to transform what was understood to be the position of sport in society.

Kelly (1988: 8) has argued that it was not until around 1900 that newspapers began to seriously devote space to covering football. He goes on to say that the twin drivers of changing print technology, which allowed substantial developments in photo-journalism, and rising educational standards resulting in more working-class people being able to read, helped to extend newspaper readerships and with it their coverage of football in particular. In many ways, the *Daily Mirror*, symbolises the beginning of the tabloid newspapers' relationship with football in the UK. Although originally launched in 1903 as a paper for women and produced by the first female editor of a national newspaper, Mary Howarth (Horrie, 2003: 17–18), it would be under its relaunched guise a year later as the *Illustrated Daily Mirror* that sports and sports photography would quickly become an important part of its 'new journalism'.

The growth of football journalism also facilitated the development of a hinterland of commercial activity, from gambling to merchandising, around sport which would not have been as extensive or national without the popular press. While the press did not invent football, they changed it by amplifying its importance and helping to create its heroes.

Of course, it is important to remember, as Brookes (2002) has pointed out, that much of the daily reporting of sport was – and is – mundane and ephemeral; with its focus on statistics and the reporting of events. However, as far back as 1905, and Britain's first £1000 football transfer, football journalism was extending beyond the remit of simple match and results reporting. Transfer dealings and the attendant speculation associated with this part of the industry started to become an established part of this element of sports journalism. Kelly (1998: 8) notes that when David Jack signed for Arsenal in 1928 for the then massive fee of £10,000, it was carried on the front pages of the popular tabloid newspapers. Indeed this fixation with statistics and facts and figures, which characterises many aspects of sporting culture, would neatly dovetail with the requirements of the emerging news agencies that would play a key role in helping to standardise sports coverage across national, and in some cases international, boundaries. The newswire services thus played an important role in the development of sports coverage and patterns of journalistic coverage. In the USA, for example, the Associated Press, United Press and the International News service all helped supply sports copy, statistics and photographs and in so doing 'produced a degree of uniformity in newspapers throughout the country' (Oriard, 2001: 26). In return, sports coverage was an important element in the establishment and success of the wire services.

As early as the 1930s, popular newspapers in the UK were cultivating the star sports columnist. The *Daily Mirror* had Peter Wilson who had originally been at the advertising agency J. Walter Thompson (Tunstall, 1996: 172). Ken Jones, who arrived at the paper in 1958 and who would enjoy a distinguished career as a sportswriter, recalls that: 'From his lofty perch Peter Wilson cast a stern eye over sport, his huge ego nourished by immoderate projection and the patronage of the Mirror's editorial director, Hugh Cudlipp. He was "The World's No 1 Sports Writer" and, more famously, "The Man They Can't Gag"' (2000: 39). In marketing terms, the *Daily Mirror* was reproducing aspects of the longer US tradition which had seen sportswriters such as Ring Lardner carry his own byline and become a star writer with the *Chicago Examiner* in 1908 (Chandler, 1996: 242). While in New York, sportswriters such as Heywood Broun and Damon Runyon held sway as two of the key journalists on papers in that city.

It was also the case in Britain that sports journalism, certainly up to the 1950s, displayed many of the characteristics evident in the American 'Golden Age' that began in the 1920s. While journalists did not roam across different sports in the way they did in the USA, most were closely associated with football, or cricket or rugby, they did play a key role (in association with radio coverage of sport) in helping to foster sporting myths and ideals ranging from the construction of sports stars to national sporting events.

Jones (2000: 42) argues that by the 1960s a more rigorous style of journalism began to be associated with British popular sports coverage, one in which, 'we [journalists] were encouraged to debunk heroes and myths that didn't stand up to scrutiny, measuring athletes as people as well as performers'. However, in sections of the British press around this time, sports journalists were still kept largely hidden away by the newspapers. The range of sports covered reflected the class-based divisions in the newspaper market, with the broadsheet press far less interested in a sport such as football, with its large working-class audience, than the popular press. When Brian Moore, later to become better known as a distinguished football commentator and broadcaster, joined the sports desk on *The Times* in the late 1950s, he recalls that the paper:

> had a style firmly rooted in the past. No sportsman or sportswomen ever had a Christian name but amateurs were allowed their initials. So it would be Matthews, Lawton and Hutton, but P.B.H. May, T.E. Bailey and Dr. R.G. Bannister. Writers had no names either. Readers were, for example, informed about football anonymously with articles from 'Our Association Football Correspondent', who was at the time the eloquent Geoffrey Green. (1999: 39)

As is discussed in later chapters, the deferential approach of this newspaper is ironic given the key role that *The Times* would play in the rebirth of sports journalism in the 1990s, signifying the extent to which sport would become a staple diet of content for newspapers across the market.

Of course, central for sportswriters and sports journalists until the age of television was the fact that one of their primary roles was to describe the game to readers who were not at the live event. Oriard in his overview of American sports writing around football in that country notes that with the arrival of television as the primary media for the sports fan:

> The sportswriting we read today is written for fans who already know the scores and probably saw the highlights on *SportsCenter*. Sportswriting has become an adjunct to

television, its primary role now to find the story behind the story, not to recreate sporting events for fans who could not attend them. (2001: 32)

In this same vain, Humphries associates this period as marking the end of what was nostalgically referred to as the golden age of sports writing. He suggests:

Traditionally, we blame television for shrinking us. Television came and made our trade less relevant. The box sucked the colour right from our cheeks. Words became less important. Punch was what counted. Punch early and punch often. We assume readers to have the attention span of babies. We assume that they'd rather be watching television. We adapted to the challenge with the appropriate pace of portrait artists struggling through the era of the disposable camera. (Humphries, 2003: 6)

However, there has always been a substantial element of mediation in any journalistic process. Sports journalism is about the interpretation of real events and making sense of them for a range of readerships. Depending on what particular section of the newspaper market one is working in, this can involve varying degrees of embellishment or sensationalism. This began to change with the arrival of substantial sports coverage on television, in the USA by the 1950s and in Britain a decade or so later, and signalled a step change in print sports journalism. As more sport became accessible to a wider audience through television, the cultural parameters within which newspapers operated were also shifting.

Both Engel (1996) and Marr (2004) have noted how there has been a long tradition of sensationalist and scurrilous journalism within the British newspaper market that stretches back into the 19th century. However, there is little doubt that the 1960s saw changes among newspapers that have directly shaped print sports journalism ever since. A growing commercial dimension in sport, the rise of the role of television and an internationalisation of the sporting arena all helped to reshape the back page of national newspapers. In addition, wider structural and cultural shifts in the print media industry saw the emergence of a more aggressive, less deferential form of tabloid journalism. Holt and Mason argue that:

From the 1960s the popular dailies went consciously downmarket and their sports coverage went with them. Sports journalism went in two directions; there was an impressive expansion of lively and serious writing about sport, mostly from the 'quality press', and a headlong rush into scandal in the 'middle market' papers like the *Mail* and the *Express* as well as the tabloids. Like the quality press they were no longer able to rely on match reports to sell newspapers. Sensing the enormous public interest in the people behind the performances, the mass press threw itself into a frenzy of speculation, gossip and sensationalism. (2000: 118)

Thus the foundations for the contemporary landscape of sports journalism were being laid during this period. For some commentators, such as Roy

Greenslade, it would be the 1980s before the final significant structural break-up of the relationship between the tabloid press and sports stars would occur; however, it is clear that these shifts were being sent in train during the late 1960s when it was becoming more commonplace for the print media to carry sports-related stories that were no longer solely confined to the back page of a newspaper.

Whannel (2002) has documented the role played by the print media in the construction of the modern sporting hero. What differentiates this process of myth-building from that outlined earlier in the chapter is the extent to which the print media became increasingly intertwined in a relationship with television from the 1960s onwards, drawing on the latter as a source of news stories. In this process they, of course, promote and build awareness among the wider public of television stars and their private off-screen lives.

While the sports stars of the late 1960s and 1970s were, by today's standards, relatively poorly paid, the elite still enjoyed a considerably higher media profile than previous generations. The creeping commercialisation of sport, which really accelerated during the 1960s (Whannel, 1992), helped to open up a new range of commercial opportunities for certain sportspeople, but only if their sport was receiving television exposure, and by association coverage in the print media. As the sports and the media industries changed, so too did the working environment for sports journalists in the UK.

THE PROFESSIONAL SPORTS JOURNALIST

In his ground-breaking study into specialist journalist correspondents carried out in the 1960s and published in 1971, Tunstall focused on football as one of the categories most identified with playing a key role in newspaper circulation. He noted that:

> *Football* reporting was well established in 1900, but confined largely to matches. By the 1950s Football journalism paid much more attention to personalities, tactics, and transfers. In the 1960s Football often led the sports pages of popular dailies six days a week – although the matches were concentrated on only two days a week. (Tunstall, 1971: 88)

The rise of the football or sports correspondent saw a shift in simply reporting the game or match towards covering events in and around football, tennis or cricket. The 1960s saw the increasing rise of sports comment and opinion as a central element of sports journalism. This process was accentuated by the rising popularity of television and the key role that sport, and football in particular, began to exert in the television schedules during this decade. For some journalists this marks a qualitative shift in the practice and nature of sports journalism.

Greenslade suggests that by the 1980s a substantive change in sports journalism and its attendant culture had taken place. He argues that during this period the tabloid newspapers began to flex their muscles in a way they had not done previously with regard to sports coverage:

> Newspapers were largely baronies, so sport would have one, features would have one and news would have one. And the editor would make sure they all had their space and that they operated separately. What you gradually saw in the popular press was that editors began to impose on the barons and telling them what they should do. And when the barons didn't do it, they would be replaced. So for instance, at the *Sun*, the sports editor from 1969, when Murdoch took it over until 1981, was Frank Nicklin who still believed in the 1960s' ethos that sports was separate from news, you were not nasty in reporting and he loved sports and the paper reflected this.
>
> If you look at the *Sun* from 1981 onwards, the editor takes the view that we must be more critical, more edgy, and you see a gradual transformation. Reporting is no longer enough, things are shown on television. Every match report now had to be about what the manager thought of the game, what you thought of the manager, what the players thought of the game, and you see the growth of quotes, which is part of the process of conflict, as often these quotes are not liked. Then you get reporters deciding to be commentators, they are encouraged to give their opinion and their point of view and slant things. This is the crucial time in the 1980s when you see the growth of the large headlines in the sports pages. Fact moves into opinion. And they set off conflict by slagging off X against Y. (Interview with author, 6 October 2004)

It is also clear that this more competitive and aggressive form of journalism impacted on sections of the broadsheet press and their sports coverage. Reflecting on the rise of the 'quotes culture' mentioned above, Williams argues that up until the 1980s:

> quotes were an irrelevance for the broadsheets, no one was interested. If you had a piece by John Woodcock in *The Times*, it was pure John Woodcock, it would not have a quote in it. *The Times* would not carry a quote from anyone involved with that sporting event. It now became much more driven by quotes.
>
> Okay, I am employed for my views and the way that I put them, but I still use quotes. Now at big events you might have three or four people there and you divide up the function, twenty years ago there would be one person there. Now there are distinct areas to be covered. So quotes become one way of differentiating out tasks.
>
> Ironically, the people watching on television will have seen more of the match than I will have, and that's particularly true of rugby matches. They have loads of camera angles, and we will not have a monitor. So there are two things you can give them. One is a view of the event; an interpretative view of the event, or you can give them voices from the event.
>
> It's the one thing we still do better than TV. They will give you the sound bites; we will be able to give a bit more depth on an event. (Interview with author, 10 March 2005)

There was another more insidious dimension to this fixation with quotes. For sportswriters such as Hugh McIlvanney of *The Sunday Times* this was the start of a process that hinted at a lack of faith in the ability of the sports journalist to trust their own judgement, He argues:

> If they [newspapers] can attach a platitude to a big name its more important than an intelligent judgement from one of their own guys. Journalists have almost lost the use of their own judgement because they've spent so much time relying on seeing the game through a prism of the reactions of a big player or manager. These reactions are almost always self-serving. (*The Independent*, 2005c)

The 1980s also marks the end of the close relationship that had existed between sports journalists and the sports stars they reported on. As money flowed into the higher echelons of professional sport from television, the cultural and financial gap between journalists and sports stars grew apace. As Patrick Collins, chief sportswriter with the *Mail on Sunday*, recalls, the days in the 1960s when the top players would happily go for a drink with members of the press pack have long gone:

> Although the players would buy their rounds, the reporters would buy more than their share, since they could claim entertainment expenses. Fast forward 40 years and we see that young Steven Gerrard of Liverpool has signed a contract which pays him £55,000 a week, that Sol Campbell of Arsenal earns more than £60,000 a week, and that David Beckham's wealth is assessed at some £50million. These people could not only buy a round, they could buy the pub, then bid for the brewery. And that makes a difference. In the smoky democracy of the Bell and Hare, distinguished footballers like Jimmy Greaves could tell football writers what had really happened that afternoon; how well they had succeeded or how badly they had failed. Sure, they would say the writers didn't understand, that they criticised with insufficient knowledge. And they were probably right. But the writers would point out their own difficulties, involving the urgency of deadlines, the paucity of facilities and the need to arrive at swift conclusions. Lobby terms prevailed, experiences were exchanged and, ideally, a kind of mutual enlightenment dawned.
>
> These exchanges are now conducted by staged press conferences or copy controlled interviews. Players can no longer confide their problems to sympathetic ears, while writers are no longer privy to the stresses of the professional game. And, since they cannot appreciate those problems, they cannot convey them to the reader. In short, everybody loses. Perhaps I simplify the dilemma. It is not quite true that a young football writer could go through an entire career without ever meeting an international footballer in an informal, social surrounding. But it is truer than it used to be. (2003: 51)

As we discuss in Chapter 5, this changing relationship between the journalist and the sports people they are writing about became one of the most significant features of the contemporary celebrity-driven sports journalism culture.

By the 1980s, tabloid editors were keen to 'bust' the cosy club between players and journalists. As Greenslade notes:

> They would say [to sports journalists] don't tell me you are one of them. So the busting open of the club meant that, say, England managers, for example, would be given a hard

time. Ron Greenwood was probably the last to just about keep the press onside. And then every manager becomes a target. (Interview with author, 6 October 2004)

For some sports journalists, such as Ken Jones, who moved from the tabloid *Sunday Mirror* to the newly emerging broadsheet *The Independent* in the mid-1980s, there was a sense that while sports journalists in the early part of the century had been too deferential to their subjects and too complicit in sentimental myth-making, that by the 1980s a cruder ideological outlook, driven by commercial imperatives, was demeaning the craft. Jones argues that this outlook:

> speaks of bias and jingoism and affiliations that would have brought a frown to the faces of people I learned from. In the last of his 63 years, a famed American sportswriter, Jimmy Cannon, made a statement that I have earnestly endeavoured to follow. Crippled by a stroke, but still hard and brave, Cannon said, 'Sportswriting has survived because of the guys who didn't cheer.' (2000: 41–2)

By the 1980s, television's influence on sport, and on football in particular, had substantially increased. This decade also saw the introduction for the first time in Britain of the regular live broadcasting of English top-class league matches (Boyle and Haynes, 2004). This intensified the pressure on newspaper football journalists that had been identified by Tunstall as far back as the 1960s. He argued that: 'The frequent televising of Football did little damage to the news reporting of the subject. It was, however, an additional pressure towards behind-the-scenes newsgathering – rather than event reporting' (Tunstall, 1971: 92).

The amount of football on television in the 1960s was tiny (with regular live matches almost non-existent) when compared to what was available by the 1990s, with the advent of dedicated satellite and digital sports channels. Thus the rise of television coverage of sport had a significant impact on the newspaper industry, and by association aspects of journalistic practice on the sports pages.

The 1980s intensified the focus on star players and managers, many enjoying a higher media profile as the result of more extensive television coverage and a newspaper market, particularly at the tabloid end, that had become increasingly competitive and driven by sensationalist tendencies. This was the decade that finally saw the blurring of distinction between fact and comment in many parts of the sports pages. Transfer speculation is a good example of a shifting in the relations between journalists, players and clubs. While clubs, and managers in particular, have long had preferred or favourite journalists to whom tit-bits of information could be leaked, thus often helping to create a climate of opinion around a particular player, this relationship became complicated by the increasing money from television flowing into the game and to the star players, and the rise of professional agents.

A situation akin to the wider entertainment industries developed, where agents, whose prime aim was to get the best deals and moves for their clients, began to exert greater influence in the management of news regarding their client. This process began to undermine the traditional vice-like grip that clubs had exercised over players and their potential movement and earning power within the industry. The 'planting' of stories about player unrest and potential interest in players from other clubs became more commonplace, as journalists found themselves being targeted by various sources, including players, agents and clubs, in a more formalised manner than the previous more informal network of contacts. In the football industry, many clubs were unprepared for the growing routinisation of news that began to develop in the 1980s and intensified in the following decade. A combination of the rise of media outlets all wanting information, increased competition in media markets for football-related news, the extension and stretching of both the news agenda and deadlines all began to alter relations between clubs, players, journalists and their audiences (see Chapter 5).

One of the key factors reshaping the wider environment within which sports journalism in the UK operated at this time was the gradual re-regulation of British broadcasting that began in the 1980s and increasingly positioned the market, as opposed to public service, at its core. As sport, and football in particular, became the 'key media product' of the 1990s this had a significant impact on print media football journalists.

THE BEAT JOURNALIST

Historically, as in other journalistic fields, the contacts book has been an important aspect in the culture of the sports journalist. As Goldlust notes:

> Most astute team owners, managers, officials and athletes themselves nurtured close friendships with selected reporters, eager to cooperate in providing them with 'inside' stories, interviews, leads and angles, well aware of the generous benefits to gate receipts that accrued from the free publicity they received from the newspapers' decision to treat sport as 'news'. (1987: 73)

Sports such as football have always enjoyed a high profile in the popular press, and the press have amplified the profile of the game's star players and managers. Yet, while the advent of television money into sport has fundamentally helped reshape the relationship between journalist and player, the culture of contacts and inside information remains an important characteristic of journalistic culture both in sports reporting and other arenas of journalism.

The rise of more formal public relations practice in sport and other areas of society, as organisations have professionalised their communication practice and attempt to control the flow of information to the media, is one of the significant changes in the culture of contemporary journalism.

Writing in the late 1980s, Kelly argued that: 'Football journalists work under enormous pressures. The daily grind of producing news to fill the back pages is never easy, but sometimes leads to excesses with over-familiar clichés, unnecessary speculation and reluctance to expose the humbug of players, managers and chairman' (1988: 9).

This period also saw the beginning of a growth in sports features, commentary and analysis as the popular press responded to the increasing control that television exerted over sport. As institutional change in the industry accelerated with the breaking of union control of large sections of Fleet Street in the 1980s, technological changes also put a relentless pressure on copy deadlines for the sporting press. The rise of the sports press pack became increasingly prominent during this period, as those members of a particular beat, such as football, found themselves not only competing with each other for stories, but also acting as a support network of gossip information and as a reference point to cross-check stories.

The beat system has been particular strong in the UK sports press and the sportswriters who have moved from one sporting milieu to another are rare. One such writer, Hugh McIlvanney, talking about his work on covering horse racing self-deprecatingly calls himself an 'occasional interloper' into the sport (BBC, 1991). Those journalists who prefer not to travel with the 'pack' are also the exception. In his overview of the racing press Magee has noted that:

> as in other branches of journalism – including politics – it is those who stand outside the pack who often make the most impact. Peter (now Sir Peter) O'Sullevan was widely known as racing's greatest television commentator, but his career as a print journalist was as distinguished. From the early 1950s onwards, his contacts – especially in France and Ireland, which few other British journalists were much concerned with – were unrivalled, and yielded plenty of long-odds winners as well as juicy stories. In those days a top-rate racing tipster was a major asset for a newspaper such as the *Daily Express*, and the handcuffs with which O'Sullevan was kept on that paper were 24-carat gold. O'Sullevan made his mark by not hunting with the pack and by nurturing the right contacts. (2004: 46)

If avoiding the sports pack was slightly easier for those journalists working at the broadsheet end of the market, those operating at the popular press end found it virtually impossible as the commercial pressures to break stories (and equally important to make sure you did not miss any) became more acute during the 1980s.

THE REGIONAL AND LOCAL SPORTING PRESS

The beat journalist has always been an integral part of regional and local press coverage of sport. This is particularly acute on city evening papers that cover major sporting teams. In cities like Manchester and Glasgow, for example, a steady stream of stories involving the big football teams is absolutely vital for the commercial success of papers in these cities. Thus journalists like David Meek of the *Manchester Evening News* will know the beat surrounding a club such as Manchester United intimately, Ronny Cully of the *Glasgow Evening Times* will supply a regular flow of copy concerning Celtic, and Daryl King will cover the beat involving Rangers. Here the beat system offers a regular and mostly predictable rhythm of newsgathering for the local papers that also have to be careful in sustaining good relationships with the local clubs.

Indeed, sports coverage has always been an important part of the mix offered by the regional and local newspaper market in the UK. Holt (1989: 307) notes the importance of the Saturday night sporting press that developed in the major cities around the UK from the late 19th century. In Liverpool, for example, the Saturday evening paper the *Football Echo* was started as the Football League began (Kelly, 1988: 7). Meanwhile, in Glasgow three newspapers competed for a readership on a Saturday night, driven largely by the carrying of football results and match reports. There was the *Evening News*, printed on white paper, the 'green' *Evening Citizen* and the 'pink' *Evening Times*, which survives today as the city's only daily newspaper.

In many ways their decline has been rapid. For example, Saturday evenings in the 1970s would see the printing presses in Union Street in Glasgow buzzing as the Saturday edition of the *Evening Times* physically rolled off the presses at about 5.30 p.m. Amidst the noise and dirt, men would wait impatiently to collect the bundles of papers as they appeared from the presses on a carousel, snatching them and rushing to deliver them around the city. Corner shops throughout the city would be full of people waiting patiently to buy 'the special' pink edition of the paper. If both the major teams in the city – the Old Firm of Celtic and Rangers – had won, shops could expect to be sold out by 6.30 p.m. Yet by the 1990s this Saturday service had disappeared, as television and radio became the immediate points of contact for results and reports. The decline of this part of the sports press also hastened as television switched key matches from their Saturday berth, meaning that it became increasingly rare for both Old Firm teams to play on the same day. The need to read a more reflective analysis on the games has since been taken up by an extended Sunday and Monday sports press and as national newspapers, using more flexible technology, have regionalised editions this has allowed them to focus on local teams.

However, the link between sports and local media remains strong. When Liverpool football club won the 2005 UEFA Champions League, the direct impact on sales of the local press covering the event was dramatic. Sales of the *Liverpool Echo* on the day after the game were up 46 per cent, while the *Daily Post* actually doubled its sales. When the *Echo* published a victory parade supplement following the return of the team, it sold an extra 36,000 copies (*Press Gazette*, 2005b). It is also worth noting the key value that sports coverage offers to the national press at a time of overall declining sales. *The Times* sold 70,000 extra copies on the day following this Champions League Final, and when they 'rested' their Monday football supplement at the end of the season in May 2005, sales dipped, which resulted in its early reintroduction with a corresponding uplift in sales (*MediaGuardian*, 2005b).

The local radio stations that became a key element in the wider sporting discourse of a city or a region have replaced much of the immediacy of the local Saturday press. Thus the rise of the post-match phone-in, pioneered by Radio Clyde in Glasgow as far back as 1978, has become part of fan culture, with radio station's often using print media sports journalists as 'pundits' offering pre-and post-match comment and opinion.

SPORTS JOURNALISM IN A CHANGING NEWSPAPER MARKET

Previous research concerned in part with the amount of space devoted to sport in the print media has tended to focus attention on the popular end of the UK press market (Hargreaves, 1986; Rooney, 2000). In his examination of media sport in the 1980s, John Hargreaves noted the volume of copy devoted to sport, and in particular to football and horse racing in the UK tabloids. This often accounted for over a fifth of the newspapers' editorial coverage. He argued that:

> The policy is quite clearly to attract working-class readers of the sports to which they are most attached. The fact that sport is classified in the trade as a 'revenue goal', rather than an 'advertising goal', that is it increases circulation as opposed to attracting advertising directly, supports this interpretation. (1986: 139)

This is no longer strictly the case, with the advertising potential of sports journalism, particularly at the 'quality' end of the press, becoming increasingly important. Although interestingly, football remains the overwhelmingly dominant sport in terms of coverage across the entire newspaper market, and is no longer viewed as solely the preserve of the working-class reader, as the game has been re-imaged to attract more affluent media consumers.

Research by Rooney (2000: 103) reinforced the importance placed on sports coverage by the tabloids. He noted that over a 30-year period from 1968 to 1998 the level of editorial space devoted to sport in the *Sun* and the *Mirror* has remained remarkably consistent in volume from 1974; on average running at between 25 and 33 per cent of editorial space in both these newspapers (with the *Sun* carrying marginally more sport).

In more recent times, it has become clear that sport remains an important element in the brand identity of the major tabloid newspapers in the UK, from the London-based *Sun,* to the largest selling newspaper in Scotland, the *Daily Record.* While sports coverage remains a mainstay of the Sunday tabloid market, to such an extent that in 2004 a national newspaper such as the *Sunday Mirror* regularly devoted up to 38 per cent of the paper to sport. This, of course, is not to suggest that the position and role of sports journalism in the tabloid market is not subject to various market and institutional pressures, with falling sales and increased competition from other media outlets in the digital age being two major concerns for sports editors in this market.

Thus in the 21st century newspaper market sports journalism remains an important part of the brand identity of popular newspapers; however, as noted in the previous chapter, the most significant development in the last decade or so with regard to the status and position of sports journalism within the print media sector has been the growth of sports journalism at the broadsheet end of the market, a previously largely under-researched area of newspaper output.

Table 2.1 shows the average percentage of editorial space devoted to sport in a number of newspapers at the 'quality' end of the UK market between 1974 and 2004. The sample looks at the month of September in 1974, 1984, 1994 and 2004. The average total pagination of the papers is also given to highlight the overall growth in the size of newspapers since 1974. Specifically, the late 1980s saw a substantial expansion in the number of supplements carried by newspapers facilitated by the new technology heralded in after the breaking of the print unions in the mid-1980s. There was also a significant step change in newspaper layout and design, and in the use of colour. Overall, part of the expansion in the coverage of sports in the 'quality' press is explained by the sheer increase in the volume of newsprint associated with national newspapers as changing work practices and new technology facilitated the expansion in the size of newspapers. As noted in Chapter 1, this expansion in sports coverage has been viewed in some quarters as part of the more general 'dumbing down' of the 'serious' press, as more attention and space is given to sports and lifestyle journalism.

The proponents of this thesis have at times seriously underestimated the impact that the growth in the size of newspapers has had on the range of

Table 2.1 Percentage of editorial space devoted to sports coverage in the broadsheet press 1974–2004

Newspaper	1974		1984		1994		2004	
	Average % editorial space	Average total pagination	Average % editorial space	Average total pagination	Average % editorial space	Average total pagination	Average % editorial space	Averate total pagination
The Times	11	22	15	32	21	44	21	102*
The Guardian	11	22	11	28	16	44**	17	60
The Daily Telegraph	18	28	22	32	25	38	30	48

* *The Times* in 2004 was available in both broadsheet and compact format. This figure applies to the compact version.
** The mixing of broadsheet formats with tabloid supplements complicates calculating the percentage devoted to sport. For this exercise and comparative purpose, broadly speaking 2 tabloid pages equate with one broadsheet page. The *Guardian* was one of the first papers to pioneer the tabloid supplement.

content now available, with some newspapers having doubled in size since 1984. There is no doubt that sports journalism is now a more important part of this section of the UK press market than at any other time in its history and the expansion in the size of newspapers is only one of the reasons for this situation.

Across the broadsheet market there has been a marked growth in the amount of space devoted to sports in this section of the UK newspaper market. While the range of sports covered has also expanded, there is no doubt that the largest growth within the sports pages has been in football coverage. This has marked a significant departure for these papers, as the coverage of football, while prominent, has not always been the mainstay of their sports journalism output. In 1974, for example, the *Guardian* was still giving the rather antiquated byline 'Association Football' to its relatively limited coverage of the sport. The sports pages still consisted of a full horse racing card, and in the month sample used in Table 2.1, a significant prominence was being given to sports such as athletics, rugby, lawn tennis, rowing and show jumping. The growth in the range, quality and diversity of coverage of a sport such as football during the period 1974–2004 has been marked.

Aspects of the role of sports journalism in the broadsheet press began to change during the 1970s. At the *Guardian*, for example, sports journalists such as David Lacy (football) and Frank Keating (sportswriter) were key figures in helping to transform the nature of the engagement of the broadsheet print media with sports. As Matthew Engel has argued: 'In the early 1970s sports reporting in the posher papers had changed little since the days of Corinthian amateurism. A fair amount of guff passed for fine writing on the basis of magisterial judgements laced with the occasional classical quote, apposite or not' (*Guardian*, 2002). Under the guidance of Sports Editor John Samuel, the *Guardian* freshened up the manner in which the broadsheet press covered sports, ensuring that some of the best writing in the paper was to be found in the previously rather marginalised sports pages. Redesigns of the *Guardian* since the 1980s have also served to emphasise the importance of sports coverage in terms of the paper's brand. September 2005 saw it relaunch in its Berliner format (between a broadsheet and a tabloid) and for the first time in its history carry a daily sports section, signifying just how important sports journalism is to the paper.

The Daily Telegraph is another paper that has for some time recognised the importance of investing in sports journalism, in this instance in order to help attract a younger professional male readership. In recent times, the paper has even used star sports columnist and former Liverpool footballer Alan Hansen to front its 2003 'Read a bestseller everyday' advertising campaign. By 2004, almost a third of the paper was devoted to sports journalism and it had acquired a reputation as the home to some of the best sports writing in the market.

Another indication of the centrality of sports in this market was seen in 2004 when *The Times*, in its 'Biggest for Sport' advertising campaign, boasted that the newspaper now had the largest sports section of any daily newspaper in the UK. A year earlier they had launched *The Game*, their dedicated football supplement, with every Monday edition of the newspaper. This supplement offered up to 24 pages solely devoted to covering a range of issues associated with football, and while primarily focused on the English Premiership, its coverage of the Scottish and European game was impressive for a London-based daily. This explosion in football journalism in particular would have been unthinkable in this section of the market even 20 years earlier. So why this massive expansion in sports journalism in the 'quality' end of the market?

In part it has been driven by wider shifts in the media market, as newspapers have attempted to appeal to new readers and in so doing stem an overall long-term decline. This has coincided with an intensification of a longer process that has seen sport, and football in particular, become a key 'media product' for television. Driven by a combination of government-inspired re-regulation and technological change this has seen the opening up of broadcasting markets to increased competition and a more commercially orientated relationship develop between sports, media and society (Rowe, 1999; Boyle and Haynes, 2004).

Stewart (2005: 443) notes how a visit to *The Times* by its owner Rupert Murdoch in spring 1996 helped drive the ongoing expansion of sports coverage at this newspaper. Murdoch, who recognised the potential for market growth through sports and football coverage, made clear that he would allocate greater funds to expand the sports section, in part as a result of the impending Euro'96 football championship.

Some sports editors view the massive expansion in sports coverage in the broadsheet print media as simply a response to the public's substantial appetite for sports content. The *Independent's* Sport Editor Matt Tench thus feels that newspapers have simply responded to the public need by filling this gap in the newspaper market. He argues that: 'A significant percentage of the public is consumed by sport and as a newspaper we have to respond to this, and as a result sport has become an important part in the selling of the newspaper's image' (interview with author, 21 September 2004).

Significantly, however, this analysis underplays the role that expanded sports coverage in the newspaper market has played in helping to fuel this interest. In short, expanded newspaper coverage of sport has helped to create a more general climate where sport and sports stars enjoy a substantially higher public profile than in previous generations. A crucial point here is the unique impact made by the expanded role of television coverage. Far from crippling sports journalism in the print media, the growth of sports broadcasting and online coverage has actually helped drive readers to the print media. In turn, this coverage helps sustain the profile of sport and stars across other non-print media platforms. The rise of lifestyle and celebrity-informed journalism and the range of commercial and cultural factors that are driving this have also helped to feed into this process (Turner, 2004).

Sportswriter Graham Spiers of *The Herald* is in little doubt that changes within sports journalism have been marked. He suggests:

> There are many changes. Huge changes from sportswriters from the mid-1970s until now. It's often unfair to judge as they operated in differing eras, but sportswriters then were much more ignorant of the scene and less European in outlook. Chief sportswriters, the No 1s on newspapers in the main, like me will write when I want, what I want, with complete autonomy. Whereas some of the tabloid guys are ordered what to write, they have copy re-written. It's a rule of thumb in tabloids that your copy can be re-written by someone. Whereas what I write is what goes into print. (Interview with author, 13 December 2004)

There is little doubt that a growing literate fan base for sports writing has also fuelled the growing commercial importance of sports journalism in the broadsheet market.

Sports such as football have seen a massive injection of television money pour into the industry since 1992 in a manner that has facilitated the creation of a generation of footballing millionaires. This group has fascinated both the 'popular' and the 'serious' newspapers, and, apparently, their readers since the mid-1990s, although, of course, it should be noted that much of this coverage has been generated not by sports journalists for the sports pages but by journalists interested in the private lives of the stars, and as such stories about them are as likely to appear on the front pages of the papers as they are on the back.

David Chappell, sports editor at *The Times* from 1993 to 2004, sees the expansion in sports coverage in this section of the UK press as partly being a result of internal changes and competition within the broadsheet market, developments in print technology and wider cultural shifts in the profile of sport, and football in particular. He notes that when a new editor arrived at *The Times*:

> His [Peter Stothard's] challenge to me was I'm not going to argue about the number of pages you've got. Make good use of them and we will take the argument on from there. In 1993, we had four broadsheet pages per day, six on a Saturday morning and seven on a Monday morning. That space will have doubled on a day-to-day basis. So we laid to rest the claim that sports journalists were less critical. I think this was always a bit of a myth.

> Add to this the arrival of Murdoch and Sky and increased television exposure and all the papers had to react. In 1993 we had two full-time football writers on the staff and freelancers. We now (2004) have 12 full time and freelancers all over the country.
>
> In addition, the Eric Cantona event [when he attacked a fan in the crowd in 1995] moved sport on to the front pages and made the news. There was a new mood and news values changed with the chattering classes talking about the Eric Cantonas of the world. *The Times* had to respond to this, and Euro 96 helped to win over editors about the editorial and commercial value of sport. (Interview with author, 8 October 2004)

During the 1982 FIFA World Cup in Spain, *The Times* devoted about half a page to coverage of the event (Stewart, 2005: 205). This, at a time when horse racing received a full page of coverage. The expansion in coverage of sport during the 1990s has been significant and dramatic.

CONCLUSION

Print sports journalism adapts and changes, as indeed does the wider newspaper market to the arrival and consolidation of each new wave of media development and its wider social impact. While television offers the immediacy of the live sports event, it is the scene-setting, the pre- and post-event analysis and any attendant scandal or controversy that newspapers are able to help sustain and run with.

In his overview of the British press since 1945, Greenslade notes the key role played by sports coverage in the creation, during the 1970s under the ownership of Rupert Murdoch, of that quintessential contemporary tabloid the *Sun* newspaper. He argues that:

> Sport was a key ingredient, despite the *Sun*'s inability to publish reports of evening matches in northern cities. Unlike its rivals, with Manchester and, in most cases, Scottish print runs, every *Sun* was printed in London. This meant that early editions were off the stone and on the trains before a ball was kicked. To compensate, sports editor Frank Nicklin developed features-based content and shrewdly hired George Best, then at the height of his footballing and nightclubbing fame, as a columnist. Such was the *Sun*'s pulling power, the absence of live sport didn't seem to matter. (2003: 250)

The last decade or so in the UK has seen the intensification of the process by which a number of elite sports have been to all intents and purposes colonised by television and organisations such as Sky, which by 2004/5 was spending over £720m a year on sport compared with a BBC budget of £290m. This expansion in the amount of sport now available on either terrestrial or satellite digital television has clearly had an impact on broadcast sports journalism. Yet print sports journalism remains a key component in the range of content that newspapers, in all sections of an increasingly competitive market, deliver to their readerships.

When Urs Meier, the Swiss referee, disallowed what appeared to be a legitimate goal for England in their quarter final match with Portugal at the Euro 2004 football championships, an incident watched live by millions on television, the subsequent campaign against him, which ran for weeks after the event, was largely sustained and orchestrated by the press. Indeed, such was the ferocity and impact that this print media campaign had, it led the doyen and elder statesman of British sports writing Hugh McIlvanney to comment that:

> Self-congratulation over the avoidance of serious hooligan activity by England support-ers at Euro 2004 has proved to be premature. The tattooed brigade may have kept them-selves in check but the same can hardly be said of the better-dressed nationalist cadres serving some of our tabloid newspapers. Urs Meier, the Swiss referee who disallowed the goal by Sol Campbell against Portugal … has been hounded in his own country, branded 'a love-rat' and casually granted the status of 'the most hated man in England'. The publicity has scarcely discouraged a flow of death threats. Poor Meier now knows that the laptop can be deadlier than the knuckleduster. (*The Sunday Times*, 2004b)

Some media commentators, such as Tunstall (1996: 194), have argued that television will emphasise the positive around a televised sports event because it has a potential vested financial interest in ensuring that the event proves to be popular with viewers and/or subscribers. He also suggests that newspapers, by way of contrast, can be more negative about an event, with a fine line existing between the role of sports journalism as a form of sports promotion and critical journalism.

The growing colonisation of elite sport in the UK by BSkyB (Boyle and Haynes, 2000: 206–20) and the aggressive cross-promotion of the satellite channel through the stable of News International newspapers, has highlighted the impact that the increasingly complex political economy of media sport is having on sports journalism. It is worth noting that by the 1990s as television rights for sporting events spiralled, driven by competition between terrestrial and satellite broadcasters for key 'media content', the sports pages became increasingly politicised with regard to the merits of the various deals. Thus the *Sun*, part of the Murdoch media empire along with BSkyB, could be guaran-teed to support the retention of live English Premiership football by BSkyB, while its tabloid rival the *Mirror* often highlighted the problems for fans that Sky's dominance of the game was causing.

With regard to the influence of the US tradition of sports writing on the UK press, it has been argued by Coleman and Hornby that:

> American sportwriters have always had opportunities to stretch out a bit, mull things over, use the room that a three-or four-thousand-word piece will buy them; our [British] best sports journalists by contrast, have traditionally been chained to the treadmill of daily journalism – eight-hundred-word responses to yesterday's or today's sporting events. (1996: 3)

Indeed, those cultural differences run deeper, not only in the differing traditions associated with journalism per se in the US and Britain, but also in the cultural position afforded sports and popular culture in general in America. The imprint of class on the British sporting landscape has shaped, and been shaped by, the sports media culture that is so symbiotically tied to sports.

However, as we have seen above, this situation began to change in the 1990s. Greenslade suggests that: 'we are in the foothills of this development because our broadsheets have only really embraced sports writing in the last ten years; I think that this will grow in Britain' (interview with author, 6 October 2004).

There may also be a certain irony that the early 21st century sees such a plethora of sports writing and journalism about sport in the UK press in an age when journalism itself appears in crisis. However, the economics of the newspaper industry is, of course, crucial for understanding the historical position of sports journalism within the wider journalistic field. As Brookes, (2002: 33) has suggested: 'Sport has been seen as economically crucial because it is a means of attracting male readers (particularly younger, affluent ones) to buy a particular newspaper title day after day, and this is reflected in the levels of investment that goes into staffing.' If sports journalism matters as never before to newspapers, part of this is down to the fact that broadcasting relentlessly promotes and profiles a core of elite sports. The impact of this process on broadcast sports journalism is examined in the following chapter.

SPORTS JOURNALISM OR SPORTS BROADCASTING?

Newspapers may have been able to make Stanley Matthews, Tommy Lawton and Billy Wright into household names, but television could turn them into stars.

Stephen F. Kelly (1988: 8) *Back Page Football: A Century of Newspaper Coverage.* **London: Queen Anne Press.**

There is print sports journalism, there is broadcasting and then there is the sports pundit.

Graham Spiers Sportswriter, *The Herald* **(interview with author, 13 December 2004).**

You have got to play to your own strengths and do the things they [television] don't do. Interviewing on television in sport is usually an absolute farce. Every question's a cap of honour. I think we [print journalists] can do better than that.

Hugh McIlvanney, Sportswriter, *Sunday Times***, interviewed in** *The Independent,* **5 December 2005.**

If the print media has been viewed as the home of sports journalism, then both television and radio coverage of sport has often been classified as a form of broadcasting rather than journalism. This chapter focuses specifically on this issue and examines the changing interrelationship between print sports journalism and the audio-visual media.

In this part of the book we look at the historical position of sports journalism within the broader context of broadcast journalism within both the public service and the commercial broadcast sectors. In so doing, this chapter traces the key role that aspects of sports journalism have played in local radio and how its importance to national radio across the UK has significantly developed, particularly in the last decade or so.

This chapter also analyses the impact that the increased competition in the television marketplace of the 1990s has had on the role and the position of sports journalism within both public service broadcasting and commercial television. At the core of this chapter is a debate about whether sports broadcasting constitutes a form of sports journalism.

BROADCASTING, SPORTS JOURNALISM AND ENTERTAINMENT

A significant distinction needs to be drawn between sports broadcasting and sports journalism. The relationship between broadcasting and sport is one that has been characterised by both a mutual distrust and a symbiotic reliance on each other. It has also given rise to a particular form of journalism. The importance of reporting sporting events and bringing them to an audience, through radio for example, has resulted in a process of mediation that often changed the nature of the event. Central to this process of transformation was, of course, commentary (Haynes, 1999; Boyle and Haynes, 2000: 36–8). However, while some of the key commentators of early radio also had connections with the print media, they viewed themselves not as journalists but, rather, as broadcasters, who were simply relaying the action and events to the listener at home. This served an important ideological function, in that it downplayed the impact that radio had in shaping the image of sport as a mediated form of popular culture.

In previous research (Boyle, 1992), the far from neutral impact that early sports radio broadcasting had on wider aspects of national identity formation in Ireland has been examined. In some ways there are clear parallels between the early sports broadcasters and the print sports journalists discussed in the previous chapter. For both, their key role was to report on events and disseminate this information to a wider audience, most of whom would have had no direct contact with the sporting event. The difference was, of course, the immediacy offered by radio and the 'liveness', colour and drama it brought to an event for the listener. Reflecting on the impact that a commentator such as Michael O'Hehir had on his audience when covering Gaelic Games in Ireland for example, writer Tim Pat Coogan remembers his relative disappointment on attending an All Ireland final at Croke Park in Dublin for the first time. He argued: 'Michael O'Hehir had made it all seem much more patriotic, large-scale, significant somehow' (Coogan, 1976: 52). Thus, while people like O'Hehir viewed their role simply as relaying events to the public, they clearly were part of a process that transformed sport and helped inflect it with a wider cultural and, indeed, political significance.

In the context of television, Whannel (1992) has clearly outlined the problematic position that broadcast sports occupy within production practice techniques and the ideological frames of journalism and entertainment. He argues that both television and radio coverage of sport involve the broadcasting institutions in representing often 'live' and 'actual' events, clearly involving elements of what would be recognised as journalistic practice. This also comes with an attendant concern about impartiality, balance and objectivity. It is also clear that while historically these aspects of journalism practice were applicable to sports broadcasting, in more recent times a range of commercial and cultural pressures make adherence to these principles less common, even among public service broadcasters.

RADIO DAYS: SPORT, BROADCASTING AND IDENTITY

From the outset of radio broadcasting in the 1920s, sport has been an important part of the portfolio of both public service and commercial broadcasters, so much so, that an interesting aspect of these early broadcasts was the extent to which sport was classified as 'news'. It was because of this that it was the Irish state broadcaster 2RN, (later to become Radio Eireann, and then RTE) rather than, as one would have expected at this time, the BBC, that carried the first live radio sporting event in Europe in 1926 (Boyle, 1992: 627). (The first outside broadcast in sports radio history is thought to have been a boxing event broadcast by a radio station in Pittsburgh, USA, in 1921.) Indeed, the BBC may well have been the first had it not been for the fact that it was not allowed to broadcast news before 7 p.m. in the evening as it was feared this would directly impact on sales of newspapers. While this convention was quickly changed, it is interesting to note that from the outset sports radio broadcasting was originally seen as news output, rather than simply entertainment.

The overarching institutional structure within which radio evolved and the wider political and economic framework that shaped broadcasting institutions was, of course, important in influencing attitudes to sports coverage. Gorman and McLean (2003: 61) have argued that: 'The development of radio as a commercial mass medium in the United States was also intertwined with expanding consumerism in the twentieth century. Advertising and sponsorship provided the financial basis of American radio broadcasting, and the audiences received "free to air" services as a result.' Thus, in the USA this more commercially orientated approach dovetailed with an equally commercial sporting environment that saw sports as being part of the entertainment industry, many years before this would be an accepted location for them in the UK. Therefore, the notion of impartiality in sports broadcasting was less pronounced, and, in keeping with other areas of radio output, the key driver was to secure an audience for advertisers and sponsors. By way of contrast, the BBC's radio coverage of sport was framed within a different ideological paradigm; one that positioned sport as an integral part of a particular view of national culture that the BBC was bound to promote, protect and reflect back to the 'nation'.

There were also other impacts that the commercial environment had on the BBC's style of sports broadcasting. Dan Maskell, who commentated on tennis for both BBC radio and television and was famous for his sparse but informed style of commentary, noted that:

> Our BBC style of commentary is very different from the Americans where, on all the major networks except the Public Broadcasting Service, there are commercials. Therefore the commentators in the USA have to cram all their information in to the periods between the points of a game – and sometimes even during the play which tends to irate viewers. … By BBC standards there's far too much talking and it is all far too busy – although the American public is conditioned to this approach. (1989: 303)

Other factors, such as class and cultural difference, also helped to inform the sports and sports broadcasting culture in both the USA and the UK. However, it was not until the 1960s that the commercial links between the media, sport and commerce, commonplace in the USA, would begin to transform the media–sport relationship in the UK.

RADIO SPORT AND NEWSPAPER RIVALRY

As sports radio broadcasting became part of the national sporting landscape, the negative impact on the print sports journalist was not nearly as great as had at first been anticipated. The actual number of sporting events broadcast was small in today's terms, so the written match report of, say, a football match, remained a key component of the sports pages of the national and local press. Indeed, it soon became clear that there was a mutually beneficial relationship emerging between radio coverage of sport and that of the print media.

The build-up to an event was something that the daily newspapers could amply reflect on, while unable to compete with the directness and the immediacy of the live coverage of the sporting event itself. In addition, it was the press, rather than radio, that carried the key post-match coverage and reflection on an event. Thus, it was the sportswriter in particular who helped create a wider understanding of sport and placed it within the broader sporting and cultural narratives of the day. By way of contrast, radio sports broadcasters were more concerned with the sporting moment and communicating the drama, spectacle and excitement of sport to an audience often primed for the event by newspaper coverage. It was often the case that both radio and, later, television would leave a sporting event very quickly after the result had been decided. In the UK, it was only with the advent in the 1990s of sports channels, with hours of airtime to fill, that sports television programmes stayed on air well beyond the end of the sporting contest.

However, while sports broadcasting required particular skills and ability, it was not always viewed as being part of sports journalism. In many ways being a sports broadcaster, rather than sports journalist, was an important part of giving legitimacy to an area of broadcasting that was often viewed within the BBC as slightly ephemeral and trivial. The distinguished television football commentator Brian Moore (1999), who worked initially as a football reporter with *The Times* in 1958, before moving to sport at the BBC during the 1960s and finally to ITV, noted how broadcasting controllers with little interest in sport were the bain of his life. To be identified too closely with sports journalism and sports journalists would have had an even greater impact on their perceived institutional status. In addition, while print journalists could be partisan in their outlook, the wider parameters of radio broadcasting suggested a greater degree of detachment and professional engagement with sport that was simply not associated with print sports journalism.

The Irish broadcaster Michael O'Hehir, whose career spanned radio and later television coverage of Gaelic Games between 1938 and 1985, was clear about the role of the sports commentator. O'Hehir, who also commentated on sports both for the BBC and for the US networks ABC, CBS and NBC, argued that:

> commentators must strive at all times to be neutral – no matter how deep felt his affiliations to a particular county or how strong his friendships with members of a team. This is essential if you are to convey what is happening to listeners, or viewers, without imposing your own prejudices, as distinct from critical comments, during the broadcast. (1996: 40)

Yet, as we noted with the earlier quote from Coogan (pp. 58–59), O'Hehir also transformed the event through his ability to convey and enhance the dramatic dimension of the event. Recognising this dimension, Moore (1999: 75) argued that: 'Commentating, whatever the medium, is no more than finding the right balance between describing the action, imparting the information, and adding that dash of drama and urgency that draws it all towards the realms of entertainment.' This raises an interesting debate about the relationship between sports broadcasting and sports journalism. While the role of broadcast news journalists is to convey and report on events for their audience, in sports coverage the nature of the event (sport) shapes the perception about the value of the journalism being delivered by the mediator. In the broadcasting industry, to be classified as a sports broadcaster, rather than a sports journalist (with the connotations it has with the print media), has over the years been deemed more respectable.

Despite the fact that O'Hehir's voice became synonymous with radio and television coverage of Gaelic Games and he is best remembered as a consummate broadcaster, for most of his media life he was actually a freelancer with the Irish state broadcaster Radio Eireann. His 'day job' was as a racing journalist with the *Irish Independent* newspaper. Later in his career, following a time as Head of Sport at RTE, he returned to sports writing with the Dublin-based *Sunday Press* newspaper and recognised that while sports broadcasting remained his first love, it was print sports journalism that gave him the opportunity to express his own opinions free from any constraints of impartiality or balance.

The history of BBC radio sport is populated with people, such as the Irishman Eamonn Andrews, who enjoyed a career in print sports journalism while also working in radio. Indeed Andrews, after just a few boxing commentaries for Radio Eireann in the 1940s, remembers how he went out and got business cards printed with 'broadcaster and journalist' proudly displayed on them (Andrews and Andrews, 1990: 76). Unlike many of the colleagues he worked with, Andrews saw the two professions as closely interlinked, with his journalism informing his broadcasting.

The history of television sport presents a similar mixture, for example, the cricket writer Jim Swanton, while primarily known for his cricket journalism with the *Daily Telegraph*, was also working in television giving summaries of England Test matches as early as 1953. Later, some of the key individuals who would shape British television coverage of sport, such as ITV's Head of Sport during the 1980s/1990s John Bromley, would begin their careers in print sports journalism. Bromley worked at the *Daily Herald* and later on the sports pages of the *Daily Mirror* with Michael Grade, who went on to become Chief Executive of Channel 4 Television and Chairman of the BBC.

While the print media are given licence to be partisan, the overarching framework of public service broadcasting, which informed radio and television coverage of sport in Britain for much of the 20th century, stresses notions of impartiality and balance in broadcasting output. These are difficult concepts to apply regardless of the cultural form being covered, but are especially difficult in the case of sport that inevitably is based on competition, rivalry and the joy and pain of winning or losing. This problem becomes more complex when aspects of national identity become deeply entrenched in sporting discourse when the broadcasting of sport involves international competition (Blain et al., 1993).

One of the significant changes in this area of sports broadcasting from the 1990s onwards has been the increasing abandonment of any pretext of neutrality in sports coverage as this has grown in volume, and competition between media outlets, either public service or commercial, has intensified. The proliferation of sport on both television and radio, and football in particular, has heightened this process. The increasingly regular coverage of European football competitions, such as the UEFA Champions League involving British teams on ITV and later Sky, has seen notions of broadcasting impartiality more or less abandoned in favour of support for the British team(s) involved. This process is as marked in radio's coverage of sport as it is in television's and is particularly acute in coverage of international sporting events with a British interest.

For example, when the England football team had been knocked out by hosts Portugal at Euro 2004, a decision compounded by the disallowing of an apparently legitimate England goal, Garth Crooks, a former player and BBC reporter, began his post-match interview with the England manager Sven Goran Eriksson by asking, 'Did you feel you were up against twelve men – and one of them was Swiss?' *The Sunday Times* (2004b) in its review of the tournament caustically added, 'And the BBC bill him as a "reporter"…' It is not at all clear how this line of questioning fits with any BBC notions of impartial journalistic reporting. Others have been more careful in their pronunciations. The doyen of cricket commentators, Australian Ritchie Benaud, both a trained journalist and a former sportsman has recalled how in all his years of covering Test match cricket for television and occasionally radio, he has never once referred to the Australians as 'we' (*The Sunday Times*, 2005b).

Despite such blatantly leading questions, there are clearly aspects of what we would now see as journalistic practice underpinning areas of broadcast sports output. For example, in 1948 BBC Radio launched *Sports Report*, which carried reports from up and down the country in a 30-minute slot. Such is the journalistic relevance of such a programme that it is still running in the Saturday 5 p.m. slot on BBC Radio 5 Live.

As the radio broadcasting of sport developed in the UK through the 1940s, the 'brute force of monopoly' meant that it would be the BBC who would become synonymous with sports broadcasting. As a result, the particular identities of commentators became closely associated with particular sports, for example, John Arlott with cricket and Raymond Glendenning with football and horse racing. In so doing, of course, these voices inspired the subsequent generation of sports commentators. Moore (1999) has recalled how he wanted from an early age to follow in the footsteps of Glendenning, then the major sports broadcasting voice in the country.

Eventually, of course, the growth of broadcast sport did impact on the print media and force them to bring something different to their sport's coverage. They did this by becoming a key source of information about the stars behind the events, by providing a range of narratives associated with sport that helped to build expectations in the run-up to an event, and by helping make sense of the result in the sporting aftermath and defining how it fitted into broader sporting narratives. To this extent radio and, later, television coverage of sport became interlinked with the print media; both bringing something different, but related to the reader and the viewer.

A NEW RADIO SPORTS JOURNALISM

The pre-eminence of television from the 1960s onwards in the UK saw radio coverage of sport remain important, particular at local level, but overshadowed by its more dominant visual companion. Yet by the 1970s, local radio was becoming an increasingly important element in the sporting ecology as the regulatory framework controlling the provision of radio services began to change. Scottish Radio Holdings secured only the third commercial radio licence granted in the UK (and the first outside London) to broadcast to Glasgow and the west of Scotland in the early 1970s.

By 1974, Radio Clyde was broadcasting football and this became a key element in building the station's identity. Paul Cooney, managing director of Radio Clyde, remembers the importance of football journalism in developing the station's success:

> As a local station we are driven by local content, but aware of big international events. Football is both a local and worldwide currency, and I think we established the importance of football very early on. In the 1970s there was no radio voice for, say, the west of Scotland, and when Richard Park and myself came together we realised that football could be a massive driver for the station. We knew there was a hunger out there and it was a type of soap opera.
>
> We had a twin approach of live games and we got print sports journalists into the studio and on the radio. Up until then there was a reporting of the sport by broadcasters, but not really with sports journalists offering comment. We also had the first phone-in when we put print sports journalists Gerry McNee and Jimmy Sanderson on air (in 1978). (Interview with author, 11 April 2005)

Here we see an early example of demand-led media. In this instance, a radio station with an intimate knowledge of its audience, tapping into an interest in football and its attendant culture, which up until then simply was not addressed by radio, or even to a large extent by television. In the process, of course, radio is not a neutral medium that simply brings events to the audience, it transforms the event and changes the nature of that experience, but more so than established stations, such as the BBC, Cooney and Park were acutely aware of the importance that print journalism played in football culture, and the centrality of comment and opinion in that culture. They wanted to use radio as an extension of this environment. In so doing, they recognised the commercial value that this would have in driving audience share on a newly established commercial radio station; but during this period – the late 1970s – they were also giving a legitimising space to an overwhelmingly working-class pursuit long before the sport would undergo its cultural renaissance in the early 1990s.

From the very start Radio Clyde had an agreement with the *Scottish Daily Express*, which in the 1970s was a major newspaper in Scotland, that two of the paper's journalists, Bobby Maitland and John Mackenzie, would provide football reports on a Saturday afternoon when the station went on air. Thus Radio Clyde immediately had links with the newspapers, and was among the first commercial radio station in the UK to establish long-term links with the print media in the realm of sports journalism.

In the history of radio sports journalism, *Radio Clyde* is also important for introducing the concept of the radio sports phone-in to the UK. Cooney notes how:

> The phone-in started around the time of the 1978 FIFA World Cup. Richard Park had been in America and had seen the rise of the radio phone-in and sports phone-ins. We also wanted to come on at 2 p.m., well before the game started. So *SuperScore-Board* in 1977/78 came on at 2 p.m. I was keen that we would speak to managers and players and get them involved and on air.
>
> We were the first to do it and it was very successful and we would go on until 6 p.m. We did what Sky does now on television, and, interestingly, when we started people asked what are you going to fill the time with, but we had interviews, news and comment and it was very successful. (Interview with author, 11 April 2005)

Thus, here we have an example of UK broadcast sports journalism being heavily influenced by what US radio was doing at that time. Indeed, it is interesting to note that while the radio phone-in was, by the 1970s, an established part of US sports culture (Eisenstock, 2001), in the UK it would take until the 1980s to introduce the idea onto national radio. Until then, it was left to local radio to play a significant role in developing a broadcast sports journalism culture that pre-empted the explosion in media coverage of sport in the 1990s.

Up until this point, those who wanted sports journalism turned to the print media, while those who preferred immediacy and the reporting of live sporting events turned towards radio, and, increasingly, television.

TELEVISION AND SPORTS JOURNALISM

As pointed out earlier in the chapter, something central lies at the heart of and implicitly shapes the relationship between radio and television broadcasters and the sports they cover. The broadcast organisation that has bought the rights to cover a sport has a far from neutral or unconnected relationship with those involved in the game. So, for example, ITV, the main publicly regulated commercial broadcaster in the UK, will ultimately be concerned with audience ratings and promoting its sports portfolio as part of its entertainment output. The BBC, while not as driven by ratings, recognised during the broadcasting duopoly era of the 1970s and 1980s that sport, while part of its wider national cultural remit, was also an important area of output in terms of attracting an audience, often outwith of peak viewing times.

The former Director General (DG) of the BBC and former Chairman of ITV Sport Greg Dyke (2004: 233–4) has argued that 'television broadcasters traditionally avoid making controversial programmes about sport for obvious reasons. If you expose wrong doing or inefficiency in a sporting organization they are unlikely to sell you the rights again.' The point he makes is directly relevant to the history of the relationship that has evolved between broadcasters and the sports they seek to cover. As sport became key 'media product' during the 1990s the links between certain sports and media outlets grew closer, creating a vested interest in promoting and presenting sport in a positive light. But the impact on mainstream television news journalism goes further than this. The accompanying access to pictures secured by organisations has increasingly helped shape the impact that sports have on mainstream news agendas. In other words, if a particular terrestrial or satellite television station has exclusive access to, say, a world heavyweight boxing title fight, it is likely to include this in its news agenda. When the BBC secured the exclusive highlights rights to show English Premiership football matches it was notable that stories related to this competition were more likely to find themselves covered in mainstream news programmes, than when the rights were held by their terrestrial rival ITV. This process has also been accelerated with the proliferation of 24-hour rolling news channels across the BBC, ITV and Sky, all eager for content and happy to carry sports news not only within their designated slots, but also often as a standalone story in the news section.

This process also often acts as a form of cross-promotion, as sporting events highlighted in a particular organisation's news progammes are often then being covered by that organisation. Thus when the satellite broadcaster Sky secured exclusive live UEFA Champions League Wednesday night football, related news stories about the competition regularly appeared both on its Sky News Channel and, more explicitly, on its Sky Sports News Channel. The normal rules of journalistic engagement become slightly trickier to negotiate in this type of relationship. As the BBC's Andrew Thompson argues:

> I think there will be some live sports broadcasters who will feel a little uncomfortable by stories that are covered in the news, it has happened in the past and it does on occasions. By and large the sports broadcasters and the rights holders realise that the BBC has to provide impartial news coverage and it needs to be accurate and it needs to be the best in the UK. That is recognised and while there may be moments of debate or uncomfortable moments, people are grown up about this and that the credibility of the BBC is to a large part based on the credibility of its news organisation. (Interview with author, 18 April 2005)

It could be argued that while both the BBC and ITV developed an international reputation for their broadcasting of sport, their engagement with, say, investigative sports journalism was almost non-existent. At the height of the duopoly between the BBC and ITV in the 1980s, sports historian Tony Mason, commenting on the lack of investigative journalism associated with television coverage of sport, argued that: 'Anything on which BBC TV is prepared to spend almost half of its summer schedules' budget deserves the sort of penetrating analysis never found on *Sportsnight* (*The Listener*, 1986).'

By the 1980s, sport had changed, in no small part as a direct result of its relationship with television and the increasingly important role that sponsors and other commercial interests were exerting on what was becoming an increasingly international cultural form. Of course, sport and its attendant culture are heavily shaped by the era that produces it. In this respect it is difficult, with the benefit of hindsight, to be too critical of the early years of broadcast sports journalism, when a certain deference to sports stars and organisations was clearly evident and the commercial side of the industry was very much in its infancy. However, by the 1980s the business and commercial dimension of the sports industry had grown substantially, while television's view of sport appeared not to have significantly changed. Indeed, the increasingly complex ties between sport, media and business were going largely unreported by broadcasters who clearly viewed sport as a form of entertainment and had a vested interest in portraying sport in a particular light and context for a range of ideological and commercial reasons (Whannel, 1992; Boyle and Haynes, 2000).

News about sport and sports stars has always been central to broadcast coverage of sport; however, the issue here has been about the scope of that news agenda. Broadcast sports journalism has been concerned with reporting results, team news and the live action events as they take place. In other words, the range of news historically covered by broadcasters has been relatively narrow and focused on staged events taking place, or about to take place, on the pitch or in the stadium. This reporting of results, scorers, etc., has a routineness about it. Despite this, some involved in sports broadcasting resent the claim that they are not involved in a form of journalistic activity. Brian Barwick, a producer at BBC Sport for a number of years before becoming Head of Sport at ITV and then Chief Executive of the Football Association, discussing this issue in relation to his colleague and noted sports broadcaster Des Lynam, responds by arguing:

> One of the things which used to make his blood boil, and used to make my blood boil, was when people used to say occasionally of our output together that there wasn't enough journalism in it. In truth, you are interpreting live events on the air and you are actually being journalistic about something that people have a real feel for and understanding of, and if you interpret the wrong way people will soon tell you. ...
>   It's quite a clinical and difficult art, live sports broadcasting, and you are interpreting the facts as they are appearing before your very eyes. A good example of that would be the two major Grand National situations – the false start and the IRA bomb threat – where Desmond had to interpret on the air as those events unfolded. So I think he is a very strong journalist and I think he is a great preparations man. (Purcell, 1999: 132–3)

Thus Barwick argues that particularly this form of live television – and by extension also live radio – involves specific journalistic skills allied to those of the professional broadcaster. A point that the BBC's Head of Sports News agrees with:

> In a way covering live sporting events is about live broadcast journalism. It's about revealing events as they unfold, and there is nothing more dramatic than an exciting live football or rugby game. So covering it live, and then analysing the story, getting to the truth of the story of what happens behind the action seems to me to be about journalism and that is what we are about. (Interview with author, 18 April 2005)

Even within sports broadcasting, distinctions exist in the division of labour associated with sports production practice. Bob Wilson, the former Arsenal footballer, reinvented himself to become one of the key faces of sport on terrestrial television from the 1970s through to the late 1990s. Wilson, who worked first for the BBC and later ITV, was always clear that his ability lay in presenting and anchoring sport on television, rather than acting as a news reporter, which he did with difficulty during the 1982 football World Cup when he followed the England team across Spain during that tournament (Wilson, 2004: 217).

Yet, as the amount of live sports broadcasting (as opposed to edited highlights packages) increased substantially from the early 1990s onwards the requirement that sports broadcasters be able to respond to the unexpected at sporting events also increased.

There is also little doubt that wider shifts in television practice helped to benefit sports broadcasters who enjoyed a journalistic background. A growing space for broadcasters to express themselves, often in order to enliven the coverage, became more commonplace during the 1980s. The cricket broadcaster Tony Lewis worked with the BBC presenting light entertainment programmes before moving to the Corporation's cricket coverage in 1986. Lewis recalls that:

> I was brought up in the old fashioned BBC presenting way, like Des Lynam – we were contemporaries in the radio sports room when we did *Sport on Four*. We were taught to get absolutely everything you could from interviewing somebody. It was the original, unselfish job. You were merely presenting, whereas now you can stop and talk to camera and get your point over. (Broad and Waddell, 1999: 162)

This ability of the broadcaster to editorialise became even more prominent in the 1990s. Lewis, whose background after a career in cricket had been in journalism, was in little doubt he saw himself first as a journalist, and then as a television performer. In 1994, when Lewis was commentating on the incident that appeared to show England cricket captain Mike Atherton illegally tampering with the ball, it was his journalistic skills that came into play. He made sure the pictures were reshown, effectively telling the story. Lewis notes that: 'It was the journalist coming out in me, being aware of the libel laws and the problems you can get into if you accuse someone of doing something without any proof' (Broad and Waddell, 1999: 166).

The same can also be said of radio. Football commentator Alan Green, for example, began his career on a BBC broadcast journalism course, cutting his teeth as a broadcast news reporter, before by his own admission stumbling into commentary (Green, 2000). His opinionated style of radio commentary marked a break with the more circumspect and deferential style of BBC commentary and was clearly informed by his journalistic background and eye for a story. While not universally popular, there is little doubt that his style of commentary was more in tune with the comment-led sports journalism that was well established by the 1990s. Alastair Campbell, the former Labour Party communications director and Prime Minister Tony Blair's former PR advisor, and himself closely associated with the growing professionalisation of the relationship between politics and the media, or the growth of 'spin' in public discourse, commenting on Green's style of commentary during Euro 2004 wrote:

> I've caught a couple of games on radio while travelling and I have joined the fairly sizable 'can't bear Alan Green' club. I want a commentator to tell me what is happening, not stuff his opinions down my ear hole. Fusion of news and comment – now sport gets the bug. (*The Independent on Sunday*, 2004)

(Campbell's direct involvement with sport and sports journalism, through the British and Irish Lions rugby union tour of New Zealand in 2005, is directly discussed in Chapter 5.)

Early 2006 also saw Green attacked by both the Bolton manager Sam Allardyce and other sports journalists for his comments about Bolton's style of play. What this highlighted is the extent to which, Green apart, most sports broadcasting remains an adjunct to the sport it is covering.

Despite individuals, such as Green, it is true to say that while stories of scandal and personal tragedy involving sports stars would be reported or news stories broken in sections of the popular press commented on (although issues of corruption in sport remained less exposed) broadcast sports journalism remains a pretty toothless beast in these areas. The parameters of the sports news agenda on television have always been relatively narrow. It was very rare that a major sports-related news story during the 1960s, 1970s and 1980s broke from broadcasting sports departments, as opposed to being simply reported once the print media had broken a story. Even today, sports stories tend to be broken by the print media, and then picked up and developed by the broadcasters.

As a result, for many print media journalists the extent to which broadcasting has been a key element in the wider sports journalism culture is open to debate. Graham Spiers, chief sportswriter with *The Herald*, suggests that:

> Print journalism remains the engine room of the whole sports journalism business. Broadcasting is a form of journalism, although it is a different type. I find there is still respect for print journalism because we sit down and talk with people such as Martin O'Neill and Alex McLeish, which broadcasters don't get. When Martin O'Neill sits own at a press conference in front of cameras he will always be slightly guarded. With print journalists it will be slightly different, he will say things off the record, it tends to be a bit more relaxed, so we get a bit closer. (Interview with author, 13 December 2004)

Many print sports journalists are also regulars on the range of radio and television sports programmes that have proliferated as the broadcasting environment has become more market-orientated. Indeed, as is discussed in more detail in Chapter 8, one of the characteristics of sports journalism from the 1990s onwards is the increasing lack of a clear boundary between print and broadcast sports journalists as many regularly cross what was once a much more significant trade boundary.

THE RISE OF TELEVISION SPORT AND THE RETURN OF RADIO

The BBC began to see its portfolio of television sporting events eroded in the 1990s as a buoyant ITV and the satellite broadcaster BSkyB pushed the cost of sports rights out of the reach of the Corporation. In the national radio market, however, the BBC continued to occupy a central role. The launch of Radio 5 as a dedicated rolling news and sports station evolved from the rolling news coverage the BBC had devoted to the first Gulf War in the early 1990s. Its subsequent successful development into Radio Five Live has been one of the most significant step changes in radio coverage of sport and sporting issues by broadcasters in the UK, helping to bring sports news out of the ghetto and not only exposing it to a dedicated sports audience but also legitimising its place in a changing mainstream news agenda.

However, an ongoing tension existed between strands of investigative and uncomplicit journalism and the more cosy world of much of the broadcast sports environment, where balancing contacts and access are important parts of the equation for many sports broadcasters, as both sport and radio coverage of sport began to change. Elite sport was now driven by the massive influx in television money and the growth in media exposure that particular sports enjoy, while the BBC adapted to the loss of a number of high-profile television sports events and began to find the audience for sports and news radio growing. This tension is illustrated by looking at the initial success of the *On The Line* Radio Five Live investigative documentary strand. *On the Line* began its days as a BBC television journalism programme in the late 1980s. It marked the beginning, however tentatively, of a more robust turn in the attention that television was prepared to focus on the sports industry and its growing hinterland. Driven by journalists primarily drawn from outwith of BBC Sport, the programme probed some of the issues, such as cheating and drugs, that television sports coverage had traditionally largely ignored in favour of a more entertainment-orientated approach to sports. As the programme's investigative team noted:

> When some of our investigations were broadcast they did not make us very popular in some quarters, even within the BBC. Two investigations in particular – 'Swansong', which looked at Ken Bates's business past and present stewardship of Chelsea, and 'Double Agents', which exposed Celtic manager Martin O'Neill's shareholding in a company controlled by one of our biggest football agents – caused some problems for our colleagues elsewhere in *Five Live* and *BBC Sport*. (Conn et al., 2003: 8)

Significantly, some of the journalists involved in the series were also investigative print journalists and writers, for example David Conn. Conn has argued that:

> Pre-1992 and Sky, television news treated sport in a humorous manner, it wasn't treated as serious news, even when the stories were about finance. That all changed in the 1990s when they woke up to the fact that sport, and football in particular, was a serious business, involving a lot of money and in which a lot of viewers were interested. In many ways it has now swung the other way, where they will now cover a transfer or a major story around a club. There is still a perception that it is show business

and box office and that is why stories about players transfers and contracts is given coverage, but there is still very little serious digging about other issues. I think there is a growing audience for examining these issues, but television will say football is box office, but documentaries about the underside of the business aspect of the game are not. (Interview with author, 14 December 2004)

Related to this, and looked at in more detail in the following chapter, is the shifting in the range of news values associated with sports. By the 1990s a sports-related story, such as a transfer of a football player, or the proposed takeover of a football club such as Manchester United, would quite likely appear as a mainstream television news story, often covered by a non-sports journalist. Sports-related stories became part of a less well-defined news agenda in which entertainment-related stories were given prominence with 'harder' political, social and economic news. Of course, sports stories related to takeover bids and such like were in fact often economic stories that clearly had a wider social relevance for sections of the audience. Nonetheless, the growing willingness to carry sports stories as mainstream news items became more marked and common during this decade as 24-hour rolling news, with its insatiable appetite for content, became an increasing part of the media environment.

The advent of digital television and the expansion in capacity also saw the launch by Sky of a rolling sports news channel. Sky Sports News and the impact that this sports news channel has had on the wider sports environment is discussed in more detail in Chapter 6.

Applying journalistic rigour to sports coverage and its growing business and media hinterland is not something that is often found in broadcasting sports departments. Indeed, forms of investigative journalistic enquiry into issues relating to sport are more often carried out by mainstream news and current affairs journalists, clearly positioned outside of the sports department. Examples include a number of investigations carried out by the BBC current affairs programme *Panorama* over the years into sports-related issues, for example drug abuse, and the growing role and influence of sponsors and television on sports such as Formula One motor racing and the FIFA World Cup.

There are signs that aspects of this culture are changing as the BBC recognises the growing importance of sports news. Andrew Thompson, BBC Head of Sports News, Interactivity and Digital Media, argues that:

BBC sports coverage has to have a journalistic spine shot through it. It's central to our coverage. There needs to be a boundary between our sports news team and our live sports coverage team. Our SNT works very closely with the rest of the BBC news-gathering operation and is charged with providing the best possible impartial news coverage be it drugs in sport, Olympic bids or whatever. We would never ever shape our sports news agenda in terms of what we deliver to the news bulletins to reflect any rights that we hold or do not hold. (Interview with author, 18 April 2005)

As noted in the previous chapter, there is not a strong investigative tradition among print journalists, and among the print fraternity it has been a relatively recent shift in the parameters of the field that has seen any sustained investigative sports journalism given prominence.

Some, however, working within the sports broadcasting industry argue that complicitness with the major actors is not as prevalent as has been suggested. Thus, while print journalists feel that the relationship a broadcaster such as Sky has with the English Premiership means they are always going to get better access, this is something that sports broadcasters appear less sure about. Former football player Andy Gray has worked with Sky as a football analyst and broadcaster since the start of its Premiership coverage in 1992 and he suggests:

> We don't make the kinds of demands of the clubs we might feel entitled to given the money we've paid for the rights. In the US, for example, access to players and coaches is not something TV asks for, but something it demands. The US broadcasters are guaranteed to get interviews with whichever players they want because that helps promote the game. It's not the same here. We're constantly denied permission to speak to players. Sometimes that is retribution for something that's been said or done that has upset the club. Quite often that has little to do with the sports arm of Sky. At the start of the 2003/4 season, for instance, we were banned by Sir Alex Ferguson because a reporter from Sky News had approached him while he was on holiday in France, stuck a microphone in his face and asked him about Beckham. I can understand why Alex was annoyed about it. It's unacceptable behaviour. But it was nothing to do with Sky Sports. However, we were the ones who suffered most as a consequence of it. (Gray, 2005: 253–4)

However, the reality as noted earlier in this chapter, is that relationships with rights holders will always be problematic for broadcasters. As Irish broadcaster and journalist Eamon Dunphy argues:

> You are very inhibited if you are in a contractual arrangement with an organisation. You do not hear the idiosyncratic voice on television as much as you ought to. It's not cultivated. The media should be working for its readers and viewers, if that leads you into direct conflict with managers and players, then you have got to do that. But, of course, rights to events are important as well. So there is a fine line to walk on this. (Interview with author, 30 May 2005)

Michael Robinson, another football player turned football broadcaster, also advocates this position. Robinson, a former Liverpool player, now lives and works in Spain where he finished his playing career. He writes, directs and presents *El Dia Despues* (The Day After), one of the most popular football programmes on Spanish television. He is scathing of the way football is presented in Britain, with its closed shop of ex-players talking about the game. He argues: 'There is a screaming necessity for a journalist, because they all speak now in a certain argot, they all sit down comfy comfy … and there is no journalist saying, "Why?"' (*The Observer Sports Monthly*, 2005a: 33). It is this cosy consensus that exists between a lot of sports broadcasters and the sports that they cover which has always neutered television sports journalism. Sport on television is set within a frame dominated by entertainment, rather than journalism values, and this process and lack of scrutiny has not been helped by the rise of what is called pundit sports journalism.

THE RISE OF PUNDIT SPORTS JOURNALISM

The growth in television and radio coverage of football has also seen the development of the football 'pundit'. This is normally an ex-professional player who has turned broadcaster and gives his 'expert' opinion on the game or related events. The origins of this form stretch back on television to coverage of the 1970 FIFA World Cup, when ITV became the first television station to use a 'panel' of managers and players to discuss and analyse games in the studio. The panel, comprising managers Malcolm Allison and Brian Clough and players Paddy Crerand, Derek Dougan and Bob McNab, broke new ground in television coverage of the sport and proved a ratings hit with the audience; a new sports format in British television had been born.

As noted in the previous chapter, the rise of 'opinion' and 'speculation' in the print media, often featuring ghosted columns by current and past players and managers had become a feature of the sports press during the 1980s. The massive rise in salaries within the football industry from the early 1990s has all but ended this practice, certainly among current players and managers who have no financial need to host a regular column in the national press. However, by the turn of the new century there had never been more media outlets talking about sports and sports-related activity across a range of media platforms from digital television, through radio and the Internet. All have space to fill and no shortage of former players (in particular those whose playing days ended before the boom times hit English football) who are happy to use the media to voice opinions and supplement their incomes.

While not strictly journalism, the rise of 'punditry' and 'expert opinion' has become an important part of the wider journalistic discourse that surrounds sports such as football. It should also be noted that punditry has become an established part of the wider television news landscape, in part as a response to the rise in rolling news channels.

As the newspaper coverage of sport changed as a response to the expansion in the sheer volume of the press and the size of newspapers, thus the rise of dedicated sports channels also extended the space devoted to sports chatter. By the 1990s, some of the shows on Sky Sports, the *Footballers*

Football Show, for example, featured former players passing comment on current issues associated with the game, and football journalists from the print media began to enjoy a higher television and media profile.

There has also been a debate about entry into the world of sports broadcasting and whether a background in journalism or one playing sport at the highest level best equips you for the pressures of sports broadcasting. There have always been former sports professionals who have become established broadcasters, former Arsenal and Scotland goalkeeper Bob Wilson and more recently on the BBC the former England footballer Gary Lineker are two such examples. Wilson's move from former football player to BBC sports presenter in 1974 was marked by the unusually short amount of time it took him to become established as a television sports presenter. Wilson himself notes that despite a difficult start to his television career, what saved him 'was my inside knowledge of the game' (2004: 202) as he was competing with other presenters who all had backgrounds in journalism.

Yet, while earlier broadcasters may have had a sporting background of sorts, often not having played at the highest levels of their sport, other key sports broadcasters were at least as likely to have come through print sports journalism. Some of the issues this development raises around debates about uncomplicit journalism and the image associated with the sports journalist and broadcaster are discussed throughout the rest of the book and examined in more detail, specifically, in Chapter 8.

CONCLUSION: SPORTS BROADCAST JOURNALISM

There remains an institutional and cultural distinction to be drawn between *sports journalism* and *sports broadcasting*. As Dunphy argues:

> Sports broadcasting is a different craft and some are brilliant at it, such as Ritchie Benaud (cricket) who is insightful without shouting from the rooftops. There is some very good work on the racing channels, very informed about the sport, in contrast with McCoist or Venables on ITV's football coverage, which is poor. Even Sky, whose coverage of sport is good, suffers in its punditry as they have to stay onside with the clubs. (Interview with author, 30 May 2005)

Benaud, as commented upon above, is unique in that he began his journalistic training with the Australian *Sun* newspaper in 1956, before his cricket playing career was over. He also cut his teeth, not on the sports desk, but rather on the News and Police beats (Benaud, 1998: 121).

For historical reasons, early sports broadcasters, although often from journalistic backgrounds, positioned themselves as broadcasters rather than sports journalists, as they perceived the latter to be associated with the newspaper industry and to be held in relatively low esteem by the broadcasting fraternity. Even today it is common for, say, a sports radio presenter to be referred to as a journalist-turned-broadcaster, as if the two are mutually incompatible. Often this categorisation comes from the print media itself, which continues to view newspapers as the true home and natural medium for sports writing and sports journalism.

One of the key aspects of the differing relationship between broadcasters and journalists is that of mediation. Historically, the broadcaster was simply relaying the sports events to the listener or later the television viewer at home. Of course, we are now aware that this process if far from neutral and is in fact a key element in the ideological transformation of the sport into a mediated event. By way of contrast, the sports journalist, in part as a response to wider sports coverage from radio and then television, began more routinely to offer analysis and opinion with regard to sporting matters, rather than simply factually reporting sporting events.

In more recent years as competition in sports broadcasting has intensified and the need to attract and retain viewers and subscribers has grown, so has the level of editorialising that takes place in sports broadcasting. While relaying the event is still crucial, concerns about editorialising on sport have lessened as controversy and conflict have become increasingly important elements on the sports broadcasting entertainment mix, driven by wider commercial pressures and also a changing sports media landscape in which the popular press continue to play an important role in shaping sports news agendas.

Part of this is also driven by an apparent increase in the importance that sport has acquired in the media itself. When the proposed cricket tour of England by South Africa in 1970 looked like it would go ahead accompanied by anti-apartheid protests at the grounds, the BBC prepared by making sure that a news journalist would be inside the grounds to report on the off-the-field activity. It was also made clear to the sports commentators that they were not to pass comment on the protestors unless they impinged on the field of play: a clear division of labour between sports and politics, and also between sports broadcasting and journalism. The tour was cancelled, but over 30 years later there is a growing recognition that sport and sporting events are increasingly important cultural and often political events, while the notion that a sports commentator or other broadcasters would be unable to deal with a similar situation today suggests that journalistic values in sports broadcasting are shifting and, crucially, a more general recognition that the sports audience is more media aware than it may have been previously.

Thus sports broadcasting remains a form of journalism, but informed by a hybrid of values drawn from television entertainment conventions and those of broadcast journalism. When Bill Hagerty interviewed members of the BBC radio *Test Match Special* (TMS) cricket commentary team in 2005, no clear consensus existed between them as to whether their coverage of cricket constituted journalism. While some, like Jonathan Agnew, clearly viewed BBC radio coverage as journalism, others, such as Henry Blofeld, argued that:

> It may be very wrong of me, but I don't regard myself as a reporter at all. I regard myself as a broadcaster and commentator. I know the two things are in a way synonymous and of course my job is reporting, but I don't look upon myself as a reporter ... I don't regard myself as a journalist, really. (Hagerty, 2005: 84)

So, even for those working within this area of sports media, some of the historical tensions between broadcasting and journalism remain unresolved.

In other countries, of course, practices do differ slightly. In Ireland, for example, journalist Bill O'Herlihy has fronted major sporting events for RTE television since 1972. O'Herlihy's background is as a current affairs journalist and he is convinced this has given an edge to the studio discussions that are part of RTE's television coverage of sport. He argues:

> The difference between me and the others [sports broadcasters] is that I had a hard-nosed current affairs training and that has been my great strength ... I regard myself as a journalist. ... as against Gary Lineker [BBC], Gabby Logan [ITV] or Richard Keys [Sky], the difference is I'm a journalist and I ask much tougher questions and can get a debate going – and sustain it. (*The Irish Times*, 2005)

This is in contrast to the UK, where over the last number of years sports broadcasting has become less journalistically driven and increasingly populated by former sports stars with little or no background in journalism.

From the other side of the Atlantic, veteran American sportswriter Leonard Koppett, whose work straddled both the print and the broadcast media, encapsulated a particular sense of a golden era of sports writing, when the print media, and newspapers in particular, were the dominant medium for the translation and interpretation of the role of sport in American popular culture. He argued that:

> The rise of the press box paralleled the development of large scale commercialized spectator sports. It made possible the impact that radio and television could use for their purposes. It created, magnified, disseminated and established the romance and detail that made sports so appealing, and indoctrinated children in their formative years to that kind of pleasure, creating life long addictions. It did so as an integral part of the complex culture that marked America through the 20th century, one that always did change rapidly but took off in radical new directions during the last quarter of it. The scene now would not be what it is without the press box having been what it was. But this is now and that was then. (Koppett, 2003: 274)

It is an examination of the position of sports journalism 'now' to which the rest of the book turns its attention.

SPORTS JOURNALISM IN THE AGE OF 24/7 MEDIA

Like everything else in the post-war years, sportswriting had undergone significant change. The determined romanticism of a more innocent age had yielded to higher standards of journalism. The best of the old-timers, who saw their roles primarily as drama critic and bards, were facile essayists. Some of them may not have identified an unscheduled news story if it had come with a letter of introduction, but with their quills they could tell you who got the game-winning goal or run while they tickled you. They told a mean fairy tale.

Ken Jones, Sportswriter (2000: 40) Decline and fall of popular sportswriting, *British Journalism Review*. Vol. 11 No. 1.

Sports Journalism now is more emphatic and dramatic than it was in the past. It's about comment, analysis, reaction and reflection.

Paul Hayward, Sportswriter, *The Daily Mail* (2005)

News is a relatively recent, made-up human commodity.

Andrew Marr (2004: 58) My *Trade: A Short History of British Journalism*, London.

Defining the boundaries of sports journalism has never been more difficult. The following three chapters examine the key factors that are shaping these more fluid boundaries, from changes in the media–sport relationship, through the rise of public relations and image management in sport, to the implications of a digital media environment. Although these processes are looked at across differing chapters, they are interlinked and part of the wider structural shifts in the sports and the media industries that are reshaping sports journalism.

This chapter examines how the ongoing commercialisation of the sports industry and its ever closer links with media corporations is impacting on sports journalism. It looks at the extent to which contemporary sports journalism practice has changed and developed in the light of a 24-hour rolling news agenda, technological developments and the growth in the volume of sports coverage across a range of media platforms. It also investigates the impact that increased competition among and across media outlets is having on journalistic practice as, for example, newspapers increasingly position sports coverage as an important part of their wider brand identity in the marketplace.

TELEVISION AND THE RISE OF MEDIATED SPORTS JOURNALISM

As we have already seen, the impact of television on print sports journalism has been considerable. However, the ramifications for the sports journalist of the increasing colonisation of elite sport by television are more widespread and often less obvious to the reader of sports copy than might be imagined. One aspect has been the internal tensions that exist within sports journalism, often, but not solely, between print and broadcast journalists. Graham Spiers has suggested that:

> The explosion of football on television and its exposure has changed the boundaries of the sports journalist. Newspapers have been gazumped by television; as a result there is a lot of stuff that appears in newspapers that has been made up. They saw it on TV last night, so we need to give them something different. (Interview with author, 13 December 2004)

While from the tabloid end of the market, sportswriter Stewart Weir from the Scottish *Daily Mirror* argues that:

> The biggest change in sports journalism over the years has been newspapers finding they are going head to head with radio and television. We have had to respond by becoming more sensationalist and by often trying to fill in the gaps or add to the stories that have already been told by television or radio. (Interview with author, 6 April 2005)

Spiers also notes the lingering ill-feeling that exists among the print sports journalists towards broadcasting colleagues with the rise of a 24/7 news culture:

> There is to this day resentment among print journalists towards broadcasters. Television was the midwife of tabloid journalism, because it came on the scene and told the world what was happening 12 hours before it appeared in print. So they came up with something different. Newspapers have to be almost artificially protected, because 24-hour news has changed the rules of the game. To some extent we are an anachronism. The key aspect for me is that as a columnist my work is not as deadline-orientated to the same extent as breaking news stories. There will always be a market for reading what someone thinks. (Interview with author, 13 December 2004)

This tension between print and broadcast sports journalists is also based on an assumption that it is the print journalist who remains the true custodian of sports journalism. For some, broadcast sports journalists work in the 'soft' side of sports journalism; their safe questioning of sports stars and players protecting the vested interest a channel has in promoting a sport whose broadcast rights it has paid substantial sums of money to secure.

As television has become the financial underwriter of professional sport (Whannel, 1992; Rowe, 1999; Boyle and Haynes, 2000) and a deregulated broadcasting market has facilitated the expansion of the amount of sport being broadcast on both free-to-air and pay TV, the impact on the sports journalist has been marked. More than at any other time in the history of sports journalism, the readers of print media are likely to have experienced a mediated version of the sports event being discussed by the journalist. In other words, the days of the sportswriter being the major mediator of sports events has long passed, and with the sheer volume of broadcast sports coverage now available to the committed fan, literally no event now appearing in print has not already been mediated by either television or radio.

However, something else has also happened that remains largely hidden from the reader. At many major sporting events, the journalists themselves are not actually watching the sport live, they are simply watching television feeds of the action and basing their copy, in part, on this. Obviously, this is applicable primarily to those sports that geographically and physically are difficult to cover, in particular golf and Formula One motor sport.

For example, in Formula One, the print media journalists from all countries watch the race in a media centre, following the action with television pictures of the event that are carried on a silent feed. Put simply, the television viewer at home has a better and more informed experience than the journalists who are there to cover the event for their newspapers. The journalists are then interpreting for the print media an already heavily televisually mediated event. Of course the main thrust of the copy filed by these journalists will centre partly on the race itself, but will be filled with quotes and comments from the main drivers and teams involved, which will be garnished from a combination of carefully controlled press releases and pre-and post-race press conferences.

As we see in the next chapter, such is the extensive influence exerted over the media in this sport by public relations and corporate concerns, that individual access to key personnel by particular journalists is heavily controlled. Motor sport journalism has always been more concerned with adding colour and glamour in reporting the characters that risk their lives behind the wheel. Interestingly, despite a history of great drivers, such as Jim Clark, Stirling Moss and Jackie Stewart, the UK print media only began to give concerted coverage to Formula One in the 1970s. Former Formula One broadcaster Beverley Turner (2004: 124) suggests: 'The *Daily Express* was the first to take an interest, with the *Daily Mirror* close behind in 1973. Ironically, the sport had to become commercialized before the press became involved: a reversal of today's relationship in which high-profile media attention attracts sponsors.' There are few other major sports events that singularly do not allow either the fans at the event or the television producer covering the sport the chance to 'get close and personal' with the main players. Cars pass in a blur, drivers' expressions are hidden away behind helmets, leaving little opportunity during the race for close-up reaction shots, which are a mainstay in creating drama and individual identification in sports coverage (Whannel, 1992). Thus the role of the sports journalist in Formula One is less one of reportage, and more one of embellishment.

Most print journalists associated with Formula One tend to focus solely on that sport and to be enthusiasts, thus their level of detachment from the surrounding commercial circus that follows the sport around the globe throughout the season is limited. As Turner notes:

> The journalists have mortgages to pay, families to feed and a job that is perceived as glamorous and rewarding. There is little incentive for them to write anything that will jeopardize their place in this world. But the result is a sport that often goes unchallenged. Stories too often skim over unpalatable truths ... That's not to say that Formula One doesn't receive bad press, it's just that those writers are rarely given access to the drivers in the paddock. (2004: 122)

Sportswriter Richard Williams, who has covered the sport for the *Guardian* newspaper, is well placed to comment on this aspect of journalistic practice. As a journalist with a wide sports portfolio, he is able to position the Formula One journalist within the wider promotional context of the sport:

> While television coverage provides the bare bones of the narrative structure the newspaper journalists, led by the representatives of the tabloids, will add layers of dramatic meaning by telling you exactly how much the two drivers concerned hate each other because one of them stole the other's girlfriend or, of even greater emotional impact, stole his seat in the best car in the field. (1998: 2)

To illustrate this point, much of the 2004 Formula One World Championship press coverage in the UK focused not on yet another championship success for the German Michael Schumacher but, rather, on the apparent imminent move of the British driver Jenson Button from the BAR team to Williams, with much being made of the apparent personal rivalries both between and within Formula One teams, all of which helped to add intrigue to the story.

Other sports, such as golf, offer plenty of opportunity to see the tension and drama of the occasion being played out on the faces and in the body language of the competitors. Yet once again, given the geographical problems faced by one journalist attempting to cover multiple contests taking place across an 18-hole course, it is television, rather than watching sport live, that is the key resource for the golf journalist. Tom Humphries, who has covered the sport as part of a wide portfolio for *The Irish Times*, is unequivocal in his analysis of the working environment of the specialist golf correspondent:

> On the one hand, covering golf is the easiest gig in sportswriting, everything is spoon fed and you have the day to mint your words and build your piece from the bottom up. Yet it is the most dispiriting job – the job that requires you to travel the most to see the least, the job where the depressing sameness of the environment must gnaw at your soul. (2003: 95)

Journalists at the major tournaments sit in the media centre watching live television feeds from the course. In addition, they are given updates, quotes from the players and information about the action taking place on the course, all of which are delivered to their desks. The major task of dexterity involved for the journalist is switching between the television screens and the large leader board that is constantly updated.

This detachment of the journalist from the event is rarely revealed to the reader in coverage of the sport that appears in print. The occasions this does happen are rare. Sportswriter Simon Barnes was part of the team covering the 2004 Ryder Cup between the USA and Europe at Oakland Hills for *The Times*. He opened his piece with:

> The shot of the tournament was played by Tiger Woods, with an assist from the cameraman. All square on the final tee and Phil Mickelson, Woods's playing partner, sent the ball on a wild curling fight [*sic*] deep into the trees. The director, brilliantly, chose to show us not Mickelson's face but that of Woods. Loathing, weariness, dismay, incomprehension and a kind of fastidious distaste chased each other across his face.
> Missing expressions included compassion, fellow-feeling and fist-clenching determination to rescue the situation. This magic moment, this perfect vignette of the inner Tiger, might be summed up as 'What the hell am I *doing* here?' It was so perfect a piece of self-revelation that the entire press tent exploded into hilarity. (*The Times*, 2004)

Barnes offers a fascinating insight into the extent that the print sports journalist is simply mediating an already mediated event. The key decision by the television producer to use a cutaway of Woods in a reaction shot, provided a heightened moment of televisual drama for what is already a compelling piece of carefully choreographed television narrative. Those watching the event live at the 18th green in all probability missed the reaction of Woods, but those watching at home would both see this moment and have it emphasised and made sense of by their television commentary.

Barnes also gives a sense of the group dynamic among sports journalists all watching the same mediated coverage together, and how the 'pack' forms a key part of the environment within which sports journalists operate. Again for the sportswriter as opposed to the sports correspondent, in particular those working at the tabloid end of the market, where breaking news stories are all important, the pressure to be part of the 'pack' is less intense. Richard Williams reflects on this aspect of journalistic culture:

> The pack is a feature of all sports, particularly football. I know of one of the best correspondents in another sport, who will be with the pack doing the interview with a big name. This man will always detach himself as the player is leaving for the dressing room and follow them and he will get five minutes and he will get a different piece. That doesn't make him popular, but he is respected because he is going the extra mile to do his job.
>
> I'd rather polish and refine my own impressions; I don't have to travel with the pack in the same way as a football or cricket correspondent. In some ways I don't like to talk to someone about a game I've just seen, because I don't want my views qualified by exposure to theirs.
>
> I am writing about opinions, and this is also competitive, as we all look at each other and are critical of each other, to the point of scorn sometimes, because we all like to think that we are right and we can be quite argumentative about things. (Interview with author, 10 March 2005)

Of course, a sportswriter such as Williams or Barnes, as opposed to a dedicated sports news correspondent, has a greater degree of licence to be open about the largely hidden production process of sports journalism. A writer like Barnes is then able to go beyond simply reporting the event, with obligatory quotes readily supplied by the players, and offer the reader his particular idiosyncratic take on an event that most readers will have already watched on television. It is here that the quality of the writing, the insight offered and the often slightly left field angle taken by a sportswriter such as Barnes can make for such compelling copy. As journalist and former editor of the *Guardian* Peter Preston has noted with regard to sports writing, '[There is] not really something called sports writing, only great writers describing sport in the same breath as they tackle life itself' (*Guardian*, 1996).

THE 24/7 SPORTS JOURNALIST

One of the major shifts in journalism more generally over the last decade or so has been the rise in rolling 24-hour news (Hargreaves, 2003; Campbell, 2004; Allan, 2005). While both television and radio have driven this process, the print media have also found that new technology has enabled them to shift deadlines and given a greater degree of flexibility to the ability of newspapers to change and update stories. Inevitably, it has been the broadcast and online media that have excelled at breaking news stories. However,

Craig Tregurtha, sports editor of the *Sunday Mirror* argues that within the realm of sports news it is the print media that still play a key role in this process. He suggests that:

> The rise in Sky and live feeds from news conferences has changed our role. However, I believe that it's newspapers that still break the stories. I mean this in two senses. There is the announcement of a new manager and Sky might carry this live, but we or other papers will have had the story in the lead-up to the announcement. I hope we are not driven by television's agenda, of course we are aware of it, but I still think that it's the papers that break the stories that are often picked up by television. (Interview with author, 28 September 2004).

It is also the case that while it is now much more common to have sports stories incorporated into mainstream broadcast news agendas, it will often be the print media that fans will turn to in order to get the extended analysis and comment which will be carried following a major story. It is also true that in many cases it will be a story originally broken by newspapers that broadcasters will then pick up and develop.

There is no doubt that the growth in the range of sports news outlets available also act as a source for other sports journalists, and, as is a feature of other areas of journalism, stories feed off each other, as reaction or, increasingly, opinion is then sought to move a story forward. Often this process happens over a relatively quick period. In the UK, the rise of BBC Radio Five Live and its commercial national sports radio rival TalkSPORT are important sources for breaking stories, as is Sky Sports News, the only dedicated British sports television news channel. These media outlets draw on both the BBC's and Sky's own journalistic network and supplement this with news from a range of wire services such as the Press Association (PA). News is also carried by these outlets directly from clubs and sports organisations themselves as they utilise a range of public relations and communication practices. As is examined in more detail in the following chapter, other sources of news in the increasingly commercialised world of sports include the City, other financial institutions and media corporations themselves.

Newspapers, such as *The Times*, are aware of the limitations imposed on them by the speed of the Internet as a vehicle for breaking stories. They will often seek a reaction from a specialised sportswriter to a breaking story and post the resulting copy on the newspaper website, before it appears in the print version. In so doing, they feel they can also drive readers to their print platform, while consolidating the paper's reputation as not only one that is a home to good writing, but also one that is breaking stories in a dynamically changing era of sports news.

This is a significant change in the traditional battle lines between the two areas of the newspaper market in Britain. While the broadsheet/compact press will never compete directly with the popular tabloid press for sports stories, put simply, they are operating to different agendas, the lines are not as clear as they once where. Richard Williams argues:

> There is this thing called convergence, which is affecting every area of every news-paper. I used to think it was convergence towards the *Daily Mail*. That is still to some extent true. I think the broadsheets and their coverage of sport has gone towards the tabloids, I don't think the tabloids have moved at all. We have found ourselves work-ing to their agenda a great deal more. So when Beckham gets hit by a flying boot from Fergie, we will not only acknowledge the story, we will cover it. And as far as that plays a role in his eventually leaving the club, then fair enough. There are stories I don't want to write about, such as Beckham's marriage. We don't have to write about that. (Interview with author, 10 March 2005)

Indeed, such is the increasingly ubiquitous nature of sports news, the extent to which it impinges and seeps into, and onto, other mainstream news arenas, that, as David Chappell suggests, it is no longer an option to simply leave the field open to the tabloid press to cover sports news. As sport has become increasingly linked to celebrity (for example, the rise of Beckham the brand), a nation's cultural life (for example, the interest in the 2005 Ashes cricket series), business (note the coverage of the take-over of Manchester United and football clubs floating on the stock exchange), and politics and public policy (note the extensive coverage of London's successful 2012 Olympic bid), it provides a range of stories that interest and touch a broad readership. Chappell argues that:

> The tabloids are terrific at what they do. They have a very developed sense of what is important to their readers. But they are writing to a formula. We have a greater range, where the writers can lead us, in a way that doesn't happen on tabloids. The broad-sheets now also compete more with them at the sharp end. So someone like Matt Dickinson our football writer came from the tabloid newspaper the *Daily Express,* but was frustrated that he couldn't express himself in the length that he wanted to there. But he has a very good sense of what is an important football news story and breaks a number of good stories. We don't have deals with agents; this is good old-fashioned contact-based journalism. (Interview with author, 8 October 2004)

Thus, one impact of the growth of sports news in both the online and the broadcast media has been to help change the nature of the relationship between parts of the print media with regard to the importance of sports news more generally. As Graham Spiers argues:

> I actually think that the media has caught up to the wider impact and significance of, say, football in Scottish society. For many years football was actually underreported in the press, given its significance. Radio coverage has become more professional as they realise that people are interested in listening to this. I am also convinced that there is a growing, more literate fan base of supporters who appreciates better quality

broadcasting and better quality writing about the game. Which partly explains why broadsheet coverage of sport has flourished in the last ten years. Tabloid sports journalism has also attracted a lot of cynicism as well, although it does contain some great sports journalism. (Interview with author, 13 December 2004)

The relationship between technology, media market change and sports news values is looked at in more depth in Chapter 6; however, one issue relating to technology and sports news values is important to highlight at this stage. This is the *pace* at which change is taking place.

In the digital age, the range of material available to the sports fan (if you are prepared to pay for it) continues to grow. Thus by 2004, Sky Digital had introduced the service *Football First: Match Choice* whereby you could watch extended football highlights (52 minutes) of your team's match in the Premiership at 10.15 p.m. that Saturday evening (assuming they had, of course, been playing that day). This complemented Sky's *Football First: Game of the Day* programme that went out at 8.25 p.m. and carried full delayed 'as live' coverage of an earlier match. One impact of this new service was to erode the traditional audience for Saturday night football highlights on the BBC's *Match of the Day* programme, which saw a drop of 8.9 per cent in the audience that ITV's *The Premiership* had been securing in 2003 (*The Observer*, 2004). However, this extended and interactive service also intensifies the pressures on Sunday newspapers to offer something distinctive and different to their readers, as Craig Tegurtha is only too aware:

Our coverage has grown because there is more sport on television, through Sky in particular, and this has fed the public's appetite for sport. In newspapers we have responded to this shift. However, the pace of change is dramatic. Sky Digital now means that people can watch highlights of their team on a Saturday night if they want. So people don't want a match report on Sunday. Sunday papers used to be filled with match reports, that was our main task. That has all changed. We need to have more analysis, reaction and additional material that they haven't seen on Sky or heard on the radio. It's very difficult and we have to evolve all the time in this job, to keep pace with the changing needs of readers and the way sport is covered in the media. It's a challenge for the Sundays because in the longer term we are losing sales. (Interview with author, 28 September 2004)

This is acutely felt in the popular tabloid end of the Sunday sports journalism market, traditionally driven by sports personalities and controversy. While all sports editors recognise the challenge that television coverage of sport, and football in particular, poses, other sections of the Sunday market have responded differently.

Significantly, in the broadsheet/compact market the rise of sports comment, opinion and columnists has been as marked as in other areas of journalism. However, Jon Ryan, sports editor of *The Sunday Telegraph,* is clear what its readers expect from the sports section of the newspaper. He argues:

> The Sunday is a particular market. Our agenda is really to reflect on the week's events in sport and set up the agenda for the coming week. So we have more space to expand on issues rather then chasing and breaking stories, although of course we will do that as well. We also think that some of the best writing in the paper will be found in the sports section, so it has to be in keeping with the rest of the paper. We have a bit more space to breathe than the dailies and I think our readers expect something different from a Sunday as well. (Interview with author, 13 October 2004)

In this sense the immediate pressures of increased media coverage of sport and its direct impact on the print journalist are more acutely felt at the popular end of the market. Here, the need to break stories and carry exclusives drives the shape of the sports news agenda, rather than analysis and reflection. Although the latter will be much in evidence following coverage of a major sporting event, increasingly one that will have been extensively covered by television.

Aspects of both continuity and change inform the environment of the 24/7 sports journalist. The beat journalist has been and remains an important part of the wider sports journalism landscape (not least in the key local press markets, where specific sports knowledge and contacts are crucial). Yet, while there has been a flourishing of sportswriters plying their trade in the broadsheet sports journalism market, the environment for the traditional sports beat journalist has got distinctly tougher. Sportswriters (often referred to as the No. 1s on a paper) are in part paid for their comments and opinions on sport. This does not always require access to players or managers and is certainly not reliant on quotes to sustain their copy. As Eamon Dunphy recognises, there is a growing difference between the world of the sportswriter and that of a sports news journalist. On taking up his post as a sportswriter at the Irish Sunday broadsheet the *Sunday Tribune* he recalls how:

> I went for it with zeal. I started by attacking all the other sports writers for not doing their job properly. The issue was complicity with their subjects, they should be writing for their readers, not to make their lives comfortable when travelling with players etc. I took the view that the sports journalist should be the outsider, they should represent the readers, and if you were dependent for information on the clubs you could not do your job properly. Now that was all very well for me. There were news journalists who are in that position and that is very difficult; I was essentially a columnist and I felt free from that conflict. (Interview with author, 30 May 2005)

Access to players and those associated with the sport remains a central aspect of the beat reporters trade; they report what has happened and what key individuals have said. Squeezed by the immediacy of television, radio and Internet coverage, they find sporting organisations and agents and sponsors attempting to exercise more and more control over access to players and officials (see next chapter).

THE CHANGING PRINT MEDIA MARKET

It is important to recognise the diverse range of journalistic activity and practice that takes place under the umbrella of sports journalism, from the beat reporter through to the sportswriter employed primarily to offer their comments and thoughts on sport. One of the challenges faced by those sports journalists working in the print media is how to deal with the increasing amount of live sport carried by television and radio. This issue is, of course, not new, and the relationship between different media is one that is continually evolving.

A series of research projects carried out by the Newspaper Marketing Association (NMA) in 2003 and 2004 attempted to illustrate to media buyers the continued commercial value that sports journalism offers in terms of awareness for advertisers. The research (NMA, 2003; 2004) demonstrated the central role that sports coverage played in the newspaper reading habits of male readers, particularly across both the 'popular' and the 'quality' markets. It argued that newspapers were crucial in setting the scene before sporting events and building levels of expectation among supporters. While it recognised that broadcast media came into their own during the actual live event, the post-event media most often used by sports fans were newspapers. As Patrick Barrett of the *Media Guardian* notes in his analysis of the 2003 research:

> Before the match or race, fans seek out news, views, speculation, gossip and transfer talk. Readers enjoy sports journalism that heightens expectations and anticipation, writing that fans the flames of their passion for the action to come. ...
>
> But it's after the event that newspapers really come into their own. While 39% of tabloid readers and 35% of broadsheet readers agreed that newspapers were very/quite important in building anticipation before an event, this rose to 49% and 50% respectively for those who agreed that papers prolong the excitement afterwards. ...
>
> Newspaper coverage after an event is seen as particularly valuable because of journalists' expertise and because of the time lapse, the depth of analysis and considered opinion they can offer. The ability to cover post match incidents is also valued: 'what's gone on once they go down the tunnel – the rollicking they got from the manager – almost like a gossip column' said one fan. 'You know the headlines – but it's a habit to compare your own opinion with what you saw' and 'the analysis is more considered, they've got more breathing space – they add something extra' were other comments. (*Guardian*, 2003a)

Obviously, the NMA have a vested interest in raising awareness among media buyers of the value of advertising in and around the newspaper sports pages. Nevertheless, the research carried out by Davey Bioletti Planning and Research and BMRB does highlight the continued key role that sports journalism plays in attracting a particularly male audience to newspapers – with

54 per cent of male tabloid readers and 39 per cent of male broadsheet readers turning straight to the back page, while this figure rises to 70 per cent and 61 per cent respectively when it comes to readers who scan the front page, and then turn to the sports pages (NMA, 2003).

However, even if some advertisers and media buyers remain to be convinced of the growing appeal across the print media market of sports coverage, a number of broadsheets/compacts are already placing their sports journalism within an increasingly sophisticated marketing and commercial context.

THE GROWTH OF COMMERCIAL OPPORTUNITIES IN THE SPORTS PAGES

As the late 1990s saw an expansion in the popularity of sports coverage across the print media, the opportunities for the cross-promotional development of sports output also increased. For many newspapers this meant a much closer relationship developing between editorial, commercial and sports departments, and for the broadsheets in particular a chance to exploit their position in the market.

At *The Times* during the summer of 2004, for example, the sports department produced its normal sports copy and its regular sports supplements, plus dedicated handbooks for major events, such as the Olympics and the Euro 2004 football championships. In addition, the paper developed its own *Football Year Book*, which published the best of the football writing in the paper, and it also regularly liaised with a sponsor to produce a dedicated handbook for a specific sports event. Thus in October of that year it produced the *HSBC World MatchPlay Championship Handbook*, which carried extensive writing from *Times* journalists on this prestigious golf event, while offering ample opportunities for HSBC to be associated with both the event and *The Times* brand. A similar arrangement was struck with the telecom company O_2 (sponsors of the England national rugby team) in producing *The Times Six Nations Championship Handbook* to accompany the start of that major rugby tournament in February 2005. There was also a link-up with Guinness to produce the *The Lions Handbook,* a free supplement produced to accompany the British and Irish Lions rugby tour of New Zealand in the summer of 2005. This newspaper is not alone in striking such deals, but *The Times* remains the most sophisticated in realising the extent of the commercial value that enhanced sports coverage offers.

While such publications are relatively commonplace across the print media, particularly in the age of extensive newspaper supplements, in sport until recently they have been rare. They signify an increasingly sophisticated relationship between the commercial, marketing and sports departments. As David Chappell has argued: 'Once advertisers were not interested in sports coverage. Now advertisers are queuing at the door to get involved and that is a change from when advertisers were shy of sports coverage. There is a commercial imperative from the paper to develop these relationships' (interview with author, 8 October 2004). As an example he cites the paper's relationship with the England rugby player and key member of the 2003 World Cup winning team, Jonny Wilkinson:

> He is a good example of the changing commercial climate. In the old days he would have had a column in the paper; however, by building in other aspects into the Wilkinson deal we create other commercial opportunities. In addition to reading his column, readers can go along to see him in person at *Times* events, they can have a webchat with him and he will appear in *Times* television and print advertising campaigns. In sports we work with a range of editorial and commercial departments in a much more intensive manner. So we are more creative and *The Times* has led the way in doing these deals and the readers have enjoyed this. Five years ago this wouldn't have happened, and sports agents see how this works and we have both adapted. (Interview with author, 8 October 2004).

In many ways this synergising of sports content and the wider commercial aims of the newspaper are another example of the increasingly ubiquitous nature of the growing relationship between commercial sponsorship, the media and content providers. It also raises a number of issues connected with the boundaries of sports 'newsworthiness', and the potentially complicit nature of some of this journalism.

At one level this close relationship between sponsors, with particular commercial aims and aspirations, and editorial content is, of course, not new. Such is the commonplace nature of the commercial relationships within a media system that has broadly migrated over the last few decades from being one concerned with public interest to one much more concerned with profit, that these developments largely occur without any particular scrutiny or apparent concern. Yet at a time when sports fans are often heard to complain about the negative impact that corporate interests are having on live sport, it is odd that a similar process is also altering the parameters within which such sports journalism increasingly operates, as corporate business strengthens its ties with media outlets.

In the case of *The Times*, does their close link with Jonny Wilkinson, for example, make criticism of him more difficult? Are major companies, such as British Airways and Guinness, more likely to be favourably reported as they enjoy a corporate relationship with newspapers? Or, indeed, are name checks for such companies likely to be increasingly part of the narratives that sports journalism tells about particular sporting events? Simon Hughes of *The Daily Telegraph*, covering the build up of the England rugby team for the 2003 World Cup, was able to wax lyrically about the benefits a new Lucozade sports drink was apparently having on the team (*The Daily Telegraph*, 2003). While on another occasion, the PA's rugby correspondent Andrew Baldock could tell fans in October 2003, that the England team would arrive in Australia for that tournament well rested:

> The squad could relax on fully-flat Club World beds aboard their British Airways flight, making cramped airline travelling – something their predecessors might have endured – a thing of the past.
> And apart from the usual in-flight movies, England's finest could also look forward to a few culinary treats. Main course menu items included braised beef with red onion and mushrooms, mustard mash, roast carrots and broccoli; fisherman's pie with glazed potato topping; or chilli chicken with fragrant rice. For those players preferring something lighter, a roast vegetable salad with mozarella cheese was available. (icwales.icnetwork.co.uk)

This was not so much sports journalism, more the sort of promotional PR material you would expect to find in an in-house British Airways magazine.

These commercial relationships are occurring not simply between the media and the corporate sector, but also across media platforms and organisations. Newspapers are, on the one hand, inviting sponsors to collaborate with them; on the other, they are also developing relationships which offer them the opportunity to extend the awareness of their brand through the central role that sport plays in that identity.

In 2004, for example, *The Times* was able to tie up with TalkSPORT, the only national UK commercial sports radio station, to sponsor that station's drive-time programme, renamed *The Game* (named after the Monday football supplement that the paper produces). This form of cross-promotion allows the newspaper to expose its brand to a broader audience that is not part of the paper's natural readership, while TalkSPORT gains credibility from being associated with a newspaper such as *The Times*.

We will return to this particular issue in the next chapter, but these synergies with other media outlets and commercial interests raise issues about the uncomplicit nature of sports journalism in an age of a more commercially orientated media environment; it also forces us to address the shifting boundaries of sports news values.

SPORTS JOURNALISM AND NEWS VALUES

Historically, sports journalism has had a relatively narrow set of parameters within which it has been located. For while stories of sports scandals make high profile news, Brookes (2002: 32–3) suggests that:

'Most journalism concerning sport is much more routine and everyday. There is a danger that in focusing on the most spectacular news related to sports we ignore what sports journalism does day in, day out.' This may be true, but it is also the case that wider shifts in the sport/media ecology have also helped to reshape agendas. The head of sport at *The Times,* Keith Blackmore, has argued that: 'The role of sport has changed significantly in the past ten years. Around ... 1990 sport, and in particular football, became something more than an account of the activities and results of the weekend. It became a branch of the entertainment industry' (*Guardian*, 2003b). While Colin Gibson, former sports editor at the *Sunday Telegraph* and the *Daily Mail,* and also former communications director with the Football Association, has suggested that:

> Sports and papers have both changed. Gone are the days when sports just meant filling up a couple of pages at the back. Sport is now high profile. It's a serious business involving corporate finance, so papers have to treat it with more seriousness, while appreciating that it's part of the entertainment industry as well. (*Guardian*, 2001)

It is these two factors, sport as a commercial industry and a major international enterprise, and sport as a form of media entertainment, and the tension between them that helps shape the parameters within which contemporary sports journalism operates.

We have already seen the ways that the expansion of sports coverage on television and, increasingly, radio has shaped and impacted on the print media. Immediacy and liveness are not two qualities associated with the print media, thus the massive expansion in the volume of their sports coverage has focused on areas other than simply reporting events that have happened, although this still has a place. However, even when you report on these events, you need to take a fresh angle, bring something else to the reader who has already watched or heard the event anyway. In short, the expansion in sports journalism has been driven by the rise in comment and opinion pieces or in the reporting of speculative information about what is about to happen. The latter it must be said is increasingly the staple diet of the tabloid newspapers and inevitably centres on some form of football-related rumour, often involving a player's proposed move to another club.

The rise of editorialising by sports journalists across the spectrum, from reporters and correspondents through to the No 1s, the sportswriters, is perhaps one of the most marked developments in contemporary sports journalism. While the sportswriter has traditionally enjoyed the freedom to intervene and shape sports discussion, the wider expansion in the amount of media space devoted to sport has helped fuel the volume of comment and opinion pieces from both journalists and former sportspeople. The challenge facing print sports journalists filing copy for the Monday paper, covering a match that may have taken place on the previous Saturday and which has already been extensively covered by both the Sunday press and other media, results in an inevitable amount of comment and editorialising in their match report.

This is not a new aspect of sports journalism; however, the volume of coverage and the range of media platforms keen to air opinion (such as the ubiquitous radio sports phone-in) is different. As discussed further in Chapters 5 and 6, the advent of the digital age also means that the speed with which information gets disseminated has impacted on both journalism practice, and attempts to manage and control this information for commercial purposes.

When Walter Smith took over as manager of the Scotland football team from the German Berti Vogts in 2004 he was acutely aware of the key role that journalism plays in his high-profile post. Speaking with the chief sportswriter of *The Herald* newspaper, Smith noted that:

> The relationship between a manager and the media has changed over the years. Nowadays, you've got opinion-makers and columnists, such as yourself, who make their feelings known. The press is free to pick on someone like Berti and have a go. It's just the way it is. (*The Herald*, 2004)

In much the same way that a political climate can be shaped by extensive media coverage of an event or individual, the relentless negative coverage of Vogts' last months in charge in 2004, helped give an inevitability to his final departure. While Wagg (1984) has argued that the press have always exerted an influence on the hiring and firing of England national football managers, what has changed in the last decade has been the audible increase in the volume of such campaigns, their fixation with the personal as well as the professional lives of those involved, and the extent to which this often relentless comment extends across media (each outlet feeding off the other) and is no longer the sole preserve of the tabloid press.

As noted in the previous chapter, 'pundit journalism' characterises an increasingly large amount of what passes for sports journalism in the digital age. Clearly, commercial pressures help fan the flames of controversy in sports journalism; however, the twin rise of both celebrity culture (which has pulled sport into parts of its orbit) and the celebrity journalist/columnist, help ensure that comment and often speculation are increasingly a central aspect of contemporary sports journalism, mirroring, it must be said, wider changes in other areas of journalistic practice. The celebrity journalist/columnist is no longer simply a feature of the tabloid sports journalism market. When the *Daily Telegraph* began to restructure itself under new management in 2004, among the casualties who departed the paper was David Welch, sports editor from 1989, and the man the industry recognises as having helped to revolutionise sports coverage in the broadsheet market through the launch of the daily sports section. However, in the later years of his tenure, *The Daily Telegraph* had increasingly been seen to rely on celebrity columnists as a staple part of its sports output, and had become less known for its journalistic tradition of breaking sports news stories.

TV NEWS AND SPORTS STORIES

It has only been since the mid-1990s that television news has covered sports news as an increasingly legitimate area of interest to viewers. Previously, news about the sports industry had been viewed either as not worthy of incorporating into the main news agenda, or as relatively trivial and unimportant. However, the massive expansion in the profile sport (and, since the early 1990s, football and its elite performers above all) was offered through coverage by BSkyB and then most other mainstream media outlets, has seen sport established as part of the wider news beat for reporters.

In this process of raising the profile of news events related to football, organisations such as the BBC and Sky did more than simply tap into an existing interest in such stories among their audiences, although this was certainly one aspect. They also helped to legitimise the profile given to football and other elite sports as part of the wider news landscape, sitting cheek by jowl with other areas of domestic and international news.

One might argue that the broader commercialisation of the media that occurred during the 1990s, set in train by changes laid down a decade earlier, has actually benefited sports and given its supporters a commercial value that most broadcasters recognise they can only ignore at their peril. In other words, the broader shift from supply-led media to a more demand-led media culture has provided sport with a space and opportunity that it had previously been largely denied. To this end, while there is no doubt that a greatly expanded, more commercially orientated and ratings-driven media environment has not been universally beneficial for all areas of popular culture, sport has benefited from the relaxing of the regulations that have policed the parameters of popular culture. Of course, this shift in news values and profile takes certain distinctive forms, driven as it has been by the opening up of sport to increased intervention from both markets and media corporate control.

As the sports terrain has expanded, so newspapers have had to respond. In particular, the broadsheet/compact print sector has viewed the increasing importance of the business aspects of the sports industry as an area that they cover better than other sections of the sports media. Donald Walker, sports editor of the Scottish compact newspaper *The Scotsman*, has suggested:

We are able to cover areas related to the business of sports that others simply don't in a Scottish context, in particular this is true with regard to the tabloid press. The proposed take-over of Hearts, for example, which has rumbled on through 2004, we were able to cover in detail, because we had journalists who understood the complex financial aspects of the situation. Some of the tabloid reporting on this issue was simply misinformed. This is something that sports pages were not covering in any great way, say, ten years ago. (Interview with author, 19 October 2004)

However, *Guardian* journalist and writer David Conn has argued that there has never been an investigative tradition in British sports journalism, and that despite the massive expansion in the field since the 1990s, this strand of journalistic activity remains largely absent from both the print and the broadcast sectors of the media. He argues:

There is actually very little investigative sports journalism being carried out. In the *Daily Telegraph* you have Mihir Bose and David Walsh on drug doping in the *Sunday Times,* but apart from that very little in the press, given the scale of the business. In many ways even the broadsheets are driven by a celebrity treatment of sport as box office and show business. For some papers the answer is humour, or an offbeat approach, but they still fail to address the real issues that lurk below the surface. Sport is, of course, entertainment, but there are other issues which a growing number of fans and readers are also interested in. There is no tradition of investigative journalism in the sports media. There is some great writing about sports, but in terms of digging away and breaking news stories there is no great tradition. While there is more sports journalism now than ever before, the investigative element of this journalism is still largely undeveloped. (Interview with author, 14 December 2004)

This does, however, also raise the issue of the role played by public service broadcasting (PSB) in exposing aspects of the wider sports industry to a national audience. While having a 'box office' or a sure-fire ratings hit are, of course, important for all broadcasters, they are surely not the only criteria that organisations such as the BBC or Channel 4 should be concerned with or indeed the sole factors that drive their editorial policy. If these broadcasters are not going to invest in this type of investigative sports journalism, then areas that often involve exposing commercial wrongdoing are unlikely to find expression in an increasingly commercially driven broadcasting system, where vested interests play a significant role in the sports industry. Richard Williams suggests that:

There is not the same tradition of sports journalism in television. Television does football like showing movies, it's show business. It's ratings-driven, so it's not surprising. I mean, what level of investigative journalism does television do in any area, really? So it is our [print media] responsibility to do it, so things like the Ashley Cole tapping-up story was a newspaper story. So a handful of journalists do work in this area, such as David Conn, Andrew Jennings, Mihir Bose and Duncan McKay, but they are very much the exceptions. (Interview with author, 10 March 2005)

Indeed, investigative work into sport remains the terrain of those who tend to work outside of the sports departments in media organisations. A clear division of journalistic labour takes place. As David Conn suggests:

> The key issue here is the way that television slice off the sports investigations from the sports department or regular sports journalists. It is normally other journalists, often who are not steeped in the issues, who will come in and deal with issues which are completely ignored by say the BBC's *Match of the Day* and *Football Focus.* (Interview with author, 14 December 2004)

Dyke, commenting on the outcome of previous BBC rights deals for sport, and football in particular, laments the lack of analysis given to these deals by journalists. He argues that after a deal in 2000 that: 'The BBC and I were both savaged in the press for losing *Match of the Day.* No one was interested in our rather good FA deal, and the fact that ITV had massively overbid was ignored: most journalists know little about money but sports journalists know the least' (Dyke, 2004: 246). One assumes his fire is aimed at the print media; however, broadcast sports journalists stand equally open to this charge. In this respect not that much has changed from the situation discussed in Chapter 3, when Tony Mason could lament the lack of analysis of the business side of sport by the BBC as far back as the mid-1980s.

Thus news and current affairs journalists will from time to time investigate certain aspects of the sports industry, such as allegations of race fixing in horse racing. However, as David Conn has noted, this strand of journalism remains largely absent from mainstream sports journalism, even that occurring in the broadsheet/compact end of the market. In part, this is explained by the sports journalist's reliance on sources in what at times can be a very closed world (we examine this aspect of sports journalistic culture in more detail in the following chapter). As the sportswriter Graham Spiers at the Glasgow-based *Herald* explains:

> There are many complexities and tensions within sports journalism and one of them is trying not too hard to bite the hand that feeds you. *The Herald* wants me to interview Alex McLeish [manager of Rangers], but they also want me to be very robust editorially about Rangers. You then try to get an interview and Rangers say no because of the coverage in your paper. (Interview with author, 13 December 2004)

Thus, while sources remain crucial for the tabloid sports press driven by a quotes culture, even the more reflective broadsheet sportswriters are aware of the in-built tensions that exist across the journalistic spectrum between sources and journalistic integrity.

The lack of a critical investigative sports journalism is also framed by more ideological notions about the separation of sport and society, despite an increasing awareness that you cannot in reality keep politics out of sport, and that sport is an arena saturated with power relations (Whannel, 1992; Rowe, 1999; 2004; Boyle and Haynes, 2000). In other words, while journalists like to present sport as being of cultural and political significance to their readers, they also view it as a form of entertainment, and as such something not always subject to the journalistic rigour that might be brought to other areas of public and national life.

There is also another factor that helps account for the lack of investigative sports journalism that emerges from sports departments; and that is a lack of knowledge about the business world. Previous research (Boyle et al., 2002) identified how most sports journalists were simply ill-prepared to deal with the financial and business aspects and issues thrown up by the contemporary football industry. Eamon Dunphy views the lack of knowledge among sports journalists as a more general issue across much of this area of journalism. He suggest that:

> The problem with sports writing is knowledge of the subject. I always get worried with, say, football, where the knowledge deficit is huge. No political or economics writers are as wrong about politics or economics as sportswriters are about sport. I think the standards are low, but there is some good sports writing in England. Even in specialist publications such as the *Racing Post* there is someone like Paul Haig who is excellent. There isn't anyone like Paul Haig writing about soccer who simply does not follow conventional wisdom. Jeff Powell (*Daily Mail*) writes well, but he's not as good as he used to be. McIlvanney (*Sunday Times*) was always on the side of the powerful. (Interview with author, 30 May 2005)

Another key element that should not be underestimated is identified by Richard Williams:

> Investigative journalism is a small part of sports journalism. Why? It's hard work and not as much fun as going to a game and writing about it and because generally speaking editors don't really encourage their sports writers to do that, they don't discourage them. But there is no drive to do that. It's the legacy of the toy department and because there are matches all the time, there are stories all the time, such as the recent coverage of Mourinho or Wenger or Ferguson. So there is no lack of activity in this area. So in a sense you don't need it for the mix, but you do need it for the good of sport. (Interview with author, 10 March 2005)

The sheer range of stories that swirl around sport often mean that sports journalists are not forced by the dearth of material to dig for stories in the same way as you might in other areas of journalism. The drama and human interest element of sport, and its year-long cycle, often means that journalists are frequently moving from one story to the next, and unless instructed and funded to run with a more in-depth investigation, most do not. For many journalists the issue of time is also a factor, with both a 24/7 sports calendar and increasingly rolling media deadlines, some feel they are not simply given the time required to 'dig around' on possible investigative stories.

Thus changes, mostly driven by the demands of television and commercial considerations, have resulted in a sporting calendar that is global in scale, diverse in sports – although dominated by football – and all-year round. The summer of 2005, with no major football tournaments or an Olympic Games, still had Formula One motor racing competing with tennis from Wimbledon, golf from the Open at St Andrews, a five-week Lions rugby tour of New Zealand and an Ashes cricket series in England for space, while the ubiquitous football had Liverpool competing in a qualifying round of the UEFA Champions League in early July. As Paul Cooney argues:

> The pace of the game (and sport in general) means that there is no shortage of stories. Sport is about results and stories move on. But it does have a financial dimension that some sports journalists cannot deal with. But it is such a part of the, say, football now that it is something that radio sports journalism needs to be equipped to address. (Interview with author, 11 April 2005)

As is discussed in the next chapter, the rise of public relations and the ability of the media and sections of the sports industry to embrace a wider 'promotional culture' have also often helped to conspire to distort or discourage a more rigorous examination of the industry at a range of levels.

This, of course, is not to distract from a wider argument that runs through this book, which suggests that in many ways in Britain we are currently enjoying a golden age in the range and quality of sports writing. Or indeed to disagree with Welch when in 2003 he argued that there is a greater audience for sports journalism than had previously been imagined: 'The attitudes of writers and editors has changed, you are now getting some of the best journalism in newspapers at the back. We regard the sports section as a newspaper in miniature' (*Guardian*, 2003b). Rather it is to highlight the gaps that still exist in this journalism and to suggest that a growing audience does also exist for a form of uncomplicit investigative sports journalism. These gaps have become more acute as the sports and media industries have undergone an intense period of commercialisation since the late 1980s, which has seen significant change both in the sporting and media landscapes and in the related field of sports journalism.

Commercial pressures are never far from the continual reshaping of the media terrain. For example, late 2004 saw *The Financial Times,* under considerable wider financial pressure, drop the daily sports page that it had introduced in 2003 and relocate the seven staff members who worked on it. Given the very specific market position of the paper, its significant investment in sports coverage did seem to suggest a diversification from its core readership. Indeed, the growth of broadsheet/compact coverage of sport in the UK means breaking into this market is particularly difficult.

The struggle to emulate other European sports papers with a stand-alone successful UK national sport daily remains largely unrealised, despite a sustained attempt by *Sport First* to break the market in the late 1990s. Unlike Spain, Italy and France, for example, where a clear journalistic and commercial division of labour sees 'serious' newspapers carrying little sport, while sports dailies corner that market, the UK market has become much more hybrid. Across the print market, sports journalism has moved increasingly centre stage in the mixed range of journalism offered to readers from the tabloid through to the compact newspaper.

CONCLUSION: AN EVER-CHANGING MEDIA LANDSCAPE

One of the major changes that has taken place since the mid-1990s as the volume of sport on television has expanded has been the need for other media outlets to adapt and change in response to the evolving media landscape. This is particularly acute for the print media and specifically the popular press. The sports editor of the tabloid *Sunday Mirror* has noted how that paper has expanded its sports coverage to devote 37 pages out of 96 to sport. However, he is aware of the challenges the print media face, as in general terms sales decline and the influence of television on the sports industry intensifies. He suggests that: 'Because of the pressures from the amount of sport available on television, and due to falling sales, we constantly have to reinvent ourselves. It's difficult and you are competing with people who will pay for stories as well' (interview with author, 28 September 2004).

The drive to offer something distinctive and different from television coverage of sport has also led to increased competition between sections of the print media. The culture of the popular press, which has viewed exclusivity of news as one of the key selling features in that market, means that access to elite sports stars and exclusive stories relating to them remain an important element of its business.

There are also the wider structural changes that are shaping the print media and its journalism more generally. A declining readership and an increasing concern with costs, as well as challenges from emerging media such as web-based journalism and blogging have resulted in an industry in an apparent permanent state of change and flux.

As large sections of the broadsheet press migrated to a compact size or similar during 2004 and 2005, this has presented a new challenge for sports journalism at this end of the market. As David Chappell at *The Times*, which dispensed with its broadsheet edition completely in 2005, has suggested:

In simple terms do you allow the size of the page you are working on to dictate your editorial policy? Well, the answer to that is no. The strength of *The Times* is in its writing. The tabloid *Game* section was about approaching a busy Monday of football writing in a different and lively way. The distinction between broadsheet and tabloid journalism as we would know it in the 1960s and 1970s has blurred now. Generations have grown up with tabloid papers. We are halfway down the road of repacking things. There are clearly editorial challenges for us, but we can't simply replace the *Sun* and the *Mirror*. *The Times*' strength is in comment and analysis, business and sports writing. (Interview with author, 8 October 2004)

While this blurring of journalistic boundaries is without question one of the key characteristics of the print media industry in the 21st century, differences do also remain.

Oliver Holt, a former *Times* journalist, now chief sports writer at the tabloid *Daily Mirror*, began his two-page spread on the 2005 Open golf tournament with the following: 'As Tiger Woods prepared to hit his opening shot of the 134th Open Championship yesterday, a swallow swooped in front of him and skimmed and dipped a few inches above the smooth grass of the first tee in joyful cycles' (*Daily Mirror*, 15 July 2005). Such an opening paragraph, and indeed his whole piece would not have been out of place in the sports pages of a compact such as *The Times*. Yet, despite someone like Holt, there remain distinctive differences in the style, approach and agenda of the sports journalism found in the popular press and that at the broadsheet/compact end of the market. They may increasingly cover the same events, many of which would not have been covered by the 'quality' press of, say, 20 years ago, but as research carried out on coverage of the Euro 2004 football tournament clearly illustrated, the tone and interpretation of these events remains, for the most part, distinctive (Boyle and Montiero, 2005).

The tabloids remain committed to sensationalist stories and the building of stories from often the most meagre of scraps. For example, when the Scottish *Sun* (7 July 2005) carried a back-page splash on how former Celtic manager Martin O'Neill wholeheartedly endorsed the appointment of Neil Lennon as Celtic captain, the paper appeared to have secured an exclusive interview with the former Northern Ireland international. On closer inspection the piece was put together not from a one-to-one interview with the manager but, rather, from comments he made, promoted by specific questions from journalists, as he accepted an honorary degree from Queen's University Belfast. This part of the story was carried by the same reporter, Derek McGregor, on page 15 of the paper and widely carried in most other Scottish papers that day. Put simply, O'Neill, such a dominant figure in Scottish football culture for over five years, made good back-page copy, but in truth this was a non-story on a quiet sports news day for that paper. Yet the demands of this part of the market require drama and news, regardless.

This is not to deny that it will often be this section of the market that will break the major sports stories, which the compacts and other media will then happily follow through on.

As the sports industry continues to develop and the media restlessly alter and change form and structure, so the boundaries of sports journalism will continue to shift. The take-over of Manchester United plc by the American Glazer family in 2005 was a story to be found on mainstream news bulletins and across the news, comment, features, business and sports pages of the print media from the *Sun* to *The Daily Telegraph*. With its political, cultural and economic connotations the story symbolised the extent to which contemporary sports and media cultures have become closely linked, and confirmed that in reality there are no boundaries to contain journalism about sports in a media landscape hungry for content. The lack of clearly defined boundaries offers both opportunities and challenges to those journalists working in and around sports.

As argued in Chapter 2, the increase in the salaries paid to elite sports stars, primarily from television and associated commercial spin-offs, has meant that selling stories or having regular columns in the press is less financially appealing than it once was. Add to this the rise in professional public relations and image management that has accompanied the influx of money and exposure television has brought to many sections of the sports industry and you find a greatly altered relationship between journalists and those who play or run elite sport. It is this aspect of the contemporary sports journalist's working environment and the rise of a more formal public relations infrastructure that is examined in the following chapter.

5

SPORTS JOURNALISM
IN THE PROMOTIONAL AGE

In one important respect, covering sport today is not the pleasure it was for earlier generations. The possibility of establishing decent communications with leading sportsmen and women has become vastly more difficult since television took a central role in the promotion of sport, bringing global audiences, multinational sponsors, agents, marketing departments and public relations experts along with it.

Williams (2003: 6) *The View from the High Board: Writings on Sport*, **London: Aurum Press.**

The plaything of corporate public relations experts and self-servers, modern journalism is found to be not so much a public service as a public health hazard.

Ian Hargreaves (2003: 13) *Journalism: Truth or Dare*? **Oxford: Oxford University Press.**

Modern sports journalism is significantly shaped and influenced by public relations. In this chapter this increasingly complex relationship between sport, journalism and public relations is discussed. As the sports economy grows, fuelled by media interests, so too have the roles of public relations and image management in sport. As elite sports stars cross increasingly over into celebrity journalism, what impact is this process having on the scope and range of sports journalism? To what extent is this changing the relationship between journalists and the sports that they cover? This part of the book examines a number of ethical issues faced by sports journalists, as access to particular forms of information becomes more difficult as sports clubs and elite sports stars all seek to exercise greater control over their public media image.

SPORTS JOURNALISM AND MANIPULATION

A fundamental tension runs through sports journalism, and while it is not unique to this area of journalism, it shapes the landscape within which contemporary sports journalism is produced. At its core is a relationship between journalist and source. As Brookes has argued:

> There tends to be an interdependent relationship between sports organizations and journalists: sports organizations want favourable media coverage, sports journalists want access to sources. This is not to suggest that there are never tensions in this relationship; there are cases when sports organizations have denied access to particular journalists or news organizations, in these cases journalists have still been able to cover news about sports organizations from other sources. But the normal relationship between sporting organizations and media organizations is one that can be described as mutually beneficial interdependency. (2002: 37–8)

There have been high-profile instances when this relationship has broken down. For example, the banning of the Irish journalist Eamon Dunphy from press conferences involving the Republic of Ireland football manager Jack Charlton in 1990, while in Scotland there is a history of sports journalists being banned at certain times by both members of the Old Firm from their press conferences.

It was noted in Chapter 2 that the growing commercialisation of sport and the growth of a more celebrity- and television-orientated sports culture has also hastened a change in this relationship, specifically for print media journalists. Richard Williams notes how:

> There is a great deal more cynicism on both sides (sport and journalists). Fifty years ago, the journalist earned more than the participants, now, especially in the last ten years, that has all changed. They have moved into another world, especially footballers, and they no longer feel we are part of their world. So a 22-year-old has money and wealth, so there is never a chance to establish a friendship that allows you to understand a bit more about the player's way of life. It's a great, great loss. (Interview with author, March 2005)

Thus the increased wealth enjoyed by the sporting elite has helped create a barrier between journalists and sportspeople that did not exist to any great extent in the 1960s and even into the 1970s.

But even when these informal social networks formed a crucial part of the sports journalism culture, many sports journalists were less enamoured with their treatment by official sources. For example, in the Tunstall study published in 1971, he noted that British football journalists compared the level of access they had to players as poor when compared to their foreign counterparts. Tunstall notes that:

> Foreign journalists – especially from Latin countries – are accustomed to much fuller access to players before and after a match than is allowed in Britain. A common aspect of visits by foreign club teams is that the accompanying foreign journalists insist on visiting 'their' players' dressing rooms. Sturdy British officials block their way insisting that none shall pass, and – journalists say – bitter exchanges of both words and punches sometimes ensue. (1971: 176)

He also notes, however, that in the 1960s some clubs did try to develop a better public relations strategy; Coventry City, one such leading example, appointed a public relations officer, who had previous experience as a journalist. But, by and large, sports public relations remained a severely underdeveloped area until the 1990s.

Neverthless, Kelly has argued that, driven by the more aggressive tabloid journalism of the 1980s:

> The lobby which has grown up where newspapers and [football] clubs mutually feed off each other for news and exclusives has reached an unhealthy level. Journalists may not always feel free to criticize when they rely so much on clubs for access and information. Indeed, reporters and newspapers continue to be threatened by some clubs who are oversensitive to criticism. (1988: 9)

The era being discussed by Kelly is one that is largely characterised by a distinct lack of public relations or news management. Rather, personal relations with managers, journalists and players remained the key for the beat sports journalist. The wider circulation battles and increased competition within the newspaper industry, specifically at the tabloid end of the market, had increased the pressure on journalists and editors to break more exclusive stories. As the popular press focused increasingly on issues of celebrity linked with the developing television culture, thus sport, and football in particular with its growing television presence, was pulled into this orbit.

It is worth noting that attempts to manipulate the media in order to set the news agenda are not a distinctively contemporary aspect of sport's increasingly mediated culture. There has always been an inherent tension between journalism and the sports and entertainment industry. The latter view media coverage as a form of promotion for particular sporting events, a means of drumming up interest and putting numbers on the gate of the live event, a function of the sporting press that has served sports promoters and sports clubs well over the years. Conversely, journalists view their loyalty as being to their readers or listeners/viewers, and to scrutinise the sport they are covering on behalf of the paying fan. In reality, of course, an uneasy symbiotic relationship has developed between both parties with the realisation that mutual benefits could be derived from it.

Journalist and broadcaster Archie MacPherson recalls the impact that the Celtic Football Club manager Jock Stein had on Scottish sports journalism when he arrived at the Glasgow club during the 1960s. He and other media colleagues remember how Stein displayed the intuitive instincts of a newspaper editor as he strove to set the sports news agenda in a way simply not previously seen in this media market. MacPherson notes how Stein:

> Was the first manager to phone individuals from the media at home, on a regular basis, to take issue with them. He would travel late at night from his home on the south side of the city to a late-night newsstand to get the first editions of the newspapers, and with that ammunition to hand he would go back home and reach for the phone. ... Across the whole spectrum of the media there would be arguments, fall-outs, bannings from Celtic Park, mending of fences, ridicule, cajoling, baiting, good-natured jousting, spectacular rows and superb humour as we [journalists] were all sucked into the vortex of his own making. (2004: 236)

Later in his career, as an unhappy manager at Leeds United, Stein spoke with MacPherson, then working for the BBC's *Sportsnight* programme, and suggested that MacPherson should hint that he [Stein] would be interested in the recently vacated Scotland team manager's job. The piece by MacPherson duly led the sports news on the programme that night. Next morning Stein took to the air to deny the story being carried by the media that he wanted the Scotland post and stated that he was happy to stay at Leeds. However, the wheels had been put in motion and a climate of opinion was created which resulted shortly afterwards in Stein leaving Leeds United for the Scotland job (MacPherson, 2004: 256).

Over 20 years later, and the planting and leaking of stories through the sports press have become a common feature of much sports journalism. The significant difference these days is that it is agents who play a key role sourcing information about players and their desire to move from and to particular football clubs or who provide inside information on the progress, or lack of it, of contract negotiations. Football managers are not averse to using an, at times, all too eager media to plant stories. Crystal Palace Chairman Simon Jordan was upset by comments from West Ham manager Alan Pardew who told journalists that he was on the look-out for a striker in January 2006 and then named a Crystal Palace player as a possible target. Pardew waited two days and then apologised through the press for naming a player who was under contract at another club. But the process of unsettling a player had begun. In this process a public relations battle for the hearts and sympathies of the supporters is often played out in the sports press. There are other impacts on the relationship between players and journalists of the intervention of agents. Humphries (2003: 27–8) recalls how, during his time covering the Irish national football team, there was an occasion when the Irish player Robbie Keane would only turn up at a press conference if a particular Dublin evening newspaper, the *Evening Herald*, was not present. It transpired that the source of his grievance was a piece that the paper had run about a Nike soccer school involving Keane without first getting final copy approval from his agent.

In the digital age, the other change, as is discussed in more detail in the next chapter, is the pace at which such information circulates as media outlets feed off each other, reproducing stories that are often unchecked. In the summer of 2005, for example, when much of the back pages of the print media and sports radio broadcasting was taken up with whether the Liverpool captain Steven Gerrard would stay at the club or move, behind the scenes public relations activity was important in shaping the climate of opinion about any possible move with the public. In the end Gerrard made a dramatic last-minute decision to stay at the club, despite having signalled his desire to move only 24 hours previously. Real Madrid in Spain had been adding to the media pressure on Liverpool by using the top-selling Spanish sports newspaper *Marca* and other papers in that country to continually suggest and hint that Real would like Gerrard to come to Spain. Real's selective off-the-record briefings of journalists all helped to add to the level of coverage of Gerrard in Spain, which was then eagerly reported in the UK media. Indeed, the inability of Liverpool Football Club to present a clear and consistent message on the issue to the media over the summer simply fuelled the speculation, and the club's poor public relations handling of the situation, in part, almost led to the departure of its captain.

These examples, of which there are many, of what today would be called public relations activity, or 'spin', serve to illustrate that there is a long history in sports journalism of cosy (and not so cosy) relationships between players, managers and officials and particular journalists or editors leading to stories appearing (or being pulled), all which serve particular interests and help shape particular sports cultures. However, it is also clear that such relationships, which have often resulted in complicit forms of sports journalism, are not unique to this area of journalism. Indeed, the relationships sketched out above could easily be replicated in other areas of journalism, for example politics, where the leaking of stories or the 'flying of kites' have become commonplace (Marr, 2004). In sports journalism, the latter is often a story encouraged by an agent about player unrest at a club to test the water about possible interest in his client from other clubs, while in politics a leaked story about possible government policy is often 'put out' into the public domain to gauge both media and public reaction to it. Adverse reaction from either can often result in this policy being quietly dropped.

THE RISE IN SPORTS PR

What has ratcheted up the tension in such relationships is the increased role of both the market and public relations in shaping news values and agendas; allied with technological developments in a digital age that have increased the pace of information exchange and seen sport (and specifically football) become a key element of 'media content' (Boyle and Haynes, 2004). The latter has seen a range of stakeholders other than the traditional newsgathering organisations attempt to exploit digital systems to deliver exclusive sporting content for primarily commercial return. Inevitably, this has raised issues of control and access to players, images and information as clubs, players, agents, sponsors and a range of journalists attempt to mobilise media content for a range of often competing commercial ends. Former *Financial Times* journalist and then Director of Communications at Manchester United Paddy Harverson realised the potential impact of this situation on the media. Harverson, when at Manchester United, argued that in the digital age, football clubs were going to exert more control over access to information as they attempted, using new media, to set up their own communication channels with supporters:

> There's no doubt the media is not happy with it and I don't blame them for being unhappy with it. There is an issue here about delivering the news to our fans unhampered and untainted by the spin of the media. The perception of us in the world is shaped by the way we are delivered and portrayed by the media, which is often negatively, so the tabloids will take something a player says and turn it around into something he didn't say, quite happily because it's a much better story. It's sensational and the newspapers know that a negative story about United is always a more attractive story than a positive story because there are a lot more anti-United fans than there are pro-ones. So all that gives us good reason to use our own media to deliver as well as the commercial reasons which is [sic] to obviously drive subscriptions and sell things, but it's about striking the balance and I think it will take some time before everyone works it out. (Interview with author, 25 April 2002)

Central to reaching this stage of the relationship between sports and journalism has been the explosive growth of television coverage of sport since the early 1990s, the erosion of a public service culture and the increasing commercialisation of sport, driven by pay-TV. As the money flowed into football, and in reality it was football that dominated all others sports in the UK sports market, and the game was more aggressively marketed by Sky Television in particular (with the Premiership becoming synonymous with the Sky brand), sponsorship and the commercial profile of the game and its stars mushroomed. The 1990s were a boom time not only for football but also for those covering the sport as its profile across the media got significantly higher (Boyle and Haynes, 2004).

However, while the increasing colonisation of elite sport by television clearly benefited those organisations directly, it did little to strengthen the depth and quality of television journalism's engagement with sport. Richard Williams notes that for the print journalist:

> Football is the hardest to cover, facilities for the press are not great, this is not true in Europe but it is here. Access to the players after the game is restricted. I mean the *Premiership* [my emphasis] is so rich because of television, and then television takes precedence over everything. They don't quite recognise that we do have a role, television provides the narrative, we flesh out the characters. (Interview with author, 10 March 2005)

The point raised by Williams that most of the major sports organisations are not that interested in providing top-class facilities for the print media in an age when television is the major financial underwriter of elite contemporary sport is endorsed by the American sportswriter Leonard Koppett. He argues that in America, the focus of the sports promoter in the USA has shifted from the print to the electronic media, partly facilitating the decline in the power and 'aura' of the press box. He suggests that:

> Newspapers remain an important element in delivering the free publicity the product needs [however] television not only reaches more people with more immediate impact, but also pays the promoter lavishly for the privilege. The 'news media' always were and always will be an essential ingredient in making commercialized sports (or any entertainment) work. But the primary medium now is electronic: radio, television and, more recently, elaborate message boards and web sites (2003: 7).

THE ISSUE OF COMPLICITNESS

Throughout the book we have noted how the growing influence of television, within the wider sports industry as both financial underwriter and key vehicle for the promotion of sport, has changed the relationship that the print media have with differing sports.

As the media industries have become more complex and interrelated, so too have the networks of influence that help shape contemporary sports journalism. When Rupert Murdoch attempted to use BSkyB to buy Manchester United, one of the largest football clubs in the world, in 1999, Piers Morgan, the then editor of the *Mirror* newspaper, a direct rival to the

Murdoch-owned *Sun* newspaper, was clear what the impact would be of such a move on the *Mirror's* football journalism. In his diary he recalls: 'Rupert Murdoch is trying to buy Manchester United … The consequences for the *Mirror* are obvious and awful. The *Sun* would get all the access they need to Britain's biggest club and we'd get squeezed out' (Morgan, 2005: 203).

While that bid failed, other media organisations out of the 'rights loop' find access to star players has become more difficult as a morass of agents and public relations managers intervene into what was traditionally a rather straightforward arrangement. As Craig Tegurtha argues:

> The growth of PR in football is a major issue for papers. The whole issue of access to players has become very difficult. In football a club might agree to an interview, the player agrees and then it has to go to the agent, who may look for a fee or knock it back. I tend not to agree to pay fees. For example, we recently did a piece with Joe Cole (Chelsea and England) and he didn't want a fee. It was a fair piece and he knew he would get a straight run from us. If he says something daft then we will of course publish it, but he trusted us and we were happy to be fair with him.
>
> Other papers will pay, so Thierry Henry will get £15k for doing something for the *Sun*. But then they are looking for copy approval and now headline approval. Agents will fax across their comments on the copy and the headline. I don't agree with that and refuse it. But it does happen.
>
> The other issue is the informal contact is much less than it used to be, so bumping into people for a chat and building relationships is much harder to do. As a result, you see mistrust has deepened between the players and the press.
>
> I'll send a reporter to La Manga (in Spain) with Chelsea at considerable cost although I know we are not guaranteed anything. Because he is good and gets on well with players, who trust him, we will get some stories out of that and longer term we have built up a bit of trust, so it was worth the investment in the long term. (Interview with author, 28 October 2004)

Allied with this is the rise of techniques now common practice in sports journalism that are more readily associated with other aspects of the entertainment industry and its relationship with the print media (Morgan, 2005: 309). These include copy, picture and in some cases headline approval by agents working for sports stars who have sold stories to newspapers. December 2005 saw the *Manchester Evening News* turn down an interview with Wayne Rooney when Manchester United's PR agency demanded copy and headline approval.

As sport, and football in particular, has become a key 'media product' with an attendant change in the value of the rights associated with sport, aspects of image management have become more commonplace. Paul Cooney recalls negotiating the radio rights for Celtic vs. Rangers matches in the late 1970s for the princely sum of £100. Those days are long gone and Cooney notes how:

During rights negotiations you would find the authorities wanting to insert clauses that would control information. We would resist, of course, but they would say 'we are all in the same business of promoting the game' and we would say 'well that's not exactly the business we are in', we are a commercial organisation servicing the people of the west of Scotland but we are not *Pravda* and journalism is not PR. The clubs would sometimes come on with 'we spend money with you', but there is a respect there now. (Interview with author, 11 April 2005)

While the rise of a more professional approach by clubs and elite players and sports people to managing their image and media profile is clearly a significant aspect of the contemporary sports journalism culture, the print media has played a significant role in the evolution of the current situation.

It was the tabloids that introduced the concept of money for articles, bringing an unhealthy dimension to the relationship between journalists and sports stars that has increasingly been corroded over the last few decades. In hindsight this 'cheque book journalism' has in many ways now come back to haunt those papers. Reflecting on the changing relationship between journalists and football players in particular, Graham Spiers argues that:

It was the age of innocence in the 1970s. So journalists who chummed up to people 20 years ago, now only get access through official club channels. But the press is to blame. They don't trust us anymore. The age of innocence was one in which you hung around with the players, you frankly did not accurately report what they said. As journalism became more intrusive and money was introduced that age of innocence was lost. And now if I want to speak to John Hartson at Celtic I go through the PR dept of the club that has been created to protect the club from the excesses of the press. (Interview with author, 13 December 2004)

THE RISE OF CELEBRITY AND THE IMPACT OF SPORTS PR

In his book *Billion Dollar Game*, television executive Peter Bazalgette (2005) charts the rise of the *Big Brother* television format and also discusses the importance of celebrity culture in contemporary popular culture. He suggests, however, that the origins of the recent explosion of interest in celebrity culture that has characterised the media landscape over the last decade or so, has its roots in the broader shifts in the political economy of the media industries. Bazalgette argues that:

There are no new human instincts driving today's celebrity culture. What is new is the multiplicity of media channels via which it is possible to achieve fifteen minutes of fame or infamy. In the past, only a few could succeed in capturing the level of public attention that Nell Gwyn, Beau Brummell and Clara Bow did. Now, as Warhol correctly predicted, everyone can – on terrestrial TV, on digital TV, on radio, in celeb magazines or on the world wide web. What is also new is that the media, which need fresh and frequent supplies of celebrities, are creating them to order rather than relying on the courtesans, highwaymen and film stars of the past (2005: 243–4).

It is against this backdrop that the rise in the profile and media prominence of sports and sports stars needs to be positioned. While the sports industry has always had its pantheon of heroes and villains who have often been to a large extent created by media coverage, and sports journalism in particular, the explosion of media outlets and the related expansion of journalism associated with sports have helped both to feed and to fuel the developing celebrity culture. The move from a supply (regulated) media culture to a more demand-led (re-regulated) media culture has helped enable the growth and explosion of coverage in particular sports, such as football, that have been a key element of media content in this new age of plenty (Boyle and Haynes, 2004).

As money has flowed into the elite end of sport and the attendant commercial and corporate interest in associating brands with elite sports and sports stars has developed, this has been accompanied by the growth in power and influence of agents, image consultants and public relations managers. These groups act as a buffer between the star and the public and attempt to manage the image of their client across the range of media platforms which have helped facilitate the pace, scale and shape of contemporary celebrity culture. While there is a recognition (Andrews and Jackson, 2001; Whannel, 2002; Turner, 2004) that sports stars are differentiated from other areas of the celebrity terrain (in that an element of talent and skill is required to become a top star), there are also growing similarities between elite sportspeople and those in other areas of the entertainment industry.

Schlesinger (2006) has noted that these wider structural shifts in media ecology have facilitated the tensions now evident in attempts to define the boundaries between public and private spheres and the accompanying shifts in standards and morality. He argues that:

> One of the consequences of this quite far-reaching shift in the moral economy is that *image-management* becomes ever more important. Indeed, this is not only a consequence but also a cause. The recourse to public relations in its broadest sense is hardly new. But with the rise of celebrity culture it has become ever more potent. It has been at the heart of government for the past three decades in the UK and what is increasingly talked of as the crisis of journalism is closely connected to the rise of the 'spin-doctor' in government. (Schlesinger, 2006)

Of direct relevance for those interested in the mapping out of these shifts within and across the terrain of popular culture, is the extent to which public relations and aspects of the culture of spin have become increasingly central to sports journalism and the wider sports industry. As is argued here, a key aspect has been the re-positioning of sports into the wider entertainment industry and the transfer of practices and procedures relating to image management, public relations and the role of agents from other sectors of the entertainment industry into a sports business culture.

Some journalists see a more corrosive dimension to the increased power that sports stars and their agents attempt to exert on their media coverage. For example, although not unprecedented, the refusal of the England national football team in 2004 to speak with the media following the team's win in Poland in a World Cup qualifier in September of that year was interesting for a number of reasons. The dispute followed criticism from the media about the performance of the team and, in particular, its goalkeeper David James. Following a mistake by James that cost England victory in its match with Austria, a national newspaper portrayed the player as a donkey; something that the England players felt overstepped the boundary of legitimate criticism. Their refusal to speak with the media was, as one might expect, roundly condemned by journalists, who on such occasions tend to mobilise the 'we are only asking the questions the fans want answered' line of defence as their justification for seeking access to the team and players. However, underlying much of the media coverage was a growing perception among sports journalists that these elite players were increasingly acting like spoilt millionaires and that a growing space had developed between journalists and sports stars. In some respects this distance echoes some of the tensions that exist in the relationship, for example, between that of the political journalist and politician (Marr, 2004). While being generally sympathetic to the right of the players to refuse to speak to the press, Richard Williams also noted that: 'Where the business gets a little murkier is when a player's agent starts ringing up the BBC to complain about negative comments on his performance. So powerful are today's galacticos that some of them believe themselves immune to the normal pressures of assessment and criticism' (*Guardian*, 2004).

The growth of formal pressure being exerted on sports journalists from agents and suchlike is also something associated with the print media. Matt Tench, sports editor of *The Independent*, suggests that: 'You do get attempts by agents to manage your pages, they ask for things like copy approval, something we never give. The situation is increasingly like what show business reporting has been for 20 years' (interview with author, 21 September 2004).

As noted elsewhere in the book, the relationship your media outlet has with key players as sources of information is fundamental in shaping journalistic practice. Those sports journalists employed for their comment, analysis and reflection remain largely indifferent to the sensibilities of highly paid sports stars, and have the editorial freedom to call things as they see them. However, those journalists operating at the more 'quotes-driven' end of the sports market, need to continually cultivate relations with a range of sources who have become professionalised in terms of media and image management. As a result, the space for uncomplicit sports journalism, free from spin, manipulation and public relations management is becoming increasingly located in distinctive areas of the contemporary sports journalism landscape. This process is taking place at a time when the audience for sports journalism is becoming increasingly aware of the range of techniques being used by various stakeholders in sport to set and control news agendas. While the proliferation of media outlets in the digital age makes this process more important for these stakeholders, it also has become more complex.

For journalists, the impact on their ability to 'get up close' to the star has been profound. Paul Cooney recognises this as an issue that is particularly acute if you are not a significant rights holder. He notes how:

It is much harder to get close to the players. The clubs also protect the players, and some-times hinder the players in establishing a good relationship with the media. We were never in the pocket of players, we were fresh and new and a bit cheeky. And we would have a go and be opinionated, which did cause trouble. It's not just the money in the sport, the whole game has become much more transient, players used to be at the Old Firm for life, now players come and go, from down south and overseas at a much greater rate. It's also now much more press and media conference orientated and controlled, it's harder to work outside that system and get one to ones with players. It's now harder for radio sports journalism to be at the cutting edge. (Interview with author, 11 April 2005)

At the same time, print journalists such as Richard Williams argue:

Everything has changed in the relationship between journalism and sport and often for the worst, such as the rise of PR. It's much harder to get decent access. I can't remember the last time I sat down with someone knowing you had an open-ended stretch of time. The other day I did a big interview with someone and I had twenty minutes, and he was ten minutes late. Not a lot of time to see into somebody's soul. And that's much more common. (Interview with author, 10 March 2005)

While in the US, sportswriter Leonard Koppett has documented the gradual development of 'off limits' areas to which the players retreat, away from a sports media that are increasingly 24/7 and hungry for content to fill the hours of airtime devoted to sport. He argues that the ubiquitous nature of media coverage of sport has helped aggravate relationships between players and the media. In addition, he suggests that:

The old intimacy would be gone in any case. A $3 million-a-year 26-year-old has little in common with a 40-to-60-year-old writer (especially if it's a woman) living on a five figure salary. Their lifestyles and daily life experience is too different. Established players are surrounded by a coterie of advisors and gofers ... Most of all, as any human being would, they react to the presence of microphones and tape recorders as a signal that they're 'on', consciously performing and wary of the consequences, not engaging in normal conversation. They go through it patiently enough, but real life resumes only when that's over. (2003: 49)

It has clearly become more difficult for sportswriters to get 'inside' the world of the contemporary sports star. Some, like Koppett, argue that it has been thus since the advent of television specifically from the 1960s. He suggests that getting an inside track on sport has become extremely difficult: 'The idea than any reporter, regardless of experience, working in an atmosphere of active and accumulated hostility amid a public relations machine training its players to conceal their true thoughts, could deliver this any day in any circumstances, seems to me ridiculous' (Koppett, 2003: 115).

Graham Spiers, reflecting on how the changing nature of the newspaper industry has also shaped the climate of mistrust that characterises the contemporary relationship between the sports journalist and the sports star, suggests that:

> The subject of sources has become more complicated. I think the old principle of the great source has become redundant. The press has got so great and the trust between the press and football clubs has degenerated so much, and it's the press's fault, because so much is made up and distorted. Because of that clubs protect the information that comes out of them and therefore it's more difficult for journalists. If you look at how this impacts on journalists it's quite interesting. To put it at its most crude, you have two different types of market. At my paper [*The Herald*] I am told what is wanted is what I think, but if I was at the [*Daily*] *Record*, what they are interested in is what the footballer thinks. So it's a quotes culture, so Jacko [journalist Keith Jackson] needs to get people, whether they are great or rubbish he needs to get to them. He needs Martin O'Neill or John Hartson, I don't as I can write an interpretative piece, so it hurts the tabloid journalist more than me because clubs close ranks.
>
> In terms of the source itself. I can speak with a Celtic director who can brief me and he will probably think he can trust me more because it's a broadsheet rather than a tabloid. Tabloids upset the club through distortion; my type of paper upsets a club through comment. So we both upset them in slightly different ways.
>
> I laugh when people talk about having a great source, because we all have them. In some cases they are talking about the PR person at the club, we can all phone them up. For example, there is only one source at Rangers and it is David Murray. Anytime anyone utters the comical phrase: 'I've got great sources at Rangers', they mean David Murray. We can all phone Murray. (Interview with author, 13 December 2004)

Chapter 2 examined some of the attempts by editors to 'bust the cosy club' between sports journalists and sports stars in the UK during the 1980s. In the USA, however, according to sportswriter Jerry Eskenazi, who worked for almost 50 years on the *New York Times*, it was the 1970s that saw a key moment in the evolution of contemporary American sports writing. He argues that: 'The freebie world of the newspaperman – and thus, the camaraderie between the reporter and the people and teams he wrote about – changed forever in the 1970s with two unrelated events: Watergate, and a story in New York Magazine' (Eskenazi, 2003: 13).

For Eskenazi then, on the one hand, Watergate and the representation of journalism in the subsequent film *All the President's Men* helped shape the attitudes of a new generation of journalists, who saw the profession as being both honourable and investigative. On the other hand, the name and shame article in the *New York Magazine* documented all the free tickets being allocated to the media from Madison Square Garden (a major sporting venue), and resulted in newspapers introducing a stricter code of practice that attempted to distance sports reporters from the events they were reporting on. Eskenazi (2003: 14) notes how: 'This new morality had a tremendous, positive effect on the business. Most important, it forced many reporters, especially sportswriters to think of themselves as professionals and not free-loaders. This, in turn, forced organizations and teams to look at reporters in a different way as well.'

The reality for contemporary sports journalists is that getting close to a subject, on their terms, has become next to impossible. It is also clear that in some cases, journalists have taken 'ghosting' jobs they would not normally take, because it is a rare opportunity to spend real time with someone and get to know them and get to see their world. Richard Williams suggests, for example, that:

> Paul Hayward [then sportswriter with *The Daily Telegraph* and later the *Daily Mail*] did Michael Owen's book and I don't think he would have done it otherwise. So the last time we were with England Owen will come over with him to have a chat, in a way that would not have happened otherwise. So there is a wall there, which is very regrettable. I am very envious of earlier generations who did the job, bought drinks with the players and talked to the players. The ghosted column is also an issue that can raise tensions, particularly in the tabloids, where players will get paid money for rubbish basically and this also lowers the value and standing of the media. (Interview with author, 10 March 2005)

The ability to shape the journalistic output and the coverage given to a sport or individual goes beyond simply denying access, although this is often the most crude mechanism that is used to attempt to control the media.

THE EASY LIFE: PRESS CONFERENCES AND PHOTO CALLS

While the 1990s have seen a rise in the professional public relations skills of teams and sports organisations, the changing position of the sports journalist has also played a role in shaping this process. For some sports journalists, while they lament the passing of the more informal network of contacts – a theme which finds an echo among journalists in other areas such as crime reporting – it has, in other ways, made life easier for them. As sports organisations have become more media and image aware the formalising of press conferences, photo calls and suchlike have all helped to routinise and formalise a large part of the flow of information.

For some journalists this is a concern; however, as football journalist Brian Woolnough has suggested, it has also made the job easier. Discussing the challenge of covering the England national football team he notes that:

> There are too many of us [sports journalists], all fighting over the flesh that is a story or a good interview. In a way many of the clueless ones have been helped by today's system with England. There is hardly any digging needed, no need for real personal relationships with the players, no access for a night out or meal with players who become friends. The FA wheel in the players, security guards stand around waiting for interviews to stop, before the players are whisked off. (2000: 116)

Allied with this is the realisation that the print media cannot compete for immediacy with the broadcast and, increasingly, the online media. However, here again the relationship is far from simple. For while print journalists may lament the increasing exposure given by rolling sports news to areas previously the domain of newspaper journalists (for example, press conferences), most sports departments on national newspapers will have the *Sky Sports News* channel on 24/7 as this and other 24-hour rolling news media cover live sports-related media conferences. Indeed, it is not unknown for journalists to lift quotes simply from watching a live press conference on television and reproduce them as if they had been at the actual event.

We have noted in the previous chapter the ways in which some sports, through public relations and communications executives and with the tacit acceptance of a core of journalists who cover the sport, exert an extensive stronglehold on its image – Formula One motor racing is a prime example. We also noted that at other sports events, such as a golf tournament, journalists do not need to leave the media centre where they are spoon-fed material from which they can build their story. Those journalists who interlope into this sports environment from other fields of journalism are often surprised by what they find.

Alex Thompson, a *Channel 4 News* journalist and broadcaster, was taken aback by the controversy caused by his attendance at an England football press conference on 25 June 2004 following the defeat and elimination of England by Portugal from the Euro 2004 football championship. Thompson asked a question at the conference along the lines of whether the England captain, David Beckham, was considering his position, given the part he had played in a poor tournament for the team. Beckham bristled and answered curtly back, clearly annoyed that this topic had even been raised. The exchange was picked up by all the news broadcasts, and Thompson, a non-sports journalist, appeared on TalkSPORT radio the following day to explain what had happened. As a news journalist he was surprised at the uproar caused by what he deemed to be a legitimate question. He claimed he was simply asking the question being put by England supporters outside the ground after the game. He noted that these 'so called conferences are pretty deferential' and he was surprised that a basic question being asked by fans, was not being put by the other sports journalists in the room.

What this example illustrates is the complex and often fraught relationship that sports journalists, who require access to players and managers, often have with their subjects. It also suggests that the distance that can grow between professional journalists, often insulated from direct contact with the fans, and readers on whose behalf they are supposed to be asking questions, can have an impact on their ability to write for these readers, as the supposed outsider, with the insider knowledge.

Eamon Dunphy has worked across the fields of sport and politics and suggests that:

> The difference between sports and political journalism is usually the calibre of people. The sports department used to be the toy department of the paper. However, sport sells and it's become more important in papers; however, the chief sportswriter would be of a lesser calibre than the chief political correspondent.
>
> In the hierarchy of journalism you needed a guy to get stories, with the populist touch, but you didn't need someone who wrote well, that has changed and it is changing for the better. In Ireland, Tom Humphries from *The Irish Times* is outstanding. You do not see the same clichés that you used to see and there is more rigour applied. (Interview with author, 30 May 2005)

While Dunphy recognises that sports journalism has changed, it could also be argued that at times there are striking similarities between the worlds of sport and politics. Both involve journalists forging relationships with those about who they write, often in quite an intense and pressurised environment.

It would also be wrong to accuse sports journalists of being unique in becoming compromised by being too close to sources. In many ways it is an endemic problem across journalism, and certainly not unique to those working within the various terrains offered by the diverse sports industry. Political journalist and broadcaster Jon Snow of *Channel 4 News* recalls how the smooth media operations of the White House in Washington, where he worked in the early 1980s, appeared to offer greater access to the political journalist. However, he notes that: 'In reality, of course, it meant that journalists were so close to the centres of power that we were seduced by them; we rarely challenged them for fear of damaging our status, and we were frequently taken in by them' (Snow, 2005: 213).

Graham Spiers is also well aware of the complex relationship that exists between journalists and the people they write about. He is aware that the issue of compromise or journalistic complicity is one shared with journalists working in arenas other than sport. He argues that:

> The closer you get to sources the more compromised you are. I have a policy of not getting close to anyone I write about regularly. I got too close to Craig Brown (when

manager of the Scotland national football team) and David Murray (chairman of Rangers Football Club). (Interview with author, 13 December 2004)

Spiers notes how his experience with the then Celtic football manager Martin O'Neill forced him to reassess the role and responsibilities that a journalist has in balancing uncomplicit journalism with the practical requirements of working closely with key sources:

> I wrote about him probably every week of my working life for 18 months when he came to Scotland. I was then invited to dinner with O'Neill and we spent five hours in a restaurant in town. When I came to write my next column about O'Neill, my fingers paused on the keyboard, and I thought I've crossed a bridge here, I like him, this is now different. Eventually I got back to writing about him as I had done before I got to know him a bit better, but I thought don't get too close to anyone. (Interview with author, 13 December 2004)

Thus again the issue of compromise is one shared with journalists working in other spheres, such as politics. The market position of, in this case, the newspaper you work for is also important. For example, Jon Ryan, sports editor of *The Sunday Telegraph* can argue that 'PR has become a growing issue in sports journalism, although less perhaps for the broadsheet press in that we are less reliant on quotes and access to some extent than the tabloids' (interview with author, 13 October 2004). The broadsheet/compact sportswriter will often be employed for their comment and thoughts, and as such is less reliant on securing quotes from key players and managers than some tabloid sports journalists. This sector of the market is often heavily dependent on a quotes' culture to drive news stories and headlines.

There is also the growing problem for journalists of elite sports stars using the media simply as a vehicle through which to promote their brand image and the commercial interests which they endorse.

THE CASE OF MICHAEL OWEN: MANAGING YOUR IMAGE

The Newcastle United and England footballer Michael Owen began writing an occasional column in *The Times* in 2004 after joining the Spanish club Real Madrid. These appeared in the sports section of the newspaper, although in 2005 the Saturday 19 February edition trailed a major interview with the star in its weekend glossy magazine, which is not aimed specifically at its sports readership. The magazine carried a moody front page shot of Owen, headlining the inside article under 'Michael Owen: On Football, Bullfighting and Learning Spanish' by feature writer Robert Crampton. Inside, spread over four pages (two and a half consisting of pictures) and under the headline 'THE REAL DEAL', the journalist opened the piece as follows:

> He's guarded, Michael Owen. Guarded by the ever-present minder from his agents, SFX, guarded too, at a slightly greater distance, by the people from Tissot, the watch manufacturers who pay him to wear their products, and guarded in any case by a personal preference for avoiding controversy. (*The Times Magazine*, 2005)

An honest, if not inauspicious introduction, which cleverly name-checks one of the key sponsors while still suggesting that what follows will in fact be a carefully choreographed and controlled piece of access to Owen by his agents. In the hour Crampton spends with him, we learn little that is not already in the public domain, indeed many of the quotes used in the article are actually taken from Owen's autobiography (Owen, 2004) written by sports-writer Paul Hayward and published just before his move from Liverpool to Real Madrid.

Thus this piece of journalism is little more than a chance for Owen to raise his profile back in the UK (through what is called in PR a 'puff piece'), with a gentle interview that exposes him to a largely non-sporting audience. In return *The Times* gets an exclusive (of sorts) that it uses to drive sales of their weekend paper and solidifies the corporate relationship it is building with the player. However, the article actually goes beyond this simple public relations exercise and further blurs the lines between editorial and adverting in a manner more in keeping with fashion journalism. Running down the side of the article we are given a list of the details associated with the £250 watch Owen is wearing (which is clearly visible in a number of the 'portraits' that accompany the article and can be purchased 'from all good jewellers and department stores') as well as his clothes, and the various websites which sell this designer merchandise.

In short, this piece is a form of advertising and promotional journalism that is becoming increasingly common among elite stars working across the entertainment industry. The top sports stars are now playing by the same rules as their contemporaries in the music and film industries. They allow access, but it is on their terms, with a careful eye on the image they project and, if possible, a tie-up with key corporate sponsors whose brand gets associated with an elite sports star.

What this type of control and access produces is a neutered form of journalism, in which little is revealed, despite in this case the best efforts of the journalist to alert the reader to the constraints within which the interview took place.

In a postscript to the Owen piece carried by *The Times Magazine*, another article based again on an interview with Owen appeared three months later in the first edition of *GQ Sport*, a new twice yearly supplement with the men's magazine *GQ*. In a three-page article titled 'Battle-Scarred Galactico', Toby Wiseman recounts his encounter with Owen, including the obligatory reference to watchmakers Tissot, and it soon becomes apparent that this is the same media opportunity on which Crampton reported earlier in the year. The *GQ* location photograph has Owen in the same clothes featured on the cover of the *Times Magazine* article. Little is forthcoming from Owen, and Wiseman builds his piece as best he can around Owen's tightly controlled PR offerings.

Owen, like other top stars in sport, is keen to manage his image, and is acutely aware of the importance of this for his off-the-field commercial activity; however, it makes for difficult journalism and offers little in the way of insight into Owen's world, other than to inadvertently re-emphasise the extent to which elite level sport stars have become an adjunct of the world of commerce and advertising.

Of course, as the sports industry has expanded, the desire to control its media image has extended beyond simply the athletes to encompass the governing bodies of sport and the people who run the industry.

THE SPORTS INDUSTRY AND IMAGE MANAGEMENT

The previous chapter raised some issues about the role and function of particular types of journalism in the arena of sports reporting and specifically the issue of investigative reporting. As public relations and image management becomes an ever-increasing part of the sports industry landscape, there are clear challenges for those who view part of the remit of sports journalism to look beyond the action on the pitch and at the increasingly complex hinterland of sport, with its moral, cultural, commercial and often political connotations. David Conn has argued that:

> There remains a clear division of labour between investigative journalism about sports and general journalism associated with sports. These interventions are usually infrequent and investigative sports journalism is not part of the remit of broadcast sports journalism. This does not mean reporting sports news, but digging and bringing to light stories from beneath the show business and entertainment veneer which the industry is so keen to present to the world. Quite often when business issues are dealt with it will be to report that a sponsor thinks a particular club is worth x amount to their brand. While this is news, there also needs to be some digging into the story, often they are simply relaying information. (Interview with author, 14 December 2004)

A certain irony exists here, in that at a time when there has never been more to report or cover in the increasingly ubiquitous world of sport, investigative journalism remains largely peripheral.

What is slowly beginning to evolve is a degree of recognition among some sections of the media that the sports terrain requires a range of journalists who are writing about sport in all its complexity, and that often this means engaging in stories and constructing narratives that reach across traditional definitions of sport, commerce and culture. Part of the reason why a media journalist such as Ashling O'Conner moved from *The Financial Times* to the sports desk of *The Times* was a realisation by *The Times* of the need to get a grip on media/sports business stories; for example, the collapse of ITV Digital and the impact of this on the football industry. O'Conner notes how:

> It was that story that caused a problem because it sat between the sports and business pages. For sportswriters it was far too financial, while the business journalists did not really get the sports angle. So I was asked to bridge those two worlds. They also wanted someone who could read a balance sheet and work on the sports desk. (Interview with author, 19 August 2005)

The rise of the sports news correspondent in both print and broadcast media outlets is another such example of this growing recognition.

As sections of the sports industry have become rich with the flow of money from television and sponsors, so the issue of governance in sport has become more important. Often this means treating those in positions of power to the same journalistic rules of engagement that most people in public life now expect from the contemporary media. For example, much of the late summer of 2004 saw both the front and the back pages of newspapers, from all sections of the market, dominated by the revelations, broken by the *News of the World* but subsequently given extensive coverage in both the broadsheets and mainstream broadcast news, that the England football coach Sven Goran Eriksson had been having a relationship with a secretary at the Football Association (FA). As the story rumbled on, further revelations emerged, including the fact that Mark Palios, the Chief Executive of the FA had also had a relationship with the same woman. The subsequent attempt by the Head of Communications at the FA – former sports editor, Colin Gibson – to do a deal with the *News of the World* (which the paper then exposed) by giving them more information on the England coach as long as Palios was kept out of the story, ultimately led to the resignation of both Gibson and the FA's chief executive.

It appears that Gibson's background in the world of sports journalism, rather than news journalism, partly accounted for his mistake. His demise served as an example of how traditional areas governed by the unwritten rules of sports journalism, which is often about networks of contacts within the game keeping stories and people out of the papers, simply was not appropriate. In a news-hungry 24/7 media environment, sports-related stories, in particular if they involve sexual scandal and high-profile individuals, are firmly part of the mainstream news agenda, and will be pursued in the same manner as political scandals, often broken by the tabloids and then commented upon by all sections of the media.

Many of these changes have been driven by money and the rise of a media-fuelled celebrity culture, which sport often sits within. The relationship between those in the public eye and those who report on these people often appears to be founded on a combination of cynicism and misunderstanding. It could be argued that a lot of the tensions in sports journalism, in this regard, merely reflect broader shifts in journalism more generally and, indeed, that there is a growing parallel not simply between sports and more general entertainment journalism, but with areas of 'hard news' such as politics.

Thus public relations techniques commonly used in, say, the film and entertainment industries, increasingly find themselves being mobilised at the elite end of the sports industry, simply exacerbating the already corrosive relationship that exists between many sports stars and journalists. Yet to what extent are parts of the sports industry, and its attendant sports journalism, simply not an appropriate arena in which to simply transplant aspects of public relations practice or 'spin' that characterise, for example, political journalism and culture? The British and Irish Lions rugby tour of 2005 offers some insights.

SPORT, SPIN AND THE LIONS TOUR OF 2005

One of the most obvious fusions of sport and public relations in recent times occurred with the appointment by Sir Clive Woodward of Alastair Campbell to act as a consultant on media and communications issues on the British and Irish Lions rugby tour of New Zealand in the summer of 2005. Campbell was the most famous political public relations co-ordinater in British politics, closely associated with the rise of New Labour, and Tony Blair in particular, and the three successful election campaigns that had seen Blair and Labour in government since 1997.

Woodward, the Lions manager, had apparently been lobbied by rugby journalists, who had complained about the poor media organisation of a previous Lions tour. He felt that Campbell, with his experience in the political world of working in a high-pressure environment, would be ideal for the most high-profile tour in the history of the Lions. Campbell was aware of the potential adverse impact that his appointment might have with some sections of the media. He asked Woodward 'Aren't you worried some of the papers will have a go at you for getting involved with a "political spin doctor?"' 'Great,' he [Woodward] says. 'Let's stir things up a bit' (Campbell, 2005).

Campbell himself was initially impressed by his contact with the rugby journalists covering the build-up to the tour. Commenting on the press launch to introduce the squad to the media he noted that: 'I got another glimpse of how different the sports media are from the political press. One, though tough and probing, basically wants you to win; the other really do yearn for bad news' (*The Times*, 2005a). It would be an opinion he would change by the end of the tour.

On arrival in New Zealand, some sports journalists, such as Mick Cleary of *The Daily Telegraph*, felt that Campbell's influence had resulted in an overly choreographed and staged image of the Lions being projected to the host country. Cleary argued:

> The Lions have been welcome guests in New Zealand, indeed cherished. They do not need to do much to be loved. If anything, they have been guilty of trying too hard. They have forced the issue, been too overt at pushing their message. What might work in the smoke and mirrors world of Westminster is not necessarily appropriate in the land of straight talking. They want straight deliveries not spin. (*The Daily Telegraph*, 2005)

There is a crucial central element that distinguishes sport from other areas of cultural and political life and thus makes much of the 'spin' that has developed round the sports industry obsolete. Sport is almost completely driven by results, often on a week-by-week basis. Winning matches, titles and trophies is a powerful panacea for many ills. Sustained success in sport makes you a powerful player with the media, while defeat (an inevitable part of sports culture) weakens the defensive shield around you.

Martin Samuel, writing for *The Times*, with which Campbell also had an occasional sports column before and during the tour, is rare among journalists working in the UK press, in that his opinions regularly appear across both the sports and the comment pages of the newspaper. Samuel's piece on the Lions tour and on the impact of Campbell and the role of public relations was damning and perceptive. He is worth quoting at length. Under the headline 'Woodward's men may learn the hard way that being caught in the spin cycle just won't wash', he argued:

> The idea that what modern sport needs – what the world needs, in fact – is media management is being crushed under the weight of the most basic truths. As expected, the 2005 Lions no more need Alastair Campbell than the 2005 Labour Government needs a 16st hooker (insert your punchline here). What they need is to win a significant game of rugby, starting this morning. The rest will then take care of itself.
> ... Spin no more works in sport than in elementary mathematics. Sport is black and white, cut and dried, win or lose, there is nothing to massage, to mould, to turn slyly to your advantage. The agenda is not set by *Breakfast with Frost* or *Today* and the only way to nobble the opposition is to score points on a scoreboard, not with a soundbite. Campbell, as a sports fan, surely knows this. He returns to New Zealand next week in

time for the internationals and what he finds, good or bad, will be unmanageable because it will centre around a factor over which he has no control: team performance.

Sporting spin is useless because it will always be trumped by the sheer intractability of results. This is not the way in Campbell's world. The day after the general election in May all three leading parties claimed victory of some sort, even the one whose leader had celebrated his triumph by resigning. Contrast this with Manchester United's sorry little traipse around an empty Old Trafford after finishing third in the Barclays Premiership. (*The Times*, 2005b)

Indeed much of the coverage of the tour focused on the role of 'spin' and Campbell's role in this process. The fact that the Lions lost the series by three tests to nil and were outclassed in all of these matches added credence to the notion that in sport winning and positive results override everything else. Campbell himself clearly recognised this, with his *Times* column of 30 June 2005 headed: 'Spin no shield in face of poor form and spear tackles'. The reference to the alleged illegal tackle by the New Zealand captain Tana Umaga that ended the tour of the Lions captain Brian O'Driscoll within a minute of the first test match was significant. It was this incident, and its fall out, which attracted much criticism from the press in both Britain and New Zealand about the apparent attempts by Campbell and Woodward to use it to deflect attention away from a terrible performance and result. 'Nice PR, shame about the rugby' (*Guardian*, 2005a) from Britain and 'Try spinning this Alastair' (*Sunday Star Times*, 2005) from New Zealand were just some of the headlines this tactic drew from the press.

As the tour degenerated through injuries and poor results in the test matches, there was an inevitability about the criticism levelled at Woodward and Campbell. The former for getting his tactics and priorities wrong, the latter for attempting to control and stage manage a tour, and deflect attention from the poor decisions being made by Woodward.

A further issue arose around the use of a photograph of Woodward appearing to be having an amiable chat with the Welsh rugby star Gavin Henson (controversially dropped from playing in the first test). It emerged that the photo was ordered by the Lions media department and that Henson was unaware it would be taken (the photographer hid behind a car, using a zoom lens). The intention of the photograph was to show Woodward in a positive light following the criticism he received for dropping the in-form star of the Six Nations Championship. It was another example of how Campbell, with his eye for news management, was hoping to set the tone for a story that had circulated about a dispute between coach and player.

The fact that the set-up became the story was indicative of the breakdown of trust between the rugby journalists and Campbell. By the end of the series, Campbell's earlier positive views on the differences between political and sports journalists appeared to have changed. In an interview with the *Sunday Times* sportswriter David Walsh he argued that:

> If I had been a journalist, I would have looked at me and thought, 'I don't know him, so I am going to make my own judgment'. The second thing I would have thought is, 'He knows the media inside out, he knows what a story is, and he is where I've always wanted to be: on the inside'. I was ready to give them ideas . . . it just seems extraordinary they were more comfortable with, 'Well, we'll see the players after the team is announced, we'll ask a few questions, get a few quotes, store them up'. If I was a sports editor, I would be wondering was I getting my money's worth. They're a nice bunch of blokes, don't get me wrong. (*The Sunday Times*, 2005a)

This issue of helping journalists was also echoed in Woodward's retort to criticism of Campbell's appointment as the tour ended. Woodward argued that if the travelling rugby journalists had:

> spoken to him (Campbell), he would have given them ideas of how they could have written more creative stuff in terms of following the teams around and how we are operating. That's why I brought him along, to try to move everything with the media to a whole new level, but unfortunately the media has not taken up that challenge. (*The Independent*, 2005a)

In this instance, the lesson was the extent to which both Campbell and Woodward underestimated the breadth and range of rugby journalism that already existed in the British press. Clearly, undertones of the 'toy department' mentality still informed their thinking with regard to this section of the media, which included not only dedicated rugby journalists but also a number of well-respected No 1 sportswriters covering the tests. The idea that these experienced journalists would welcome being told how they might improve their copy seems to suggest a serious misreading of the journalistic culture associated with this area of the trade. In addition, as noted earlier, it also misunderstands that promoting the game is simply not what sports journalism is about, and despite the increasing blurring of the line between PR and journalism and between editorial and advertising in sports journalism, it is winning and success on the field of play that remains the most important driver in shaping journalistic opinion and comment. The newspaper coverage of the dismal Lions tour of 2005 merely reaffirmed this.

CONCLUSION: THE CHALLENGE FOR JOURNALISM IN THE PROMOTIONAL AGE

At the core of this book is a debate about the location of sports writing and reporting within the wider field of journalism. If sport itself has become more commercialised and is increasingly part of what might be viewed as the entertainment industry, then one should not be surprised if aspects of journalistic practice evident in, say, the music or film industries, are reflected increasingly in sports journalism. In other words, if sport is simply a wing of a global, commercial entertainment industry, then should we be surprised if sports journalism begins to have much in common with its related journalisms in the showbusiness arena?

What is emerging in top-level sport, financially underwritten by television and aggressively hyped by sections of the newspaper market, is the creation of a climate in which certain sports stars appear to have more in common with stars from other areas of the entertainment industry. As a result, aspects of news and image management and public relations practice are more common and widespread in this domain than has previously been the case. This, however, does not automatically mean that sports journalism is simply becoming an extension of the gossip- and celebrity-driven journalism that characterises much of the heavily expanded media environment. The nature of sports performance differentiates itself from, say, the film industry in a number of ways. Success and achievement based on a talent to play a particular sport to a high level remains, largely, an important attribute for entrance into the upper echelons of sports stardom. When this ability starts to wane, the wrath of once kindly sports journalists can be swift, biting and unrelenting. As Kram (1989) noted in his article on Muhammad Ali and his sporting decline, great men die twice, and often the end of a sporting career can be excruciatingly painful.

There also exists a difference between individual and team sports that make comparisons with other parts of the entertainment world problematic; the forms of creativity involved in sport can also be said to differ from that of a musician or, say, an actor. Indeed, on closer inspection the particular configuration of sport, which despite attempts, usually by television, to control the ebb and flow of events, still has uncertainty of outcome at its core. This uncertainty (which we saw, for example, in the Ashes cricket series of 2005, when the destiny of that famous urn was not decided until the final two hours of the last day of the final test) is one of the intrinsic pleasures of sport. Failure and even, from time to time, unexpected success, suggest that the reporting and coverage afforded a major football, cricket or rugby international differs in its narrative trajectory from that of a rock concert or film premiere.

Neverthless, one should also remember that while sports journalism now stretches to cover a wide multitude of journalistic activity, at much of its core remains a central dynamic that often constricts its ability to cut through some of the issues of image control looked at in this chapter. As Eamon Dunphy argues:

The other thing worth understanding about sports writing is that sport is in the hero business. Writing is frequently about heroic figures. It's in the hero and villain business, so it's in the hyperboly business.

It's difficult to write calmly and objectively when you are writing about things that move people very deeply. You have to take that into account when looking at sports writing. It takes a degree of fortitude to go against conventional wisdom, to take on the mob, and sometimes a journalist has to do this. (Interview with author, 30 May 2005)

Yet, as the tentacles of sport reach out in a more explicit manner into other areas of political, economic and cultural life and in so doing encroach upon the journalistic terrain of other areas of the industry, so the nature of its reporting and the stories constructed around it will continue to change and develop.

In the age of promotion and media manipulation, the challenge to produce uncomplicit sports journalism is, in many ways, simply an extension of those faced by journalists in other spheres of journalism. As attempts to control information and news management grow, as elite sport becomes increasingly politically, commercially and culturally important so sports journalists will have to work harder to get beyond the stories that to all intents and purposes simply drop into their laps and onto their laptops.

The following chapter examines how the digital media age, characterised by the pace and speed at which information flows, is also changing the environment within which sports journalists work.

6
SPORTS JOURNALISM IN THE DIGITAL AGE

I think increasingly the heart of sports journalism is going to be on the web.

Andrew Thompson, Head of BBC Sports News, Interactivity and Digital Media (interview with author, 18 April 2005)

We are too quick to look at the finish line, instead of studying or enjoying the race. We want winners, even if the losers have better tales to tell. We want controversy instead of wisdom. We live in an era of breaking news. Too much, too quick, all the time.

Sportswriter, Tom Humphries (2003: 371) *Laptop Dancing and the Nanny Goat Mambo: A Sportswriter's Year*, **Pocket Books/Townhouse: Dublin.**

Digital media are significantly changing the environment within which journalists operate. Developing some of the issues raised in the previous two chapters, here we examine the extent that the development of a digital media landscape is altering the practice, role and position of the sports journalist.

Areas of particular interest in this chapter include the rise of online sports journalism; the impact of the Internet on sports sources; and the evolving conflicts between journalists and sports clubs as they attempt to not only exert greater control over their perceived intellectual property and image rights, but also reshape contemporary sports journalism in a more corporate age of sport.

SPORTS NEWS IN THE DIGITAL AGE

Hargreaves (2003: 2) has argued that: 'The ascent in journalism's influence is easily explained. Its underlying cause is the growth in the cultural, political, and economic value of information, facilitated by the emergence of new, cheap electronic technologies to distribute and display news.' Also, a central element in this ongoing process is the extension of the news-gathering arena. By 2005, over 66 per cent of homes in the UK had digital television (TV International database), giving access to at least *BBC News 24*, *Sky News*, *Sky Sports News* and the *ITV News Channel*. These 24-hour rolling news channels now regularly carry sporting press conferences live and view the carrying of sports news as a legitimate area of their operation. So, for example, when Liverpool Football Club returned as European Champions to the city in May 2005, all the news programmes mentioned above covered the victory parade (lasting at least three hours) live. This was in stark contrast to the return of previously successful Liverpool teams from Europe in the 1970s and 1980s, which, with the exception of local television coverage, did not constitute mainstream news coverage or the allocation of substantial news resources. The expansion in the range of television news outlets over the last decade or so as digital technology has come on-stream, now renders coverage of such sporting celebrations as increasingly commonplace television news events.

Television now carries live media conferences involving sport and sporting issues in a manner unrecognisable ten years ago. In addition, rolling radio news means that another source of information is available both to fans and, importantly, to other sports journalists. The impact of these changes is to quicken the pace at which information gets circulated across media platforms, something discussed in more detail later in the chapter.

Another characteristic of the digital age is the growing synergies taking place across previously distinct media outlets. For example, while there is a history of links between some areas of the sports print and the sports broadcasting sector, digital technology, combined with a more market-driven media system, is facilitating ever closer and often more commercial links. In the UK, *Sky News* works closely with the national commercial radio station TalkSPORT, which in turn, as noted in Chapter 4, has a weekday drive-time sports programme sponsored by *The Times* in a deal worth over £1 m to the radio station. This cross-promotion is important, but in some cases the links are even closer. In Sweden, for example, March 2005 saw the launch of a new sports television channel SPORT-Expressen, a collaboration between the *Expressen* newspaper, a sports rights distribution company IEC and a technology company Hego. In an increasingly competitive multi-channel digital television environment, the brand exposure that the print media can bring to a fledgling television sports channel is important. It also allows various economies of scale to be enjoyed across journalistic resources, costs, while allowing the cross-flow of news and editorial from print to both broadcast and online outlets.

August 2005 saw the *Guardian* collaborating with Channel 4 television in an attempt to raise its profile among sports fans. The paper had been hit by *The Independent*'s relaunch as a compact paper and had resulted in the *Guardian*'s daily sale being down in 2005 by almost 4 per cent year-on-year. What was interesting about *The Guardian Sports Show* (the result of the collaboration), was that unlike a simple sponsorship tie-in, the owners of the paper, the Guardian Media Group, paid half the costs and as a result had direct editorial involvement with the show, which ran for six weeks. This also coincided with the launch of the paper's new 12-page sports section in September 2005 and an increased sales campaign to drive sports fans to its print and online sports journalism.

Of course, one of the issues these kinds of editorial relationship raise is the extent to which sports journalism becomes complicit with a range of relationships that extend across newspapers and broadcasters, with the latter being rights holders to a number of sports. Will these events be promoted above others? Do these networks alter and impact on news values? Is there room for critical, uncomplicit sports journalism that may find fault with other media partners? It would be naive to suggest that such commercial developments do not have an impact on editorial decisions. As a combination of both the digital landscape and a more lightly regulated broadcasting market allow a growing number of such synergies to develop, these editorial issues will have to be worked through. For sports journalists they suggest that some of the wider ethical dilemmas, faced by their colleagues at the so called 'hard news' end of the journalistic spectrum, about reporting on issues that are commercially sensitive to media organisations are becoming more difficult to avoid.

In the USA, ESPN, the most successful cable sports channel in the world, has also used its *SportsCenter* news and highlights programme as a key element in the range of related television and online channels that now form part of the ESPN family. Yet the channel has been criticised for using athletes in its promotional features, suggesting a cosy relationship between the channel and certain sports stars (Shea, 2000). This relationship raises clear ethical issues for journalists breaking stories about these athletes, while *SportsCenter* anchors have also been criticised for getting involved in commercial advertising, which may be viewed as compromising their status as sports journalists. In reality, this situation reinforces the issues raised in Chapter 3, that television sports broadcasting, while a form of journalism, generally has too close a relationship with the material it covers to be journalistically rigorous enough in its dealings with sport. In short, television, be it terrestrial or satellite/cable, frames sport within a paradigm that is predominantly entertainment-driven, with journalism always invariably second in this hierarchy of values.

Not that the issue of trust and journalistic integrity is one of a simple dichotomy between print and broadcast/online media. There is one area where the increased carrying of live interviews (or recorded as live) and press conferences with, for example, football players and managers is impacting on the print media. Amy Lawrence, football journalist with *The Observer*, is clear that one of the major differences between print and broadcast sports journalism has become the issue of trust. She suggests: 'If a player is speaking to camera there is a sense that it is more difficult to play with those words on the screen. This may not always be the case with the print media' (interview with author, 9 August 2005).

This theme of the breakdown of trust between sports journalists and those they write about is one that has run throughout the book. In part it comes out of the passionate hothouse, results-driven environment within which much sports journalism takes place. Where the outcome of a rugby or football match (sometimes with millions watching on television) can result in a manager losing his job. It is also often based on a fundamental misunderstanding of the relationship between sportspeople and journalists. Despite what critics may say, sports journalists are far from simply cheerleaders, although sometimes they do, of course, adopt this position. However, it is a job that often can (and should) involve criticising people you may have got close to and as a result it is not a profession always conducive to enduring long-term personal friendships.

The digital age of sports journalism is characterised by elite sports that have become increasingly financially dependent on media organisations. It operates in a highly competitive environment where the speed at which information flows and a multitude of often competing media platforms, all eager for content and comment, tend to mean that trust is often in short supply. Humphries (2003) notes how a more gentle age of trust between sports journalists and football players, for example, has been replaced by a relationship characterised by paranoia. He adds: 'The players are younger and richer and more callow now. Generally they hate us. Of course, all of them don't hate us all the time. Some of them just hate some of us all the time. That's why we keep turning up' (Humphries, 2003: 26). Often, of course, this mistrust is based on a player or manager being 'turned over' by a newspaper, sometimes by a sports journalist, but more often than not, by a news journalist.

The BBC's Andrew Thompson recognises the journalistic challenges that the digital news environment brings. He argues that at the BBC:

we have recognised that sports news is now a front page pre-occupation as well as back page concern. I don't think there is any change in the mind set towards sports news stories; the key elements of BBC journalism have always been present. There have been some structural changes that have improved the sports news coverage in recent years. This has been about creating a closer relationship between sports news teams and the BBC newsgathering teams and BBC Sport broadcasting teams, where appropriate.

The crucial point here is that it is impossible to draw a clear line where sports news ends and news begins. Which means that the relationship between sport and news has to be very good and it has to be one of trust and mutual understanding and, particularly, on big stories one of working together.

I think we have a structure that is able to cope with the shifting boundaries of sports news. (Interview with author, 18 April 2005)

There is little doubt that the blurring of traditional boundaries between news and sport is one of the most important aspects of the contemporary media sport landscape.

THE BATTLE FOR NEWS

There is no shortage of sports-related content available on the Internet. Journalists will use the web as a source for information, and, in particular, with official websites for sports teams attracting exclusive content, often this will be the first port of call for journalists looking for direct quotes from a player, manager or athlete. However, despite the explosion of material on the web, in terms of sports journalism, the impact has been towards reinforcing already existing media brands. Thus *BBC Sport* and *Sky Sports* are two of the key sites for sports news on the web. Andrew Thompson argues that:

The BBC sports website is probably Europe's biggest sports website and it's a 24/7 operation and prides itself on delivering sports news quickly and effectively. It's won a lot of awards and about 80 per cent of that website is about delivering sports news and delivering a great service. Yes, we stream coverage and do other things, but its spine is its sports news coverage, so for me it's at the heart of the BBC sports division and the BBC's sports news coverage. And as time goes on we are looking at the relationships between the web team and the Five Live team, television sports news team, what are the sensible synergies, what ways can they work together to provide content across all the platforms. (Interview with author, 18 April 2005)

While sports pieces written specifically for the web will often be shorter in length than if they were to appear in a newspaper, a lot of print material from papers such as *The Times*, the *Guardian, The Independent* and *The Daily Telegraph* will also be posted on their respective websites. In 2005, sports pieces were invariably among the top downloaded stories from the websites associated with the *Guardian, The Times* and *The Daily Telegraph*.

In addition, official football club websites will carry material that they have gathered and sourced in-house and distribute it across the range of media platforms endorsed by the club. At the height of the dot com boom, it was envisaged that the top clubs would have their own teams of in-house journalists generating content across a range of official digital media outlets for the club, with this exclusive content generating revenue through sub-scriptions and advertising (Boyle and Haynes, 2004). The reality was that the market, and in some cases the technology, was underdeveloped for such a fundamental restructuring of the sports news food chain. While research by Aura Sports (2005) indicates that 79 per cent of sports fans see their offi-cial club website as the most important source of news, with 61 per cent stat-ing that national newspapers are their prime source, the print media sports sector has not been decimated by the rise of the Internet as a source of sports journalism. The key issue is the extent to which some element of trust and lack of complicity is required to give any sort of journalism legitimacy. Journa-lists working for club publications both on- and offline are there to promote the club and pursue a different agenda to those sports journalists working for other media organisations.

However, the web has impacted on the already fraught issue of journalis-tic access to sports stars, who have developed a greater awareness of the importance and commercial value of image rights in the digital environ-ment. This has been accompanied with the rise in personal websites attempt-ing to offer exclusive comment. As sportswriter Natasha Woods of the *Sunday Herald* has noticed:

> As the big players in, say, football are now selling themselves through club television and their websites, there is a need for them to hold back and give exclusive material to these other outlets as opposed to national papers. This is a real change, as they hold back material for their own outlets. (Interview with author, 2 August 2005)

As a result, in some instances newspapers have become a less important medium for players to communicate with supporters. Of course, sports news journalists will have little compunction in lifting quotes from players and reproducing them after they have either appeared on personal websites or been carried by television channels run by sports clubs.

The web also sees a lot of sports-related material and fans websites generating considerable amounts of content, comment and information. Often this material is reacting against some comment or opinion that has appeared in the sports print media. Yet even in this unregulated market of sports jour-nalism, some element of authority remains important, and as a result, rather than any one simple source, fans use the web to access journalism not only from a range of sources, including official club websites, but also through established media brands such as the BBC and Sky.

THE PACE OF CHANGE

One key element that characterises the digital sports news environment is the pace at which sports news stories are circulated in and across a range of media platforms. At the BBC, journalists input copy that is then carried across the range of media platforms carrying sports news for the Corporation. As Andrew Thompson argues:

> People want to be able to get their sports news wherever they are on a range of different platforms. From text alerts, to the web, to *BBC News 24* for the latest sports news, to the more crafted news bulletin. The multi-platform authoring system that we have introduced over the last year, which allows people to write the story once and for it to go out across a range of platforms from Ceefax, the web and mobile texts, makes it easier for journalists, so technology has played a role in that. (Interview with author, 18 April 2005)

The pace of news is important as it not only challenges the authority of traditional print media, which simply cannot keep up with delivering breaking news to their readers, but also offers an opportunity for a newspaper to extend its brand through an online presence. Many will use their website to carry an initial story, with a view to driving readers to the more in-depth print version which may appear the following day. A newspaper such as *The Times* is well aware of the importance that an online presence has for the sporting identity of the paper. David Chappell notes how:

> We track our internet readers and on any given day sports stories are among the top ten read stories online. And sport is consistently one of the areas that get among the biggest hits to the web. It allows editorial executives to see the importance of sports to *The Times*, which is helpful for us in terms of resources. We have also put stories online before they have gone into the paper. So the Rugby World Cup [2003] was put online before it went in the papers. You would not put exclusive stories online, but we can use them to reinforce our identity and connect them to the paper. (Interview with author, 8 October 2004)

Thus the technology that allows you to monitor your online readership can, in the case of sport, also prove useful in the ongoing battle for securing scarce resources within newspapers such as *The Times*.

However, the pace at which stories get picked up and carried across media outlets also presents a challenge for traditional notions of journalistic integrity. As the race to be first with a story has increased in an age of 24/7 rolling news, the accuracy and indeed the fundamental role of a journalist in the circuit of communication begins to change. In sports news, the task of checking, filtering and making sense of stories for readers, listeners and viewers becomes more difficult as a lack of time increasingly constrains journalists. This is further complicated with the increasing use of the Internet as a news source for sports journalists. While this allows them access to the newswire services, many also use it for trawling for information and stories, often posted on fans websites, and often less than 100 per cent reliable. There is also the issue of the instant nature of the posting of information on the web, such as quotes from news conferences, which previously would have been eagerly retained and used exclusively by the print media. With the pressure on time and resources sports journalists, and journalists in general, increasingly find that the Internet has become an important source for information. This process of data gathering requires one to maintain the journalistic rigour of checking material that appears on the web for its accuracy, while this reliance on the web can often be at the expense of getting out of the office and speaking with people: a developing trend that some commentators feel is an increasingly impoverished aspect of contemporary journalistic practice (Marr, 2004: 115).

This reliance on newswire feeds, the rolling 24-hour sports news digital channels, such as *Sky Sports News*, and the web for information and stories is changing the practice of putting together a story for some sports journalists who, despite this tendency, remain among the least desk-bound of their journalistic colleagues. During the time spent researching this book, the author was aware of at least two football stories, carried by a national tabloid newspaper, that originated directly from a fan website. Both stories, which related to transfer speculation, completely unfounded, were carried by the newspaper but made no reference to their original source. In both cases, these stories were picked up and carried by other media outlets, before being quietly dropped as it become clear there was no substance to them.

The pressure of time has always been an aspect of print journalism culture, but in an age where news agencies can be posting quotes and comments from players on their websites almost as soon as a press conference (which may have been carried live on television and or radio) has concluded, the opportunities for a sports journalist to step back from a story and dig deeper have become less frequent. The media glare on particular aspects of elite sport appears to be continual, while the commercial pressure to 'break stories' has become more acute for sports news journalists. Richard Scudamore, the Chief Executive of the FA Premier League, has argued that:

> The football world and journalism share the same crowded galaxy and there are no places to hide. The rolling news agenda and the advent of instant digital media has redefined the written word and certainly our relationship. The match reports remain factual but every facet of the game provides journalists with ample opportunities to editorialise and differentiate from the immediacy of broadcast and electronic news. (*Media Guardian*, 2005a)

When this process is allied to the increasingly complex business-related stories that are part of the sports media landscape, it can become a confusing and potentially difficult terrain for sportswriters.

Natasha Woods is well aware of the pitfalls of increased use of the web, for example, but feels that its benefits outweigh its associated drawbacks. She suggests that: 'In terms of research, particularly when you are away from the office, it is phenomenal. As is the instant access to material, including your own library, so you can search previous stuff you have written' (interview with author, 2 August 2005).

This use of the Internet as both a research tool that may prompt a story and an important vehicle that facilitates the further development of this story is something that has been recognised by sports journalists. Ashling O'Connor notes how:

> The Internet is a very good resource for finding people. For example, there was a mention in a football newsletter about John Arne Riise (Liverpool and Norway footballer) being upset about a Norwegian company using his name. So I searched the web for his lawyer, was able to email him and we had then a conversation as he spoke to me from his car phone. And I was able to run a story on the back of that. Now before the Internet it would have been very difficult to get hold of him, so it can break down barriers. (Interview with author, 19 August 2005)

Koppett saw a continuing impact being made on journalistic practices by new media developments. He argues that: 'The laptop makes possible communication and instant research we never even dreamed of. Its potentialities will continue to change the way reporters, publicity people and offices interact, and press box routines will reflect them' (Koppett, 2003: 273).

He also argued that since the 1990s one of the key shifts in American sports journalism has been the extent to which it is often associated with the print rather than the electronic media; it is now the latter that drives the shape, structure and direction of contemporary sports culture, rather than newspaper journalism. In the UK the situation is not as clear-cut. For while newspapers cannot compete with other media for breaking sports news, the web versions of these papers can carry this material. It also remains the case that it tends to be the tabloid sports press in this country that continues to set much of the sporting agenda through its breaking of stories and the perceived impact they have on shaping public sporting opinion.

GOSSIP, RUMOUR AND IMAGE POTECTION IN SPORTS JOURNALISM

The impact of the pressure of time, as previously rigid deadlines have tended to collapse and sports news is carried 24/7 across more media outlets, can be an issue for sportswriters. As is the growing awareness of the damage that (mis)information or opinion can have on someone's reputation in the age of almost instant dissemination via the Internet.

In April 2003, James Lawton, chief sportswriter with *The Independent*, ran a story in which he accused the then Celtic manager Martin O'Neill of displaying a 'combination of arrogance and total ignorance of what passes for acceptable behaviour' over what Lawton perceived as a conflict of interests for O'Neill given his position both as a football manager and as a shareholder in the Proactive Sports Agency. In addition, Lawton argued that O'Neill had attempted to suppress the disclosure of this information. In October 2004, O'Neill successfully won a High Court battle with the BBC, which had made similar, unsubstantiated claims. In July 2005, *The Independent* apologised to O'Neill, who had also brought a libel action against Independent News and Media, owners of the newspaper. They accepted that Lawton's allegations were untrue and based on false information. Both the newspaper and the BBC paid O'Neill's legal fees and an undisclosed 'substantial' amount for damages. O'Neill had already won libel cases against both *The Observer*, for a story it ran in 2001 about him plotting to replace Sir Alex Ferguson at Manchester United, and the Glasgow-based *Daily Record*, again for a sports story it carried in 2003 claiming that O'Neill had agreed to become the Liverpool manager. Both stories were untrue.

The summer of 2005 also saw the former footballer and now television football presenter Gary Lineker defending a libel case brought over a column he had written in 2003 for *The Sunday Telegraph* regarding the transfer of Harry Kewell from Leeds United to Liverpool. In the article Lineker (who it transpired in court had not actually written the piece; it had in fact been ghosted for him by a journalist) suggested that Kewell had been a willing participant in a dishonorable and financially dubious transfer. Kewell sued Lineker, the publishers and the *Sunday Telegraph*'s sports editor for libel. However, the case collapsed as the jury failed to reach a verdict and was settled out of court shortly after.

What these cases illustrate is that in an increasingly image-conscious media age, where stories are picked up and reproduced across the digital landscape at great pace, sports people are willing to sue over issues raised in the sports pages. When this had occurred in the past, these stories tended to have been broken by news journalists and carried at the front end of newspapers. This tendency to extend litigation to the sports pages also gives some insight into the problems faced by sports journalists in covering sports-related stories that involve complex financial issues. In this instance, a growing willingness to sue can act as a deterrent to journalists wishing to probe parts of the sports industry that are already, as noted in previous chapters, not particularly extensively covered. Natasha Woods suggests also that:

Investigative sports journalism has all but gone by the wayside. Part of it is a resources issue and part the 24/7 rolling news culture that we have. A few sportswriters still do it, but the pressure on resources and time are such, this has become hard for newspapers, even the broadsheets, that are much more driven by the need to deliver sports news stories. (Interview with author, 2 August 2005)

In an age where large amounts of sports journalism are devoted to comment and opinion, and where the pace at which stories gets circulated around the public domain has increased, these cases are unlikely to be the last involving either sportswriters or, even, television sports 'pundits' who are able to have ghost columns carried in the print and online media. With sport and its top stars now firmly within the celebrity culture discussed in Chapter 5, a concern about the potential impact that stories have on the image of a player or team has become more acute. As one senior newspaper lawyer speaking with journalist Bill Hagerty in *The Independent on Sunday* (7 August 2005) noted: 'You would not believe the number of complaints that come in from footballers when the paper gets something wrong, no matter how slight. They demand apologies and damages and often they've got agents as well as "no win, no fee" lawyers egging them on.'

The news environment has always seen newspapers happy to run with stories of scandal and celebrity: today, these stories are as likely to involve football or sports stars as they are to involve celebrities from the world of television or cinema. In one week alone in August 2005, two football players, Keith Gillespie and Andy Johnson, accepted apologies and substantial damages from two different national UK newspapers, the *News of the World* and the *Daily Star*, for running stories involving their private lives. An over-reliance by journalists on the web for information about sports stars can be a dangerous and potentially costly business.

THE WIRELESS SPORTS JOURNALIST

If the media landscape within which sports journalists ply their trade has altered, so too has the relationship they have with technology and established patterns of working. David Chappell argues that:

The modern sports journalist is a considerable beast. Before mobile phones things were very different. For example, a London journalist going to cover an Arsenal evening match in Newcastle would get on the train at 1 p.m., let me know he was getting on the train and I wouldn't hear from him until he got off the train at 6 p.m. He would then ring me from the match and ask what I want tonight. With laptops and mobiles their output is now much greater, they can write stories on the train, make calls, so they have to be more rounded. We are looking for journalists whose range is much greater, they are more flexible and more productive. (Interview with author, 8 October 2004)

The mobile phone means the journalist can be in constant contact with the office, and potentially be directed by the sports desk. While laptops and email facilitate the sending of copy back to the desk, and with wireless technology there now exists an ability to 'write on the road' and to file copy across a range of media platforms.

While a technological divide may have existed at one stage as new digital technology was rolled out in the 1990s, most sports journalists today recognise the benefits that this technology can bring. Richard Williams suggests that:

> the new technology has helped, making people think about the quality of the words, rather than simply banging them into the paper in quite the same way. The writers and the sub-editor have greater control, and there is no printer intervention, which makes it easier to write reflectively under pressure.
>
> You can't go AWOL anymore with the new technology. It makes life easier, you don't have to stand in line trying to get access to the one phone line. New technology has made the job 24/7, but also more pleasant as well. I remember when I was 18 covering a rugby match and having to run a quarter of a mile down the road to file from a pay phone, I had to get someone to watch the match for me, that wouldn't happen now. (Interview with author, 10 March 2005)

While some of the old school sports journalists have never totally embraced the technology side of modern journalism and would rather dictate into a phone watching the game than be looking at a laptop, the reality is that contemporary sports journalism now often stretches beyond the confines of the game itself, so the modern sports journalist requires a breadth and range of skills that digital technology can help to facilitate.

It has also hastened the process by which journalists are able to work more from home, rather than be in and around the office. Sports journalists as a group tend to be less office bound than most, spending a good deal of their time on the road and out at sporting events. Ashling O'Connor notes how:

> When you have a regular column you don't need to be in the office every day. If you have a laptop and a mobile you don't need to be in the office, particularly on a sports desk, where there are so many journalists who are on the road. (Interview with author, 19 August 2005)

It also means that a new generation of more technologically orientated journalists is entering the field. For example, sports journalists who work for Teletext will find their job involves some traditional aspects of sports journalism, for example, attending press conferences, sporting events and suchlike, but they will also be expected to work more closely with technology. This can involve sending SMS sports alerts to mobile phone subscribers, posting sports copy on the analogue Teletext system, servicing the website and continually re-evaluating the sports story, and rewriting and giving added value to information carried through the newswires. Sports journalist Mark Magee who works for Teletext notes how:

> *Sky Sports News* is on in the office all the time. They may not always break a story, but they are very good at getting reactions to a story. They always seem to be able to pull that together really quickly with their good access to the Premier League. (Interview with author, 6 April 2005)

He and other journalists are also surfing the web and using portals such as the *News Now* website (www.newsnow.co.uk), which collates news from over 20,000 news sources and other websites and is updated very five minutes. They are also being constantly fed material through the newswire services, which, well over a century on, remain an important part of the landscape of sports journalism.

NEWSWIRE SPORTS JOURNALISM

The digital media landscape has also transformed newswire services such as PA Sport (www.pa-sport.com) – part of the Press Association – which has 150 staff servicing its UK operation. PA Sport now provide sports content to a range of media platforms, from the traditional print outlets, through the web, to mobile phones and pda handsets. In the digital age print-ready sports reports are a lucrative business for PA Sport. Along with television listings, this part of its business was worth £52 m in sales in 2004, as opposed to the £15 m generated by its breaking newswire service (*Guardian*, 2005b).

What characterises the digital sporting landscape is both the 'always on' nature of communication and the expansion in the range of media outlets that require to be serviced with sports content. Thus newswire services such as PA Sport have reinvented themselves and have grown in importance in servicing this expanded sports media sector. Some sports editors, however, have reservations about their overall standards of accuracy. Craig Tregurtha, for example, argues that:

> They are still very important and, of course, relate to the resources you can spend on them. What I would say, is that as the spectrum of sports covered by the wires has increased, their accuracy is not what it used to be. However, if you use web copy you should be checking the facts anyway, so that is our responsibility. But they are important to the sports section of a paper, depending on your resources. (Interview with author, 28 September 2004)

The issue of resources remains an important factor in helping to shape the coverage given to sport by various media outlets. As budgets have been tightened in news-gathering agencies, so the under-resourcing of journalism has become an important issue across the print media sector. In part it has resulted in an increasing reliance on news sources that are basically public relations outlets, and at times an over-dependency on wire copy.

Another feature of the digital age has been the growth and reliance on free-lance sports journalists. This has been marked over the last decade or so as the range of print outlets, from magazines to non-sporting publications, which may carry sports material through to an expanded wire service has developed. In addition, newspaper sports sections will, of course, often use freelance jour-nalists as regular contributors, particularly during the football season.

In the case of the financial funding of print sports journalism, the situa-tion is often uneven across the sector. While a number of sports editors indicated that compared to their rivals they were in reality under-resourced to compete, other media organisations see the sports desk as being relatively well resourced. *The Times*, for example, was able to have four writers cov-ering the British and Irish Lions rugby tour of New Zealand in 2005, and also have two columnists delivering copy (including, as we noted in Chapter 5, Tony Blair's former political 'spin doctor' Alastair Campbell). The same paper had seven sports journalists covering the Wimbledon tennis tourna-ment that same summer, and this did not include photographers and news journalists from the front of the paper who were covering the tournament. In short, the increase in the profile of sports journalism has resulted in it being one of the better-resourced areas of journalism and while, at the pop-ular end of the print media market, this has been the case for a number of years, the level of resource has increased at the broadsheet/compact end of the spectrum.

CONCLUSION: THE SURVIVAL OF PRINT JOURNALISM IN THE DIGITAL AGE

Bell (2005) has argued that over the next decade or so the decline of the print media will continue as more people turn to the Internet for news and journalism. She states that: 'It is clear to me that the future of written jour-nalism lies more in electronic distribution than it does with the printed page' (Bell, 2005: 45). One of the challenges she suggests is how newspapers adapt to the migration of readers going online in search of news. It is also clear that sports news and journalism will continue to be an important aspect of this new online news ecology. One issue that the decline of 'traditional jour-nalism' and the rise of bloggers has raised is the challenge this process has for the legitimacy of journalistic authority. Much of this discussion has focused on the reporting of politics and the impact that the web and the rise of bloggers is having on political journalism. However, in the arena of sports journalism there is a long tradition of dissent, from 'mainstream' sports journalism through media such as fanzines. Evolving out of the print fanzine movement, sports fans were among the earliest groups on the web to establish communities and networks, either to circulate information and organise themselves or to lampoon 'traditional media' coverage of their sport or team. While this tradition continues, the breaking of sports news across the web and digital 24-hour news and sports television and radio channels has not eroded the appetite, particularly at the broadsheet/compact end of the market, for more in-depth and reflective sports journalism. Thus, while the development of online sports journalism is certainly a key part of any news strategy in the digital age for an organisation such as the BBC, the market for print sports journalism has also remained strong at a time when other areas of journalism appear to be suffering. Indeed, it is striking that online web sports coverage appears not to have significantly impacted on the appetite of readers for the traditional newspaper variety.

The expansion of journalism on the web has offered increased opportunities for journalists writing about sport and helped encourage the development of freelance sports journalism. Pete Clifton, head of *BBC News Online* and then head of *BBC Sport Online* has argued that:

> With so many sports websites springing up, there has never been a better time to be a fledgling sports journalist. But with demand so high, the pool can be shallow. The need to identify a good chain of journalists – from colleges, newspapers, rivals – has never been greater. It is a crucial phase for sports journalism on the web. With the right mixture of talent, content, technical skills and partnerships, it will truly come of age. (Clifton, 2000)

Over five years on, we know that a feature of sport on the web has been the consolidation of a few key sports websites, and that it has been the major sports news broadcast organisations, such as the BBC, Sky and ITV, and print media brands, such as the *Guardian, The Times* and *The Daily Telegraph*, that have established a reputation for sports journalism on the web. Organisational change in these institutions over the last five years or so has seen not only a merger of editorial and strategic thinking with sports content, but also sports journalism being used to generate content across media platforms in organisations large enough to enjoy economies of scale.

Sports journalism in the digital age is, of course, characterised by continuity and change. It remains the case that sports fans require various types of information, and will use different media at the appropriate times to access it. In sports fan culture speed of information is of the essence, and in this traditional broadcasting, the web and mobile communications are ideal vehicles for results and breaking news stories. Ironically, it is the latter aspect of this mixture that remains one of the weakest aspects of the BBC's online profile. *BBC Sport Online* will pick up and run with sports stories, but does not have a reputation for breaking stories. The web is particularly important for fans who live abroad, allowing them to keep connected to their team or sport in a manner that was unimaginable a decade or so ago.

However, other forms of media continue to remain important for sports journalism. The tabloid print media continue to be the engine for breaking sports stories, and the print media more generally are important for the retelling of sporting stories (often carried live on television and radio). They also offer previews, speculation, comment, analysis and features, all of which enhance the sporting experience and crucially remain an important element of sports fan culture. There is also something about the newspaper form that chimes with the needs of the sports fan to read about (and relive at their leisure) a particular event or the sporting exploits of their team.

Digital media has both shifted and consolidated the balance of power among media towards television, the web and mobile communication systems, yet there remains a need and a place for the written word. Sport as a cultural form grows and develops with its retelling. Print sports journalism is about both reliving the story and building a bridge between past and present sporting narratives; at its best, sports journalism is about making sense of the wider context within which events have occurred. As we have seen in this chapter, technology has altered and shifted working practice in the field of sports journalism in ways not dissimilar to other areas of journalism.

While much about journalism has changed in the digital age, and will continue to evolve as the long-term decline of newspaper sales shows no sign of abating, that ability and power to allow people to relive sporting moments remains a powerful weapon in the armoury of the print sports journalist, whose skills also allow them to move between print and online sports journalism with relative ease.

7

GENDERED SPORT? GENDERED SPORTS JOURNALISM?

Sports news is home to one of the most intense and historically enduring gender divisions in journalism, in terms of who is permitted to cover which sports as journalists how athletes are covered as well as in terms of which genders are served as audiences.

Deborah Chambers, Linda Steiner and Carole Fleming (2004: 111–12)
Women and Journalism, **London: Routledge.**

The golf journalist, advanced in years but, alas, not in enlightenment, was in full rant last week about the pointlessness of the European Seniors Tour. 'It's not real golf is it? I mean, it's just like women's golf – just not real.'

James Corrigan, Isn't it time we took women's sport mores seriously? *The Independent*, **6 June 2005.**

At the core of the debate about the role of women in sport and in the media has been a concern about the representation of women in sporting discourse. There is general agreement that women's sport receives little prominence in mainstream media coverage of sport both in the UK and in the USA; the latter being where much of the research into this area has been carried out (Boyle and Haynes, 2000; Eastman and Billings, 2000; Brookes, 2002; Duncan et al., 2005). This lack of profile, some argue, is due to the fact that women's sport in general is less popular and thus less high profile than professional male sport. In the USA, this argument is regularly mobilised by sports editors to justify their low coverage of women's sport. Significantly, they will often argue that this decision is simply based on lack of reader interest, although most editors have had little systematic contact with their readers to substantiate this opinion.

This lack of representation takes place against a backdrop of the increasing participation of women in sports (www.sportengland.org). Of course, in some sports, such as tennis and athletics, women's sport has a profile within a mainstream sports television audience, but even here the representation of women in these sports has tended to be heavily sexualised (Creedon, 1994; Hargreaves, 1994; Boyle and Haynes, 2000; Bernstein, 2002; Brookes, 2002; Messner, 2002)

The lack of women involved in the production of media sport, again, can be raised as one of the reasons for this historic under-representation. To what extent are women, working in sports journalism for example, expected simply to cover the limited female sports beat? Related to this issue is the question of whether sports journalism remains one of the last journalistic arenas in which women have failed to make real progress, in terms of their ability both to make an impact as a sportswriter and to move upwards within the institutional organisations that shape the production of sports journalism?

In this chapter we examine the extent to which sports journalism remains a traditionally male journalistic arena. We want to see in what ways the gendered profile of the profession has altered with the increase in media outlets that have been keen to use sports coverage as an important part of their media branding? Are there particular areas of sports journalism in which gender is becoming less of an issue, as the values of sports journalistic practice evolve and develop?

WOMEN, SPORT, JOURNALISM AND SOCIETY

The range of representations of women in the sports media has historically been limited. As noted in earlier chapters, traditionally the sports pages of the print media have been viewed as a predominately male preserve, and in many ways, despite the changes in the industry that have been discussed in this book, this remains essentially the case today, specifically in the UK press. Here, the promotion of the expanded sports coverage carried in newspapers, particularly in those at the broadsheet/compact end of the market, has been aimed at attracting younger male readers. This expansion has also been closely linked with the accompanying growth in television coverage of sport, the majority of which has tended to reinforce the dominance of traditional sports such as football, rugby and cricket. There is, however, little doubt that the gendered sporting landscape is altering, as more women get involved in male-dominated sports, and the popularity of the women's game in football, golf and cricket continues to grow.[1] However, at times it does appear that a cultural lag exists in the sports media in recognising the extent to which the relationship between gender, sport and society is changing.

In the USA, ongoing rolling research carried out between 1989 and 2004 by the Amateur Athletic Foundation of Los Angeles suggests that women's sport still goes largely unreported in the sports news and highlights programmes carried on US television. In its 2005 report it states that men's sport accounts for 91.4 per cent of network sports airtime with women's sport gaining 6.3 per cent of coverage, and while Fox devoted about 3 per cent of airtime to women's sport, this figure was even lower on the ESPN SportsCenter programme at 2.1 per cent (Duncan et al., 2005: 4).

In the UK, research carried out by the Women's Sport Foundation in 2003 estimated that only 5 per cent of media sports coverage was devoted to women's sport. Within this figure, newspaper coverage of women's sport was on average 2.65 per cent , only slightly up on the figure of 2.3 per cent in 2000. While this figure did rise to 7.1 per cent when the attention was focused solely on the broadsheet press, the fact remains that women's sport remains largely absent in the tabloid sports press (Women's Sports Foundation, 2003).

In addition to the issue of the media profile of women's sport, there is also the extent to which sexism is embedded in certain aspects of the culture that surrounds some sports. Turner's damning critique of the sport of Formula One motor racing succinctly demonstrated the extent to which, from the paddock through to the boardroom, sexism is endemic in the sport (Turner, 2004: 154–73).

In many ways, despite the expansion in space in both print and broadcast media that has allowed sports journalism to enjoy greater prominence, women's sport in the UK is relatively poorly served. The BBC has been allocating greater resources to cover women's football and 2005 saw coverage given across the BBC's platforms to the UEFA Women's Football Championships that was staged in England. Internal BBC research in 2005 has indicated that considerably more women are watching sport on television than was previously thought to be the case, particularly with regard to the popularity of men's football among this section of the population (*The Times*, 6 August 2005). To what extent, then, is this cultural change impacting on the production side of sports broadcasting and on the wider field of sports journalism more generally?

STILL NOT A JOB FOR A WOMAN?

If the history of sports journalism in the British press has been little more than a footnote in academic studies of journalism, then the position of women in this area of journalism has merited, until recently, barely a sentence.

Elsewhere, more research has been done, for example Rowe's work looking at women sports journalists in Australia (1999: 53–7) and work coming out of the USA (Creedon, 1994). While other areas of journalism in which women have had a controversial history, such as war reporting, have been increasingly documented (Sebba, 1994; McLaughlin, 2002; Magor, 2002) the history of women in sports journalism in the UK remains largely under-researched.

There is, of course, work which has examined the historical struggle women journalists have had as they have attempted to establish themselves in the industry (Mills, 1997; van Zoonan, 1998; Steiner, 2005). It should be noted that various research carried out by the Women in Journalism organisation (www.womeninjournalism.co.uk) argues that sexism remains an issue right across journalism in the UK. Platell (1999: 140) has argued that:

> Sexism is institutionalised in newspapers. You only have to look around at the number of women and the positions they hold in national newspapers to illustrate this.... Why is it that so many talented young women leave newspapers in their thirties to move into magazines and freelance work?

More recently, Keeble has noted how only 22 per cent of journalists in what is still called Fleet Street are women, and he also argues that the: 'Concern of feminist critics focuses particularly on the coverage of sport. Women cricketers, footballers and golfers hardly get a look-in. And often when they do feature, their presence is heavily sexualized' (Keeble, 2004: 19).

Recent work on the relationship between women and journalism that has been carried out by Chambers et al. (2004) has begun to rediscover and give a prominence to the role played by women in the development of journalism in the UK. However, the best work on the impact of women in sports journalism has tended to come from the US. In part this is explained by the simple fact that, for a range of cultural and institutional reasons, women have made a bigger impact on sports journalism in the USA than has been the case in Britain. As Chambers et al. (2004: 33–4) note when discussing the period between 1850 and 1945:

> In both the United States and Britain, women journalists were expected to be 'different' from male colleagues in both what they wrote and the way they wrote it. ... Again, especially in the US, women could and did muscle their way into covering literally everything from sports to international affairs, although by no means in the same numbers as men.

Creedon (1994) has pulled together the most detailed historical sketch of the long history of female journalists working in sports. She notes how, as far back as 1869, Midy (Maria) Morgan was recognised as one of the first female sports journalists, covering horse racing for the *New York Times*, and that the period between 1870 and the 1930s was one in which women sports journalists made regular contributions to the outpouring of sports copy that characterised US journalistic discourse during this time (Creedon, 1994: 70). Kaszuba (2003) has argued that:

> Contrary to the impression conveyed by many scholars and members of the popular press, women's participation in the field of sports journalism is not a new or relatively recent phenomenon. Rather, the widespread emergence of female sports reporters can be traced to the 1920s, when gender-based notions about employment and physicality changed substantially. Those changes, together with a growing leisure class that demanded expanded newspaper coverage of athletic heroes, allowed as many as thirty-five female journalists to make inroads as sports reporters at major metropolitan newspapers during the 1920s.

So while this history of women working in sports journalism in the USA has been one of struggle, with women often having to battle for acceptance in the face of prejudice, hostility and even in certain cases violence from a male dominated sports culture, in the USA at least, that history exists. As a result, there have been a range of role models for each subsequent generation of women wanting to become sports reporters and sportswriters. For example, in 1978 LeAnne Schreiber became sports editor of the *New York Times*, thus occupying a position within newspapers that almost 30 years later women journalists in Britain have yet to secure.

It is worth noting that more recent research by Smucker et al. (2003) suggests that while significant advances have been made by female sports journalists in terms of their institutional position within sports media organisations since the mid-1990s or so, barriers to promotion and advancement are still areas of dissatisfaction among these journalists.

Organisations in the USA, such as the Association for Women in Sports Media (AWSM), which was established in the 1980s, have helped to promote and support female journalists working in the sports media. AWSM, with over 600 members, argues that:

> Although the presence of women in sports journalism isn't as unique as it was in the 1970s, women still must deal with many of the same roadblocks that Melissa Ludtke did as a reporter for *Sports Illustrated* in 1977 when Major League Baseball excluded women from interviewing players in the locker rooms. AWSM seeks hurdles to these roadblocks with a unified voice that ultimately will help women become more effective in their careers. (www.awsmonline.org)

The extent to which issues of access and profile remain to be resolved for women in sports journalism become evident when our attention is focused specifically on the UK sports print media.

WOMEN AND PRINT SPORTS JOURNALISM

There remains little doubt that across the journalistic spectrum, women remain woefully under-represented in sports journalism in the UK. A snapshot of the figures involved is pretty revealing. In August 2005 a survey of national daily newspapers showed that there were up to 160 journalists carrying by-lines in the sports pages of the national press in the UK. Of these, only 14 were female, of which 3 were to be found covering horse racing, 3 working as sport columnists, 5 covering football, 1 reporting on badminton, another covering equestrian sports, and the other reporting on the financial and business side of sport. Of these 14, 5 were to be found on the sports pages of *The Times* and *The Daily Telegraph*, while only one, Janine Self, a football journalist for *The Sun*, regularly appeared among the pages of the tabloid sports press. In total, women journalists accounted for just under 9 per cent of the sports journalists working in the national UK press. A survey of the Sunday newspaper market saw 244 journalists with by-lines appearing in the sports pages, with only 7 females among them, giving a figure of just under 3 per cent.[2] Clearly, even with the under-representation of women in other areas of print journalism, these figures are very marked and suggest that despite advances in the broader sports industry, women sports journalists remain something of a rarity in the UK press.

One aspect may be the culture that surrounds sports journalism, although, as has been argued throughout this book, there is no monolithic sports culture, with different sports and the journalism that accompanies them having unique features and character. Football journalism, however, does completely dominate sports journalism and is thus an important area to examine.

Some sportswriters are clear that aspects of a more traditional macho sports culture still find echoes in the contemporary working environment that surrounds sports journalism. This aspect is more likely to be found around the tabloid end of the market and in and around football journalism in particular. Graham Spiers suggests that:

> There is a macho thing that goes on with sports journalism. There is a feeling that we are hard men, tough boys, in particular with the tabloid pack. And there is still an old-fashioned old school thing about journalists. Journalists hate political correctness, they hate liberalism, they hate liberals, this is the pack, so I am looked upon as a bit of a nancy boy, It's like being in the Army, you're not really in, until you've done this or that, served your time on the *Sun* or the *Record*. (Interview with author, 13 December 2004)

For a sportswriter like Spiers there remains a difference between the journalistic culture that surrounds football reporting in Scotland, for example, and that which exists in and around the London dailies. To some extent this is informed by a sense that London-based football journalists view both Scottish football and the journalists who cover the game there as being inferior to the game and the journalism that exists south of the border. There is also a deeper cultural stand that informs Scottish sports journalism and its culture that, at its most regressive, is still happy to display aspects of a more homophobic culture that has often been associated with football in the past. Spiers suggests:

> There is a lot of very good sports writing in Scotland; however, I do think that these old-fashioned values are deeply embedded in the Scottish sports writing scene more than they are down south. When you get sportswriters together at, say, a Scotland v. England game, I am aware of references to the Scottish pack being at the bottom of the food chain. I suspect, for example, that in the hard school of Scottish sports journalism that below the surface there is a real core of homophobia. Jokes about gays and suchlike are common. (Interview with author, 13 December 2004)

Among other journalists working in the sports field, football journalism, whether Scottish- or English-based, is generally perceived as being the most macho and masculine of the journalistic beats associated with sport.

One of the key aspects of gaining entry into the cultural world of the football journalist is knowledge of your sport. There is an underlying assumption among some male football writers that, ultimately, a women football journalist, for example, lacks the inherent knowledge to adequately cover the game. Lynne Truss, then a columnist for *The Times*, began to cover football for the paper in the mid-1990s and noted that among the older male football journalists the attitude was one of, 'Women cannot write about football, because they don't play it.' As she argued:

> By the same token, of course, theatre critics start each day with a speech from Hamlet, while dance critics squat at the barre. Open hostility was rare, but Brian Glanville, a legendary polygot aesthetician of the game and erstwhile *Times* football colleague, once said in front of witnesses that had he known his spare ticket was for me, he'd have torn it up (Truss, 1999: 128).

Indeed veteran sportswriter Brian Glanville has argued on another occasion that women football journalists are:

> allegedly football reporters but they haven't got a ghost of a clue what's going on on the field ... One can be a woman in print without it noticing – you can't see the lipstick or smell the perfume. But when it comes to a woman asking questions on TV ... I would find it difficult to listen to a Miss Motson banging on ... You'd never trust a woman with something as important as a football result. (*The Times*, 1998)

This fundamentally sexist outlook has been challenged by a number of women football writers including Amy Lawrence, who works for the Sunday broadsheet newspaper *The Observer*. Lawrence is well aware of the social capital required to break into and be accepted by the rather closed culture of football journalism, and attributes her relatively smooth passage in part to her own background as a dedicated football fan. She points out:

> When people ask about getting by in a man's world, they are surprised when I say I've never really had much of a problem. It wasn't easy, but I wasn't conscious of having more problems than a novice reporter coming into the game. My knowledge and passion for the game was important, and I owe a debt to someone like Paddy Barclay [football writer with *The Sunday Telegraph*] who took me under his wing and introduced me to people as someone who really knows her stuff on the game, and that was an important in. After that it's up to you how you progress. If you have knowledge of the game and a passion for the game, then you are in. (Interview with author, 9 August 2005)

Indeed Lawrence notes that even the above-mentioned Glanville, among other football writers, appears happy to talk with her and discuss aspects of the game.

Similarly, Ashling O'Connor recognises that her specific beat at *The Times* was one that was largely unthreatening to other sports journalists at the paper. She suggests that: 'Because there was no others writing about sports business specifically on the paper, I was not a threat to anyone, as I was covering an issue that most were happy for me to cover. So, as a woman journalist I had no resistance' (interview with author, 19 August 2005). When she has been directly involved with other sportswriters and journalists, O'Connor reinforces the point made by Amy Lawrence, that it is how well you do your job as a journalist which creates the respect. At the 2002 FIFA World Cup, O'Connor suggests that her ability to stand her ground in the 'mixed zone' media scrum, where journalists from all sectors of the media compete for quotes from players, was an important part of her acceptance by male colleagues. She notes that: 'all they [the other male sports journalists] want to see is that you work hard and mix with the other journalists and get the quotes, then you are accepted. You get respected for that and they see you are not simply writing fluffy pieces' (interview with author, 19 August 2005).

Given the relatively closed world of many of the sporting 'packs' of journalists, who travel on the road together a good deal of the time, breaking into this group requires you to show you can do the job. While this gaining of respect will be part of the process of assimilation for all new journalists, the ability of women sports journalists to establish their credentials quickly appears to be important.

A DIFFERENT STYLE OF JOURNALISM?

Another issue related to women sports journalists is whether they offer a different perspective on sport from their male colleagues. In other areas of journalism there has long been a perception that women journalists have been ghettoised into covering 'domestic' 'female' issues, or 'soft news', and disregarded when it comes to being at the forefront of hard news (Chambers et al., 2004). Indeed, some new female entrants into journalism are clear that aspects of the rise of celebrity-focused journalism, particularly in the 1990s, has acted as an incentive and encouraged more young women to consider entering the profession. The *Daily Telegraph*'s news reporter Elizabeth Day, who was voted the 2004 Young Journalist of the Year, has suggested that:

> What is it that now attracts so many young women to print journalism? … I think the answer to this lies in the most noticeable shift in print journalism over the last decade: the trend towards celebrity news. In a progressively secular society, celebrities have become our new spiritual icons to the extent that even the Archbishop of Canterbury wants to draw parallels with *Footballers' Wives*. With the launch of *heat* magazine and the incredible success of the *Mirror*'s 3am Girls, the door has been opened to a new breed of female diary journalist … Celebrity gossip is a more extreme aspect of diary schmoozing and a watered-down version of the honey-trap. In both, women are able to capitalise on their assets to get a good story. Given that the readership of the gossip pages is mostly female, it also makes sense to employ women who know what other women want. (2004: 23)

If there is something in this new gendered attraction to journalism, then it should not come as too much of a surprise if the sports pages not only remain driven by male sports editors who view their primary audience as men but also continue to be so lightly populated with either women's sport or women sports journalists. Certainly, in the case of football journalism there clearly was a space that opened up for women writing about the game during the early to mid-1990s as the cultural explosion of football created a wider media hinterland of opportunity (Boyle and Haynes, 2000). However, Amy Lawrence feels that this moment was relatively short-lived and has not been sustained in more recent years. She suggests:

> The explosion in football writing which occurred after Italia 90 with Gazza's tears, the Taylor Report and the boom in football allowed me to get into football journalism. There was an appetite for football writing which opened up opportunities. In one sense that window has closed now, there was clearly a sense in the early 1990s that it was good to get a woman writing about the game, as it had become more popular with women and it also might attract female readers. I'm not sure that is the case anymore. (Interview with author, 9 August 2005)

Yet within the changing boundaries of sports journalism, with its greater focus on personality and the relationship of sport to the wider society, journalists such as Lawrence feel that women football journalists can bring insight into the emotional aspects of the sport. She notes how:

I am conscious that I will focus on the more emotional aspect of things in my writing. I am interested in the way that people in the game express themselves. We [women journalists] may be less hard in our appraisal of people and situations, and we may also be more likely to give them the benefit of the doubt than some of our male colleagues. Of course, this may just be a personality thing, rather than a gender issue. (Interview with author, 9 August 2005)

Also crucial in this aspect of the approach taken to the style and substance of the journalism is the organisational culture that shapes the nature of sports journalism. Most women sports journalists in the UK work at the broadsheet/compact end of the market and as a result they tend to be given a little more space to cultivate their own style and approach. The tabloid end of the market finds a more prescriptive news agenda being driven by the sports desk, where the parameters set by the sports editor significantly shape the tone and colour of the sports journalism. There remains significantly more difference between the style and tone of male sports journalism found in many parts of the tabloid press and that which appears (often covering the same event) in the broadsheet/compact press, than between, say, male and female sports journalists working in the same print media market, or, indeed, within the same organisational culture.

If the situation in the sports journalism print media market continues to see a significant gender imbalance in terms of journalists working in this area, does the broadcast sports media differ from this in any way?

BROADCAST SPORTS JOURNALISM AND PRESENTING

As noted throughout the book, one of the factors that has helped stimulate the expansion in sports journalism across a range of media platforms has been the increase in television coverage of sport. This development has also led to a greater female presence on screen as sports broadcasting and women no longer appear to be mutually exclusive categories for television producers. The advent of *Sky Sports* as a serious player in the media environment in the UK during the 1990s and the wider gender shifts in the relationship women have to sport in general have helped this process. It does, however, reinforce the distinction that, to a certain extent, sports broadcasting remains a subsection of sports journalism. In other words, while recognising that presenting and fronting live sporting events on television, as Gabby Logan regularly does for the ITV network, is a highly skilled broadcasting job, it is not necessarily viewed as journalism but, rather, as a distinctive form of sports presenting and broadcasting. Of course, these areas are not unconnected, and Logan also pens a sports column for *The Times*; however, crucially, the increase in the profile of women working across sports broadcasting has tended to be in the area of presenting, rather than sports news reporting. For example, 13 television presenters from the 47 used across the *Sky Sports* network in 2005 were women; however, of the 46 sports news reporters working with *Sky Sports*, only 1 was female. While Sky has been proactive in helping to change the gender profile of sports broadcasting to more accurately reflect the gender popularity of sport, the area of sports broadcast journalism remains overwhelmingly the preserve of male journalists. The latter is more in keeping and reflects the position noted earlier in the chapter with regard to the print media.

It is also true to say that, over the years, Sky has been guilty from time to time of introducing women sports news reporters whose ability and journalistic knowledge have appeared to be less important than how telegenic they appear on screen. To some extent this has mirrored the situation that has become an issue in American sports broadcasting from time to time. In 2003, the ABC network hired Lisa Guerrero as a pitch-side reporter, but dropped her after one season after criticism about her lack of sports knowledge and the growing perception that her looks, rather than her broadcasting and journalistic ability, had secured her the job. In what is still an overwhelmingly male sports culture, these interventions have done little to advance the legitimate claim that female journalists are as well equipped to be involved in broadcast sports journalism as their male colleagues.

In the UK, the BBC has also helped to change the face of sport on television, with women presenters fronting a major sports programme such as *Grandstand* and the coverage of the *Wimbledon* tennis championships. Early 2005 saw Celina Hinchcliffe become the first woman to present the Corporations's major football programme *Match of the Day*, signalling, as Gabby Logan had done on ITV, that producers accept having a woman present television coverage of a predominately male sport such as football.

The BBC's own research suggests that this feminisation of television sports presenting is part of a wider gender shift that finds more women watching sport on television than had previously been thought to be the case (The *Times*, 2005d). The research found that up to 10 million women had watched the England v. Portugal Euro 2004 football match and that the *Match of the Day* television audience was 37 per cent female. In addition, 45 per cent of the audience for the BBC television coverage of the Six Nations Rugby Championship was also female (*The Times*, 6 August 2005). Perhaps even more significantly has been the growth of women journalists covering sport working throughout local and national radio. An important breakthrough in that most distinct area of sports broadcasting, the sports commentary, was made in August 2005, when the BBC announced that it was including the first female football commentator, Jacqui Oatley, in its team of commentators for Radio Five Live coverage of the 2005–6 football season.

THE TIMES THEY ARE A-CHANGING

For some sportswriters, Natasha Woods for example, gender is not the barrier it once may have been to entry into the industry. She suggests:

> I don't think it's that there is a bar to working on a tabloid as a sportswriter, 10 or 20 years ago, yes there was. I don't think sports editors think like that now. You just need the right job to come up, and the right people to be around. There are more women sportswriters who specialise, say, in athletics or tennis, so there may be certain sports that attract women more. It may be an issue of role models or, simply, that there are more female journalists who are interested in the arts, cinema or whatever than sports. There is not a major bar to people getting into the industry. Tabloid writing and football writing are a bit more macho. But I have never experienced any problems working in sports journalism, but I have worked for progressive editors, which helps. (Interview with author, 2 August 2005).

When the *Times* football journalist and columnist Alyson Rudd recalls her first big football assignment covering Spurs v. Peterborough from White Hart Lane, she feels that she has been treated fairly as a women entering the world of football journalism:

> I am frequently asked if I feel an outsider, sat next to men in a men's world, and whether they resent my presence. Well, one or two do, I suppose, and maybe a few more just hid it very well, but that night summed it up for me. One reporter said on discovering it was my first pressure fixture that I could ask him for help if I needed it. I did not ask and he did not patronise me by offering help anyway. ... There were no sidelong glances, no cheap jibes, and to be honest I never gave and never do give the fact I might be the only female a second thought. (Rudd, 1998: 69–70)

Thus what emerges is a sense that for those women working across sports journalism, once they are on the inside, the organisational culture is important in shaping their work experience. Yet again we return to the important role of the sports editor, who shapes the working environment in which female sports writers feel they will be given a fair deal.

In the USA, there is also a sense that since legislation was introduced (Title IX) in the early 1970s that banned sexual discrimination in education and encouraged greater female participation in journalism schools, the role of women in sports journalism has been strengthened. Kerry White has noted:

> In that new atmosphere, many women have found that the sports journalism field has become nearly equal in terms of the opportunities afforded men and women. Susan Reed, the editor-in-chief for *Golf For Women* magazine feels that women today who

wish to be sports journalists face no more barriers than their male counterparts face. 'Women have been in the mainstream journalism world for twenty years. By now, we're held to the same standards,' Reed said. 'Examine women beat reporters in basketball, football, any sport – they're just as good.' (White, 2005)

Thus, despite issues of locker room access still becoming an issue from time to time, the precedent of the woman sports journalist is well established both in media organisations and in the sports industry. This does not, of course, automatically mean that prejudice has been eradicated, and sports and sports journalism in the US is still strongly shaped and driven by men.

In the UK, Emma Lindsey worked as a sports journalist at *The Observer* for three and a half years during the 1990s. In the passage below she highlights the double dimension of being both a women and a black sports journalist in an overwhelmingly male and white environment during that period:

> I was one of a very small band of women writing about sport in national newspapers. I say 'band', but actually there was no particular sense of camaraderie amongst us, born probably of the 'fighting over crumbs' phenomenon. When we did meet at events such as Wimbledon, a nod or a wave might be exchanged from a safe distance, dispersed, as we were amongst the mostly male camps of male sports journalists. Anyway, thanks to the likes of newspaper doyennes Sue Mott at the *Daily Telegraph*, the *Guardian*'s Julie Welch, and television's ace anchorwomen, the late Helen Rollason and the now ubiquitous Sue Barker, the fact that being a woman at sports events was barely an issue most of the time. Yet sometimes being black was. (Lindsey, 2001: 190)

Lindsay's account of her time on the sports desk at a national newspaper also raises an important aspect of the wider sports journalism culture in the UK. For while the focus of this chapter has been on the relative lack of representation of women as sports journalists, the absence of black and Asian journalists working in sports journalism across national newspapers is even more acute. There is no doubt that the perpetuation of particular stereotypes around gender and race that can find articulation in the discourses produced by sports journalism is, in part, enhanced by a relative lack of diversity among the collective body of sports journalists. Again, in some aspects television sports broadcasters such as *Sky Sports* have led their print colleagues, in the sense that television's on-screen sports presenters and even reporters are more likely to begin to reflect the diversity in terms of gender and ethnicity of the sporting audience they both speak to and also represent.

CONCLUSION: STILL EVERYTHING TO PLAY FOR?

In her study of the experience of women journalists working in a number of cities including Toronto, Sydney, Melbourne and Mumbai, Minelle Mahtani suggested that there existed systemic gender discrimination against women in journalism. She argued that: 'it is premature to celebrate the dawning of a new era where we are witnessing an increase in the number of women working in journalism' (Mahtani, 2005: 299). From this research there appears to be little to cheer with regard to any increase in the profile of women working in sports journalism in the national UK media.

What emerges from this chapter is the extent to which significant differences exist between the levels of representation of women in sports journalism across media organisations. Sports desks at the tabloid end of the newspaper market, tightly driven by their sports editors, are more likely than the broadsheets/compacts to be all male. In keeping with the more editor-driven agenda of the tabloids as opposed to the broadsheets/compacts, sports editors at the tabloids frame the agenda of their papers very specifically, with sports journalists entering that culture expected to adapt to the particular agendas and style required of them. Across the UK national press there are no female sports editors, despite, as we have seen, American journalists holding this post as far back as the late 1970s.

Broadcasting, both television and radio, as well as online media are all likely to have a greater percentage of women working in sports broadcasting, itself part of the wider sports journalism environment, but compromised at times by its focus on presenting the news and live sport and not subjecting sport to the journalistic gaze which one can find more readily in the print media. Sports news reporting remains a growing but underdeveloped aspect of sports broadcasting, often seemingly driven and framed by the relationship rights holders have with the sport. But in radio in particular, a greater voice has been given to women involved in the reporting of sport, and this is something to be welcomed.

One aspect of a more commercially orientated media system is a tendency to pander to what is perceived as popular, or 'box office', in appeal to readers, listeners and viewers. As has been argued throughout this book, sports journalism in general and sports such as football in particular have all substantially benefited from a less paternal media environment. However, moving to a more demand-led media system does mean that there are areas of what might be termed 'market failure', in the range and style of sports broadcasting and journalism. Women's sports coverage is certainly one area where without the, albeit at times limited, coverage given by public service broadcasters such as the BBC, then this profile would be even lower. Given the close link between the expansion in television coverage of sport and the greater space and resources with which the print media cover sport, then an organisation such as the BBC becomes a key player in any future development of the profile of women in sport. Research from the Women Sports Foundation have noted how in countries such as Australia, significant differences exist between the range of male and female sports covered by the commercial and public service broadcasters, with the Australian Broadcasting Corporation (ABC) broadcasting women's netball and basketball, the most popular women's sports in Australia (Women's Sports Foundation, 2003: 5).

As noted elsewhere in the book, sports journalism, despite initial difficulties, is one of the areas of print journalism that has actually benefited from the increased exposure given to its subject by broadcasters. However, in an age increasingly shaped by subscription television, it has been a range of male sports that have significantly gained in media exposure, while other sports have been largely ignored.

For those women working within sports journalism, few indicate being subject to any significant discrimination. They all highlight the importance of knowledge of the sport or sports you are involved with, allied with an ability to write and a foundation of core journalistic skills. Yet their numbers, when set against the wider growth of women in journalism, suggest that the culture of sports journalism, with its, at times, macho image, may act as a deterrent in attracting new journalists to this area. The issue of role models also becomes important, as they can both inspire would-be journalists, and offer a glimpse of the possibility of career advancement and development. In the USA for example, the sports journalist Christine Brennan has been an important role model for young women seeking to enter sports journalism. She is a *USA Today* sports columnist who has worked across print, broadcast and online media, including ESPN. Brennan was the first female sports writer at *the Miami Herald* in the 1980s, before moving to the *Washington Post.*

While in the UK there is a history of distinguished women sportswriters working in the print media, they remain few in number. However, as a new generation of women journalists begin to emerge from the growing number of journalism-related courses in British universities, one can expect that more female graduates will attempt to establish themselves as sportswriters.

In terms of the range of representations of women's sport, perhaps elements of the changing digital landscape discussed in the previous chapter offer the possibility of change for media coverage of women's sport. The development of the web as a source of information about sport's broad and diverse culture has certainly helped give space to a range of sports that perhaps struggle to gain profile in the more traditional media. However, even this advance is double edged, as it allows certain sports to become embedded as niche activities and remain tucked away in cyberspace, detached from mainstream media coverage. This is a trend that has been increasingly identified in the new media coverage of women's sport in the USA during the 1990s (Messner, 2002: 92).

If some aspects of the journalism culture associated with sports writing appears slow to change, there are other areas of the professional image of the sports journalist that have altered significantly in the last decade or so. In the next chapter we examine some of these issues and return to investigate the validity of the image of sports as the toy department of contemporary media culture.

NOTES

1 In the case of football see the ongoing research being carried out by the Centre for the Sociology of Sport at Leicester University (www.le.ac.uk).

2 The newspapers surveyed were *The Times, The Daily Telegraph*, the *Guardian*, The *Independent,* the *Daily Express,* the *Daily Mail*, the *Daily Mirror*, and *The Sun*. Scottish-based nationals included *The Herald, The Scotsman* and the *Daily Record*. The *Daily Star* was excluded from the survey, as a large element of its sports pages were simply reproducing copy that appears in its sister paper the *Daily Express*. A number of weekdays in August 2005 were chosen to look at the papers. The Sunday papers in the survey were *The Sunday Times, The Sunday Telegraph, The Observer, The Independent on Sunday, the Sunday Express, the Mail on Sunday, the Sunday Mirror, the News of the World*, and the Scottish nationals, *the Sunday Herald, Scotland on Sunday, the Sunday Mail* and the *Sunday Post*. There were an additional nine journalists (including one woman) with by-lines in *The Observer Sports Monthly*, an award-winning magazine free once a month with *The Observer* newspaper.

8

THE IMAGE AND STATUS OF
THE SPORTS JOURNALIST

They're just about able to do joined up writing.

Businessman and former Tottenham Hotspur chairman, Sir Alan Sugar giving his opinion on football journalists. (*The Observer* 24 April, 2005)

The British journalist is not altogether popular.

Andrew Marr (2004: xiii) *My Trade: A Short History of British Journalism*, London: Macmillan.

I think that the generation of sportswriters coming through is more cosmopolitan. I think the standard of people in their mid 20s to mid 30s is very much higher than in my experience. They are more open, they have wider interests and wider terms of reference, and more sophisticated, more judgmental. The literary style is higher, although the best writers today are not necessarily better than the best of thirty years ago. The general standard is higher.

Richard Williams, Chief Sportswriter, the *Guardian* (interview with author, 10 March 2005)

If the public has not held the wider profession of journalism in particularly high esteem, then the traditional image of the sports journalist has been lower still. This chapter addresses a number of issues related specifically to the professional context and image of the sports journalist. As sport has become more popular and more important as 'media content' across a range of platforms, has the traditionally lowly status of the print sports journalist been significantly altered?

Over the last decade or so, the media have dramatically evolved and changed. To what extent have the sources of knowledge, influence and journalistic tradition that have influenced sports journalism followed a similar path? What is the likely impact of the academic rise in journalism studies – and the particular growth of sports journalism – in terms of both graduate entry into the profession and its own self-image?

THE LOWLY SPORTS JOURNALIST?

When the then *Guardian* journalist Matthew Engel wrote a book about the history of the popular press, he began by noting how some people had compared being a journalist to being a soldier, and that to earn a battle-hardened reputation meant working on particular newspapers. If this were true, Engel suggested:

> I have spent almost twenty-five years committing journalism, most of that time on a newspaper: the *Guardian*, generally regarded as the most gentlemanly regiment in the army. For part of that time, I was the cricket correspondent, generally regarded (by non-cricket correspondents) as the cushiest of all Fleet Street billets. ... I have spent my journalistic war as the rough equivalent of a skiving Aldershot pay clerk. (1996: 9)

We have seen throughout this book, that sports journalists have historically found themselves positioned towards the lower regions of any journalistic hierarchy. Engel suggests that within sports journalism, the cricket journalist was viewed as enjoying one of the easiest beats of the sports terrain. A characteristic of many sportswriters who do reflect on their profession is to denigrate their job in terms of journalism, while paradoxically in so doing they often are able to make a case about why sports journalism matters (Humphries, 2003; Baker, 2004; Hughes, 2005).

It is important to note that this book has been primarily focused on sports journalism within the UK media sector. While sport may be a universal cultural form, often inflected with particular local regional and national variants, the journalism that covers sport is far from universal (Crolley and Hand, 2002; Blain et al., 1993). Journalism is clearly shaped by the institutions in which it is located, and in turn these media organisations are products of a wider, culturally specific set of political and economic influences. Thus the upsurge of interest in sports journalism that has occurred in Britain over the last decade or so, and its expansion and diversification (within limits of course) may not be echoed elsewhere.

In 2002 a report from the Danish think tank Mondaymorning presented a devastating critique of sports journalism and its journalists across the Scandinavian sports press. The report painted a picture of a sector of journalism in serious decline, in terms of both its popularity and its journalistic standards. By way of contrast to the findings in this book, the report argues that Scandinavian sports journalism has retreated into a narrow ghetto, rather than expanded into other areas of journalism, as has been the case in Britain. Clearly, while this Scandinavian journalism has been shaped by the particular cultural and political environment that drives media development in this part of the world, some aspects of the research does find an echo in British sports journalism.

The increasing impact of television coverage of sport in driving the print media agenda is something that journalists in the UK would recognise. However, even given the relatively underdeveloped investigative sports journalism culture that exists in Britain, this aspect of journalism about sport seems entirely absent from the Scandinavian culture. While some argue that sports journalists have improved their broader journalistic training over a period of years, the Danish report suggests that the uncritical journalist working in 'soft news', detached from their more serious 'hard news' journalistic colleagues, remains the dominant characteristic of sports journalists working across Denmark, Norway and Sweden.

By way of contrast, in Britain and Ireland a new generation of sportswriters looks with some disdain on the traditional divisions between 'soft' sports and 'hard' news journalism. Humphries argues:

> There is an old territorial arrangement in newspapers wherein it is deemed that everyone is an expert on sport, but that sportswriters only know about sport. In other words, a political correspondent may sit down and write a column on a sports issue and, even through the column is filled with laughable errors of fact and judgment, nobody will say anything. A sports columnist, however, is not expected under any circumstances, to devote a column to his or her views on, say, foreign borrowing policy. During the Michelle Smith controversy, some of the most offensive and laughable pieces I read were by people who fancy themselves as heavyweights of the news pages. (2003: 110)

Patrick Barclay the *Sunday Telegraph* football journalist, recalls that when he worked on *The Independent*, the only time he came into contact with the newspaper editor was in 1989 when he was asked to write a piece that would appear on the front page of the newspaper following the Hillsborough stadium disaster in which 96 Liverpool fans lost their lives. The meeting was to reinforce to Barclay, one of the most respected football journalists in the business, the importance and responsibility that came with someone from the back pages being given access to the front of the paper.[1] Given the changing status of the football writer within the broadsheet/compact newspaper market, this attitude would be much less likely to exist today.

Indeed, one of the most significant changes in recent years in the culture and terrain of sports journalism is the blurring of traditional journalistic boundaries. Sport and related stories no longer are played out solely on the back pages of newspapers or tucked away in the sports sections of television and radio news. Unlike, say, a decade ago, most newspapers and broadcasting organisations will have a sports news correspondent, sometimes working close to the sports desk, but increasingly more likely to be allied within the mainstream news-gathering teams.

The political and economic profile of sports and its elite stars has increased, driven by a more commercial and less-regulated media sector. As a result, high-profile sports scandals, be it focused on the love life of the England football manager or the importance and political significance of the London 2012 Olympic Games are all stories carried on mainstream news and have helped extend the range of sports-related journalism that is to be found across the print, broadcast and online sectors. This has been a process not without tensions and strains as organisations and journalists both adapt to and shape a journalistic agenda that views the narratives constructed and associated in and around the sports industry as being increasingly relevant within contemporary popular culture.

With these changes come frictions, as the boundaries of what constitutes sports journalism continually shift and develop. For some this is a natural evolution, as sport becomes a central aspect of popular culture. Graham Spiers argues:

> The scene has changed and I think there is a tension not just between broadsheet and tabloid journalists but a tension between older values and newer, more liberal values. We all travel around in this uneasy circus together with Rangers or Celtic in Europe and in the main it's fine, but you can tell there are tensions around the changing values. There is a new generation of journalists coming through and you can tell they have got disdain for the old guard. But when you say old guard, these might be guys in their late 30s, but they belong to the tail end of the Have you been in the Army son school of hard-man journalism.
>
> The start of the 1990s across the UK was when you began to see more University graduates move into sports writing, some drifting into it by accident. There was an infusion of different values that began to trickle into the scene. I see younger guys coming on the scene that I personally get on great with and I'm much more in tune with. (Interview with author, 13 December 2004)

As a result of this ongoing process the image of the sports journalist remains, at times, complex and contradictory.

Craig Tregurtha is adamant that a central aspect of the self-image of the sports journalist comes from the overall leadership of the particular newspaper that you work for. He argues that:

> It really depends on the editor of the paper. If they treat sport as important, then you enjoy a status within that paper. It really does come from the top. So I think we are quite important to a paper such as the *Sunday Mirror*. It is a great job and you don't

get a lot of movement within the industry. I would still like people to come through local papers. Working the sports desk on them is a great way to get grounding in the range of skills and issues that you are faced with. We get more people in from college and university and I don't have an issue with that. In the end it's about talent and I will take that from wherever. (Interview with author, 28 September 2004)

Among many sports editors there is a perception that a change has taken place among some of their colleagues with regard to the professionalism of the desk that they run in newspapers. They talk of how surprised interlopers into sports from other areas of journalism are about the skills involved, for example, in writing a 'runner' during a live football match for example. Matt Tench noted the high level of skill required to work in this area. He felt that part of the changing perception of the sports journalist among others working in the print media, was a growing recognition by those who came into contact with the sports desk of the professionalism and skills under pressure that were often evident from those filing copy from live events (interview with author, 21 September 2004). Richard Williams also notes how:

The odd thing is that it is quite a difficult job. Last night I was in the press box (Arsenal v. Bayern Munich, UEFA Champions League match): I had to file a 850-word piece 10 minutes before the final whistle. I had to write a piece that couldn't be invalidated by anything which happened in the last 10 minutes, sometimes that is very hard to do. I remember the 1999 Champions League final, a goal in the last minute, and we had all filed, then you have five minutes to turn the piece on its head, and then they scored again. That's when people earn their money. You can only do that if people have aptitude, experience and trade craft to do it. People say it must be a nice easy job, well at times its technically hard and that happens quite often. You are having to write about an incomplete event and then having to re-write when it's completed. The technical demands are very high, so the people who do it at the highest level are very professional. Cricket is a bit gentler, but that is why football journalism is so competitive. (Interview with author, 10 March 2005)

As the expansion in the opportunities for sports journalism, in all its various forms, has grown, so too has competition among the print media to attract the star sports journalists. Significantly, this has been driven by the rise in football coverage to the extent that some journalists can argue that:

Football's dominance was not welcomed by all sports journalists. 'Among the old boys there's a feeling that there was a time when football had its place, as did rugby and cricket,' says one. 'Now it's year-long football, with even the most boring stories getting page leads, even in the summer during the off-season, while other sports are glossed over.'

But for football writers, this is a golden era. Footballers were not the only ones to benefit from the game's financial windfall; those that write about them also saw their wages soar. Newspaper proprietor Richard Desmond reputedly offered football writer Harry Harris a £200,000-a-year package to join the *Express* and others have negotiated lucrative deals. The kudos attached to sports journalism has produced a new breed of football writer – one who is as comfortable writing about the internal politics of Uefa as he is describing England's exit from Euro 2004. (Robinson, 2004)

It is also true that this movement of star football or sports writers is not something confined to the tabloid end of the print media market.

As a result of this change in the commercial value attributed to sports journalism in terms of its contribution to both sales and the brand image of the broadsheet/compact newspaper, the profile and status of top sportswriters has never been higher within the print media sector. There now exists a transfer market among sports journalists that is more reminiscent of other areas of contemporary journalism, with star journalists being poached by rival newspapers. Thus, while the majority of sports journalists will work for wages in keeping with the general low level across the industry, a new elite of sports journalists are among some of the highest earners across the journalistic spectrum. Paul Hayward, chief sportswriter with *The Daily Telegraph*, moved to the *Daily Mail* in 2005 for a reputed salary of almost £250,000. It is also increasingly common to see newspapers, from all sections of the market, use their sportswriter as part of their front page 'puff' to entice readers to the paper. This all provides evidence of a change in the status and commercial value of a number of elite sports journalists in a broadsheet market that until just over a decade or so, paid little real serious attention to sports journalism.

Sports editors such as Jon Ryan of *The Sunday Telegraph* are well aware of the importance that key sports journalists play in establishing the brand identity of their newspaper and positioning it within a competitive market. He suggests:

Newspapers have changed as sport has changed. Take football, the game, for a host of reasons, has moved up market, it's now after-dinner conversation in a way it wasn't not that long ago. *The Daily Telegraph* carries football news stories on its front pages that would have been unthinkable not too long back. I mean *The Sunday Telegraph* has always been a cricket paper, traditionally our number one sport, but the range of sportswriters has grown over recent years to the extent that a football writer like Paddy Barclay will have a status that would not have been the case on a paper such as this previously. (Interview with author, 13 October 2004)

The growing commercial importance of sports journalism to media organisations has unquestionably helped to alter traditional ideas of value and status. When David Welch left *The Daily Telegraph* in 2004, he became an agent working on behalf of a number of high-profile print media sports journalists. His role was to help realise the increasing commercial value of his clients, who he felt in the past had given their expertise and service to other media on the cheap. He argued:

> I believe there is enormous scope to increase the commercial opportunities for sports journalists and to ensure they are more appropriately rewarded and respected. Sport has sustained newspapers and launched both TV channels and internet sites. Yet the part sports journalists have played in this continues to be underplayed and undervalued. (*Press Gazette*, 2005a).

For Welch, the diverse range of digital media carrying sports-related content and the increasing media profile of sport offers a clear opportunity for key sports journalists to extend their portfolio and their commercial value. While in America, Simons (1999) noted the growth in the coverage given to sports journalism in the print media since the early 1990s and the corresponding increase in the value of top sportswriters within the journalism industry.

THE QUALITY OF WRITING

The internal divisions that have always existed across sports journalism are still evident, but in many ways have become more complex. The expansion of sports writing and the sportswriter in the broadsheet print media sector has been one of the key changes in the UK market. To talk of sports journalism as if it were one homogenous body of work is simply to misunderstand the range of journalistic output and practice that one can find under this rubric. Graham Spiers argues that of the sports journalist:

> There are various images. The back of the book, the toy department image is still there. On the other hand that is contradicted by the growing respect for a good sportswriter. Indeed, there has always been respect for the sportswriter, sometimes perhaps beyond our status and worth. There is still a patronising attitude to the sports hack, but if you are regarded as a literate writer you do get quite a lot of respect. The growing literate fan base has fed my part of the market, broadsheet sports journalism. Sportswriters are now more important than they have ever been in this country, as sport is recognised as being important editorially. (Interview with author, 13 December 2005)

The prominence given to the sportswriter as someone often identified with some of the best writing in a newspaper is increasingly common among the broadsheet/compact sports editors. David Chappell argues that:

> Journalists are more ghettoised in the UK, where they tend to focus on their beat, their sport. In the US, the sports tended to move from season to season so you covered football and baseball and basketball. The other issue is that of space. US newspapers tended to be bigger, having a lot of space to fill, so the sportswriter had more space to breathe. We have compartmentalised our sports journalists to some extent. As sport

has become more commercial, the notion of sports seasons has disappeared here. The writing talent has given much more space in the last decade or so, and broadsheets have got a broader canvas. Although we have a compact tabloid issue. There is now a new space for good young writers and we are seeing a new generation of writers. In addition, we have a much more educated sporting public, who are bombarded with sports from television, they know the difference in tactics, they have their own opinion. So the journalists have to adapt and give something additional to this and assume that a certain level of knowledge exists in their readers. (Interview with author, 8 October 2004)

Certainly among the growing number of sportswriters who have come through some form of journalistic training, the perception is growing that sports journalists in general are becoming more professional. Natasha Woods argues that: 'I think good sports journalism is good journalism. A good sports journalist should be able to go and work on any area of the paper' (interview with author, 2 August 2005).

There are also, clearly, poor journalists working in sport, but this is becoming less so as competition for places increases and those entering tend to come from a background that involves journalistic training. As more space is devoted to sports journalism at the broadsheet/compact end of the market, this area increasingly demands that sports journalists are coming with a strong journalistic background as opposed to simply a passion for sport.

THE MEDIA SPORTS JOURNALIST

Another key factor that is changing the image and role of sports journalists is the ability of sport to provide key content across a range of media platforms. In keeping with other areas of journalism, the boundaries between print and broadcast sports journalism are more porous than was once the case. The boundaries between and across journalism are often less well defined. As Marr suggests:

Today newspaper cultures are blurred, and there is a far less clear distinction between broadsheet journalists and tabloid hacks ... People move easily between papers and papers and telly. But like plumbing or selling fish, there are certain skills without which it's very hard to be a journalist – although it's a fair bet that there are more journalists who can't write shorthand or who don't understand libel law than there are fishmongers who cannot gut a mackerel. (2004: 4)

However, while increased competition in the radio market has opened up the opportunities for print sports journalists to increasingly appear on radio, differences do exist. Bob Shennan, Controller of BBC Radio Five Live, takes the competition from their national commercial rival TalkSPORT seriously but has also argued that: 'The fact is we have totally different approaches to covering sport, and totally different motivations for doing so. Having the Premier League rights is fantastic but it's the BBC's responsibility to offer a whole raft of different sports and to support them with robust journalism' (Shennan, 2004). Thus, while print sports journalists will appear from time to time on the BBC, the commercial radio station, with less resources, is more likely to draw on print journalists, often for their opinion and comment, to augment their in-house sports reporters.

This expansion of media outlets has also helped facilitate the rise in the profile of sports journalists that we touched upon earlier in the chapter. Amy Lawrence observes:

> There are a lot of egos in the press box. Some of the press would be very well dressed coming to games, almost like the footballers. There is a sense that football writers do feel that what they say matters more than the players. Through television you can become quite well known. Sports writing is not something I would have associated with celebrity, but that has changed. (Interview with author, 9 August 2005)

Television and media exposure has added to this sense of celebrity among some sports journalists. Former newspaper editor and sports journalist Harry Reid has also noted what he calls the 'look-at-me' stridency in some contemporary football journalism (Reid, 2005: 129). Their public profile from by-lines now accompanied by a picture, through to the numerous opportunities for sportswriters and journalists to appear on television or radio, all give a greater number of them a higher profile among the general public than previous generations.

As argued in Chapter 3, there clearly still exists a division between sports journalists, whose background has always been in journalism, and those former sportsmen and women who have moved into sports journalism when their first career has ended. While for many sports stars this avenue of career development is often through television and sports broadcasting work, often involving an aspect of 'punditry', increasingly they work across the print, broadcast and online media. For example the BBC's cricket correspondent Jonathan Agnew, a former county and England cricketer, has successfully reinvented himself as a cricket journalist and broadcaster, but remains aware of the impact that his former life has on his journalistic credibility. He has noted:

> I often find my views quoted in newspapers, not least because some papers still hold the opinion that the BBC cricket correspondent should not be allowed to express a view. Rather than influence the media, I hope that my progress from player to correspondent shows that there is a role for former cricketers in the media, despite the intolerant views of some of my colleagues in the press box. (*The Independent*, 25 July 2005b)

The growth in the range of media outlets covering sport and the growth of sports-related journalism has of course increased the range of opportunities for former sportspeople to get involved in media work. For many this means sports broadcasting and presenting, rather then becoming fully-fledged print sports journalists. The obvious exception to this rule is cricket, with its traditionally better-educated middle-class players often making inroads to the more literary style of journalistic output which has characterised broadsheet cricket writing. Recent examples of players turned journalists include the former England captain Mike Atherton, who is now a cricket journalist for *The Daily Telegraph*, and worked with Channel 4 television when they covered cricket, and former England bowlers Derek Pringle (*The Daily Telegraph*) and Angus Fraser (*The Independent*).

Some other journalists are not impressed by what they view as the growth of celebrity sports journalism. The political journalist Peter Wilby has suggested that: 'I fear that sportswriting is in steep decline, not only because it has more space than it can fill but also because the celebrity culture dictates that former players should be writers' (*The Observer Sports Monthly*, 2005b). In cricket journalism especially, however, there is in fact a long tradition of former players who have moved across from playing into print journalism, and with more space devoted to the sport this trend has increased.

The above cricketers have thus become full-time cricket writers (it is a legacy of its literary and class influence that the term cricket journalist as opposed to writer is rarely used). However, there are broad differences between the groups of former sportspeople who move into that subsection of sports journalism called sports punditry. On one side there are those who will often appear on radio or television, will have a ghosted print column, will often rely on their network of relationships in the sport, and will often refrain from criticising former colleagues. For others, the trade of journalism is only to be entered if you are prepared to cross a line, which may result in you having to be critical of friends and former team mates. In the latter category one such example is the former Celtic and Scotland football player Davie Provan, who currently works in football journalism across television, radio and the print media with *Sky Sports*, *Radio Clyde* and by writing a non-ghosted column in the *News of the World*. Provan is well aware that in the age of comment, sports journalism should not be an easy ride for former sportspeople. He has argued:

> There's a big threshold you have to cross and any ex-professional who wants to work in the media has to cross it eventually; if you're asked for a comment you have to give it honestly. It can be a critical comment and you can lose friends through it. I'm saddened by that, but I don't think there's any other way to do the job. There's this feeling with professional football, we don't betray each other … Easy to criticize? It is actually easier not to, sometimes. (*The Sunday Times*, 2004a)

Many sports journalists often feel former sportspeople are compromised by their former allegiances and thus lack the journalistic rigour to ask the difficult question that is an implicit part of being in the trade. There are exceptions, like Provan and journalists such as Paul Kimmage, the former professional cyclist who is now a sportswriter for the *Sunday Independent* in Dublin and *The Sunday Times* in London. Kimmage has created a reputation for himself as sports feature writer, able to draw on his own experience as a professional sportsman to inform his writing. Writing about Kimmage, Humphries has noted:

> He's a great interviewer who uses silence and aggression as weapons. And he's a former pro sportsman himself. Lots of the players [the Irish football team] have read *A Rough Ride*, his matchless book about his cycling career. That personal history gives him an edge. Professional sports people respect him because they know that he knows what its like. (Humphries, 2003: 202)

Many former sportspeople are also considered by sports journalists to lack a journalistic news antenna, which can result in stories going unreported or simply being missed. This is a critique often applied to athletics coverage, particularly on BBC television, which appears to be increasingly populated with former British Olympic stars such as Steve Cram, Roger Black, Sally Gunnell, and on BBC radio, which employs the recently retired Denise Lewis.

As we noted in Chapter 3, it is here that the subtle differences that exist in sports broadcasting, as an aspect of sports journalism, become evident. While commenting and reporting on live events is a form of journalism, and the ability to communicate past 'insider knowledge' of competing at the highest level can be important, these former stars lack the journalistic edge to probe and dig around the sport or even to ask remotely critical questions of many of the athletes. There is too much of the 'all friends together club' about much of this form of sports reporting or journalism; this really is sport as entertainment and show business. This aspect of contemporary television sports coverage has also been commented on by veteran broadcaster Des Lynam. Lynam, who has worked for both the BBC and ITV, argues that: 'I wasn't a professional sportsman so I can't take on the aloof attitude that some professional sportsmen do when they become commentators. I think that journalism is missing from television now. It's gone the other way. Ex-players all the way through' (*The Daily Telegraph*, 1 October 2005). Exceptions do exist to this form of anodyne broadcasting, such as the use by the BBC of the US former Olympic 400-metre champion Michael Johnson, whose insightful, honest and often critical comments, simply served to reinforce the lack of journalistic edge that informs so much coverage of the sport on BBC television. This has not always been the case in the history of BBC coverage of the sport. The late Ron Pickering was renowned not only for his ability as both an athletics commentator and broadcaster, but also for his opinionated, informed and critical reporting on some of the murkier aspects of the sport such as doping and racism.

Ironically, it is also a former US sports star, who freelances for the BBC, who offers the only real critical journalistic edge to the Corporation's coverage of the Wimbledon tennis championships. Former player John McEnroe combines his breadth of knowledge of the sport – the lack of which is often a criticism made about sports journalists by sportspeople – with a critical honesty and journalistic sense of what makes a good story. He will, when he feels it is fair comment, be critical of players, matches and even the sport in a manner that has become increasingly rare in sports broadcasting, and television coverage of sport in particular.

STILL FANS WITH TYPEWRITERS?

Two other related issues are worth discussing in any debate regarding the image of the sports journalist. One is the strange relationship that exists between the individual sports journalist and the journalistic 'pack', which travel around together covering the same events and reporting from the same press conferences. On the one hand, there is a requirement to get a story, while at the same time covering basically the same terrain as your rivals, on the other, there is a fear that you might 'miss' the story that emerges from other journalists. This concern is no different to that faced by journalists in other spheres, such as politics.

Political journalist Andrew Marr has documented the extent to which those journalists attending the same event construct a story. He notes that 'often I come away (from a press conference) feeling that the story or "the line" has emerged only because one colleague had the loudest voice that morning or the most aggressive opinion' (Marr, 2004: 58). Thus sports journalists operate within the same network that both supports colleagues and rivals and constrains the parameters of the story. There exists a strange mixture of complicitness and competition between the journalists of the sports pack.

As argued earlier in the book, the predetermined story can often be an element in this process, with the journalist simply keen to get the quotes to back up the story or the line they were already planning to take. This can often be the case with those journalists working for the tabloids, where often sports editors will set and frame the agenda for how a story will be covered in that paper. This is part of what Eamon Dunphy calls the 'soft consensus' among many sports journalists, with the broadly agreed heroes and villains already having been cast before the stories are written (interview with author, 30 May 2005).

The nature of journalists' engagement with sportspeople can also exaggerate this process. As access becomes an issue, the granting of 'one-to-one' interviews is often limited, while press days are divided up to allow the dailies, the Sundays, and the radio and television journalists all to get their time with players or athletes. The sight of five journalists sitting around a table with a player, with pearlcorders whirling and notebooks at the ready, is a common part of the working environment for most sports journalists, often with an implicit element of conferring of notes after the event to make sure they have missed nothing. In some sports their Sunday newspapers colleagues will be wheeled in as the dailies journalists leave the room, in others, such as football, clubs will offer different players to satisfy the needs of the daily and Sunday papers. Occasionally, sports tournaments will offer players to the media in a 'mixed zone', a sort of media scrum, where print and broadcast sports journalists compete for quotes from a player or manager.

This formalised aspect of news-gathering, of course, does not mean that sportswriters do not form their own views and opinion, often adding depth and colour to the bare reproduction of quotes that often characterises sports news reports. There are also, of course, those who tend to stand out from the pack or travel as an 'insider', while maintaining a distance from colleagues and the culture that travels with the 'pack'. In reality these will be the No. 1s, the sportswriters who rely on their insight and opinion to construct their more reflective pieces rather than breaking stories or uncovering news. The racing journalist and broadcaster Peter O'Sullevan recalled in a BBC documentary how, on starting out in journalism, the press tent at one of the race courses was pointed out to him as a hub of journalistic activity. At which point the advice he received was to stay out of there as much as possible, something O'Sullevan, who earned a reputation as a distinguished journalist who rarely followed the journalistic 'pack', took on board throughout his career (BBC, 1991).

Central to this process, of course, is both the role of the sports editor and the wider cultural and market environment of the media organisation a journalist works for. Their immediate institutional environment shapes all journalists, and sports journalists are no different. For example, a sports journalist working for a broadsheet recalled how a tabloid newspaper had splashed with a back page story from a news conference that he had also attended but not filed a story from. When asked by his sports editor why he had not filed, the journalist informed him that this was because the footballer in question had not said what was being quoted in the tabloid and had certainly not meant what he said to be interpreted as it had been. His editor accepted this explanation, and he was put under no further pressure. At a rival tabloid this may well have not been the case, but at the broadsheet newspaper this sports journalist felt no immediate pressure to embellish his copy.[2]

The other criticism made of sports journalists is one that often calls into question their journalistic abilities to report in an impartial and balanced manner, the sports journalist regarded as a fan with a typewriter, or in the contemporary version a laptop. Roy Greenslade argues that when he began in the trade back in the 1960s:

> The difference between a sports journalist and any other was that you are really a fan with a typewriter. Even if you are not covering the team you love, you love the game. They were close to the players in a way unimaginable today. Journalists and sports players mingled with each other, shared a common lifestyle, very little conflict, and almost no conflict between players and sports reporters at all. (Interview with author, 6 October 2004)

While Rowe (2005: 127) has noted how: 'Sports journalism ... seems to oscillate between a rather sycophantic cultivation of key sports sources (such as clubs and players) and a sometimes shrill demonization of those organizations and individuals through sports scandals and *exposés*.'

There is no doubt that football journalism in particular is still populated with journalists who have come in through the fanzine movement or through specific club magazines or publications. Often these journalists come with a well-stocked contact book that helps smooth access to certain clubs and individuals. As a result, it is commonplace among supporters to assume, often correctly, that particular journalists have an affiliation with a football club that in their eyes taints their journalistic output.

While such journalists exist, others park their prejudices at the door, just as those working in, say, political journalism are supposed to. Arsenal fan and football writer, Amy Lawrence suggests that for her, football journalism is:

> A bit like getting in the zone when you are covering a game, there is so much to do and think about during a live game, that personal bias doesn't come into it. Of course you might want a goal to go in, but you need that passion. You cannot write about the game if you have no passion for the game. (Interview with author, 9 August 2005)

Also, as more people enter the industry from a university and journalism training background these issues are less acute than they once were. But Greenslade's observation remains a valid one in that sports journalists, as a rule, love sport. While many may fall in and out of love with sport over the years, its initial pull and allure can remain compelling for most (see sports journalist Will Buckley's fictional account (2004) of the football writer who falls out of love with the game). And yet many political journalists, for example, will also have a fascination and deep knowledge of the political terrain they cover, and in many ways this knowledge is an important part of the armoury of a journalist. The challenge for sports journalists is to remain in some form detached from what can be an intensely human drama, often played out against the backdrop of a seething cauldron of emotion and noise and a television audience of millions. Here, once again, we return to the role of the sports editor and the institutional environment within which a journalist is working.

At the tabloid end of the market patriotic rhetoric can sell newspapers, and sports journalists covering international events often take an unambiguous stance. For those sportswriters working at the broadsheet/compact end of the market, a certain reflective detached analysis will often be expected. As Jones notes, the golden rule of objectivity is a difficult one to invoke in contemporary sports journalism:

> The perspective of many who occupy the press and commentary boxes today seems closer than ever before to the supporters, leaving them equally vulnerable to the effect of winning and losing. Michael Owen's terrific goal against Argentina in the 1998 World Cup finals caused so much rejoicing among England football correspondents that the business of covering sport appeared to have altered beyond recognition. (2000: 42)

In this judgement Jones may be being a bit harsh. That particular goal was a sublime piece of sporting skill on a grand stage that even the most hard-hearted Scotsman could only applaud. In addition, if for too long, sports journalists have been accused of travelling too close to the sporting circus and the players associated with sport, perhaps the divisions that now exist between journalist and sportspeople are not as unhealthy as first appears to be the case. Being closer to the supporters and fans (and readers and viewers) rather than the sport may in fact be a price worth paying, but only, and here one accepts Jones's wider point, if some journalistic rigour is applied to that process. Other sportswriters, such as Tom Humphries, recognise the role that the print media play in selling sport, but Humphries also argues (2003: 349) that he thinks 'a large part of sports journalism should be about the extinguishing of flammable hype by whatever means come to hand'.

For those working in that section of sports journalism called sports broadcasting, selling the event has become an unfortunate by-product of sports mutation into television entertainment. Despite the notions of impartiality and objectivity that frame television journalism, these are rarely observed in sports coverage of international sporting events, and add credence to the claim that, ultimately, sports broadcasting is a narrow and partial form of sports journalism.

Thus sports journalism and notions of journalistic impartiality remain a problematic area; however, perhaps no more so than it is for the wider field of contemporary journalism, which is saturated with comment and opinion as well as factual reporting.

ENDPIECE

For some in the industry, the image of the sports journalist as simply a 'fan with a typewriter' should not be overplayed. Sports journalism, like other areas of the trade, has become much more competitive and in many ways more professional. The back pages are no longer where journalists go looking for an easy time. David Chappell, then sports editor of *The Times* and now a senior executive at the paper argues:

> With the new sports journalism, we are journalists first and sports lovers second. It might not always look like this, but as a sports editor the people I employ are good journalists, they know a story, they have good news antennae, good contacts, are good listeners, in other words they are good hard-nosed journalists. I'm not fussed about people who can name every FA Cup line-up since 1957, I want people who can question and where they have to, fall back on their journalistic skills. Football writers tend to specialise in that and are busy. Others, such as our golf writer John Hopkinson, can go to rugby, squash, and can approach these sports not as a fan, but as a journalist. And this is crucial. (Interview with author, 8 October 2004)

This sense of the need for the modern sports journalist to be more journalistically equipped, than previous generations, to deal with the range of issues they may have to face is echoed by Pape and Featherstone (2005: 105–6), who argue that sports journalism has become an important specialism within contemporary newspaper journalism.

There have always been sportswriters who have featured in the pantheon of great journalists and writers, particularly in the USA, where sports journalists like Grantland Rice was, arguably, more famous than many of the sports stars that he wrote about (Fountain, 1993). As the range of media outlets have increased, driven by changing technology and, equally as important, a more commercially orientated and less-regulated media environment, so has the range and profile of those directly involved in writing about the sports industry. However, as stated in the previous chapter, it is also important to note that despite the range of changes that have characterised the UK environment that sports journalists operate within, in terms of both their individual organisational culture and the wider sports industry, as a group they remain almost exclusively male and white. They are also under-represented in terms of the number of black and Asian sports journalists, particularly in the print media, who are plying their trade at the highest level.

The final chapter offers some reflections on the contemporary challenges facing sports journalism and pulls together some of the themes that have been examined throughout the book.

NOTES

1 This interview took place in 1992 at the European Football Championships in Sweden as part of another project.

2 This was an off-the-record conversation with a journalist and is used to illustrate the important role that the type of newspaper you work for has in shaping journalistic output.

CONCLUSION: SPORT, JOURNALISM AND SOCIETY

So the skill and privilege of a sports journalist, it conveniently struck me from the outset, is to be present at an event, be alert to details, and then describe it with immediate effect, or (a luxury which doesn't always pay off) recollect it in tranquility, with de Tocqueville open on the desk. Uniquely in journalism, its appeal to the reader is entirely in the presentation of the simple fact: 'I was there; I saw it with my own eyes; it happened once and it will never happen again.'

Lynne Truss, 'On the Terraces', in S. Glover (1999: 127) *Secrets of the Press: Journalists on Journalism***, London: Allen Lane.**

The columnist Alan Watkins once noted that political journalists have to pretend to hate politicians but actually rather like them whereas sports writers really loathe sportsmen but dare not admit it.

Matthew Engel, *The Guardian***, 7 October 2002.**

THE CHANGING LANDSCAPE

Leonard Koppett has reflected on the changes in sports writing over the years. He argues that wider changes in the newspaper industry, including increased competition from television and new media, have all impacted on the journalistic culture of reporting and writing about sports. He points out that:

Overall, today's sports pages are better written – in the literary sense – than 50 years ago. But the change in content and purpose is much greater. Our idea, then, was 'get the story, tell it as clearly as you can, avoid being wrong, look for the most interesting angle, don't worry about the stenographic reproduction of quotes.' Today's formula is 'make (not just get) the story, be entertaining at whatever cost to accuracy, aim at getting the reader's attention (which will draw attention to you), and move up the ladder as fast as possible'. (Koppett, 2003: 262)

Among UK sports journalists there is also a perception that their field has changed dramatically over the last decade or so and that change will continue, as sports journalism appeals to a new generation of people entering the industry. Richard Williams argues that:

There has been a very big shift in values. One of the issues is that a lot of people appear to want to be sports journalists, particularly young men. Now, 10 or 12 years ago nobody wanted to be one. In that time a massive shift has taken place. The key element appears to be that football has become fashionable. There is much more space, more competition between papers, thus key writers get much more projection. Although this has always been the case in the tabloids, but in the broadsheets they now get a big push. (Interview with author, 10 March 2005)

As part of that process he also argues that the boundaries of sports news will continue to expand and develop, increasingly pushing at traditional notions of what constitutes sports journalism. Williams suggests that:

The generation of people who are coming through now into jobs like mine just accept that popular culture is now more pervasive and more a part of people's lives. They see sport as a natural part of life. While 20 or 30 years ago news stories in sport were pretty non-existent, this is not so anymore. (Interview with author, 10 March 2005)

Sports journalism now not only offers an opportunity for those interested in entering the industry not simply to tell stories or impose a narrative frame on the chaos of events in and around sport, but also the chance for some to express themselves as writers.

As Eamon Dunphy argues:

Sports journalism is now a much richer field for someone who can write. There are more spaces to write, it's not a ghetto anymore. It's something you can aspire to now. If you want to write about contemporary life and culture then sports journalism gives you that opportunity. Sport is reflective of society, of what is right and wrong in contemporary culture, the good and the bad. This is a rich and interesting area for a writer and a journalist, they can now think I can do good work here. It excites and engages me as a journalist and its popularity is part of the natural expansion of sport in popular culture, through television, radio and newspapers. If I were an American writer I would love to write about Tiger Woods or about Beckham. (Interview with author, 30 May 2005)

This sentiment is echoed by Amy Lawrence who argues that it's part of the ability of sport to speak to wider aspects of society that forms part of its appeal to a journalist. She suggests that:

Football has become more pervasive in society, so you are writing about finance, about much bigger things than just the sport itself. If you think you will come into this area and just write about the game itself, then you are kidding yourself. You will find yourself writing about all aspects of life. (Interview with author, 9 August 2005)

And yet at its core the central paradox of sports journalism remains. Is it simply, as many have argued (Jennings, 1997; Sejer Anderson, 2000), a wing of the entertainment industry, immune from the ethical rigour apparently required of other fields of journalism? Or is it an increasingly disparate discipline, which demands to be recognised and respected as a legitimate area of journalistic output?

Throughout this book the tension between sport as part of the entertainment industries and sport as an increasingly central aspect of contemporary culture has been evident. In reality, these two concepts are not mutually exclusive. As sport has mushroomed, it has been inevitable that what gets reported should also change. Both sport and journalism have been shaped by technological change and the adoption of digitisation as an important characteristic of contemporary media culture. While it may still be true, as Brookes (2002: 39) has argued, that sports journalism remains distinctive from journalism in general, it would appear that as the terrain of sports journalism has expanded and the boundaries at which it operates have become less well defined, so too this distinctiveness has become less marked.

The issues and debates that surround the tenor, tone and content of sports journalism's range are increasingly the same as those that concern journalism more generally. They are shaped by the organisational culture and values that inform the media institution that produces this journalism. As a result, the term sports journalism encompasses journalism that can be, at times, lazy, poorly written and lacking a rigour or ethical core, through to journalism that is well researched, rigorous, enlightening, insightful and illuminating, and everything in between.

Factors such as commercialisation and the global nature of communicative developments have all helped shape the changing relationship between sports and journalism. For print sports journalism in particular, its expansion has come at a time when the commercial pressures on newspapers and journalism has been intense. The pressure continually to break stories, the temptation to 'spin' a story and 'puff' its importance through a more sensational treatment, all exist not just in sports journalism, but across journalism more generally.

The rise of the Internet and alternate sources of news have, as we have seen throughout the book, changed what print journalism now views as its natural terrain; to some extent it has become less concerned with news and more focused on comment and analysis. Yet the Internet and the continued dominance of television have not impacted on sports journalism to the same extent as other areas of the industry. While it has changed aspects of print sports journalism, overall, not least by encouraging some younger journalists to use it as the key source for information rather than actually getting out and speaking to people, television and the Internet have been good for those working in sports journalism, not least because it has driven an audience to the print media and made sports journalism commercially important across the market.

The growth of television coverage of sport has helped fuel both the expansion and the increasing resources that have been targeted at sports coverage by the print media. Rather than be viewed as unproblematic evidence of a 'dumbing down' of culture, as outlined by critics in the opening chapter, the rise of sports journalism across media platforms, and the print media specifically, is more about wider structural changes in the media industries and the increasingly complex interplay between media forms in the digital age. In a more demand-driven age of media consumption, sport sells and remains of interest to a large section of society, while the digital infrastructure of contemporary media help facilitate a more speedy and ubiquitous distribution of this material.

Commercial and public service media have recognised the cultural appetite for sports-related content, particularly among younger readers, viewers and listeners, and responded to this. The rise of the popularity of sport is partly explained by the extent to which it is sustained and constructed by the media, and sports broadcasting and journalism in particular. What we have also seen is a wider cultural shift in attitudes to sport and the emergence in society of a middle-class audience, which remains influenced by aspects of a more traditional working-class cultural milieu. This has helped shape newspaper coverage of sport. As part of this process, the coverage of sport, and football in particular, in the broadsheet/compact market has helped to legitimise this area of cultural taste and has actually given it a voice and a dynamic of its own making. It is also clear that a range of wider cultural, political and, indeed, economic factors have shaped the rise in the popularity of a sport such as football (Boyle and Haynes, 2004). Football's long-term popularity and the extent to which it has become embedded in the individual and collective everyday lives of many people in society is the result of deeper social and cultural factors not necessarily created by the media. What has changed is the commercial desire of media corporations to service and develop this longer-term relationship. Journalists working in and around the sports industry have benefited from this change.

THE GOLDEN AGE?

The sports journalism industry has, in keeping with other areas of journalism, been one characterised by change. The so-called 'golden age' of sports journalism has long gone, and despite the protestations from journalists of limited access to contemporary sports stars and the apparent negative impact the rise of public relations and a promotional culture has had on the trade, its end should not be lamented too much. In his thoughtful analysis of Scottish football Harry Reid views the 1960s and 1970s as the golden age of football journalism (Reid, 2005: 130). However, while there was undoubtedly outstanding sportswriting during this period there was also for many years large trenches of sports journalism that was sloppy, inaccurate, poorly researched, badly written and woefully informed. It was the soft end of the profession, an easy street for 'fans with typewriters'. While there was also brilliantly written and informed sports journalism, this was often hidden away in corners of the media market, and read by an informed minority of fans. While the legacy of the sports journalist as myth-maker can still clearly be seen today, it is also accompanied by a more enquiring, hard-nosed and, perhaps, even honest relationship between journalist and public.

As this book has attempted to map out, sports journalism in the 21st century encompasses a multitude of activity and practice across print, broadcast and online media. From the expanded, more reflective and literary sports writing of the No. 1 sportswriters, through to the rise of the sports news correspondent of most broadcasting organisations, part of the contemporary terrain of sports journalism remains that of market-driven sensationalism. This area of popular journalism remains informed by speculation, gossip and, often, ill-advised comment. However, it would be wrong not to acknowledge that this also sits side by side with a more cynical journalism, which seeks to expose and question aspects of the sports culture in a less deferential manner. In other words, the range of what constitutes sports journalism or journalism about sports has never been greater, and for all the lacunae that still exist, has never been more diverse in range.

The increasing economic and political importance of the public relations practice that is growing up around the sports industry presents a challenge to journalists working in this field. But the challenges they face are similar to journalists in other areas. There remains a need to get out of the office and look beyond the neatly crafted media release and to question on behalf of readers and viewers. Sport, with its mixture of entertainment, drama and news values, offers a particular challenge for journalists in their need to both inform and entertain in an increasingly fast-paced news environment while addressing, in many cases, an increasingly knowledgeable audience.

Sport continues to offer a range of compelling narratives for the 21st century, and despite the rise of television sport, sports journalists remain one of the key narrators of that ongoing story. As sport remains a central aspect of contemporary popular culture, thus the commercial value of sports journalism, and selected sports journalists, will continue to escalate. The challenge for these journalists is to offer uncomplicit, informative and entertaining journalism against the backdrop of an increasingly commercial and privatised media system. In such an environment the need for some parts of sports journalism to question, investigate and call to account the powerful within sport and its attendant political and commercial culture will become even more acute. And while sports journalism has correctly been criticised for its lack of investigative edge over the years, it should be noted that this area remains a small, but growing aspect of the wider culture of sports journalism. Again, the decline in investigative journalism is not unique to sports coverage and is a concern across news journalism more generally.

This book has suggested that the next generation of sports journalists are as likely to be journalists writing about sport and its cultural impact as they are to be very narrowly focused sports journalists. For while sport, at its core, remains an essentially banal, trivial and ephemeral pursuit, it also exposes in a very public manner, some of the wider narratives and stories that sustain communities, identities and a society's sense of itself at both a local and a global level. This process of identity-formation is not unimportant and should not be underestimated or lightly dismissed as such. It is also a process that in a more commercially driven media has been recognised as an important driver in sales and subscriptions across media platforms. As a result, unlike some other areas of journalism, sports journalism continues to thrive and develop despite, or indeed because of, media change and technological innovation.

Sports journalism remains a strange occupation, which for the elite sportswriters involves travelling with the 'pack' in a strained relationship of camaraderie and competition, of late night working, and of hanging around in airports, press conferences, media centres and hotel reception areas in an attempt to snatch a word with players, managers and athletes. It is a job that involves telling stories, making sense of the nonsensical, making entertaining the mundane, and deflating the egos and self-important pomposity of many who run the sports industry. It can be both, at times, trivial and important.[1]

Among the growing formalisation of university-level journalism 'schools' in the UK, sports journalism is becoming a popular part of wider journalism studies degrees, as well as a distinctive stand alone course.[2] While these programmes predominantly attract male students, they also have a growing popularity with female students. A combination of the increasing high media profile of sports journalists, the ubiquitous nature of sports broadcasting and journalism across a range of media outlets, and the associated 'glamour' of getting close to the celebrity world of elite sports-people all appear to be part of the allure. As more university-trained journalism students enter the field in the UK, it is worth recognising that sports journalism offers a microcosm of many of the wider challenges and issues being faced by journalists and journalism in general. These include debates about the rise of public relations, the challenge of impartial reporting, the impact of the economic on the cultural, and the continual reinvention of what we understand journalism to be about. All of these issues can be found in any study of the expanded terrain of contemporary sports journalism.

It also raises issues about the breadth of training and education required by sports journalists. For while the doyen of British sportswriting Hugh McIlvanney has always been associated with the more literary end of the sports journalism spectrum, he has always viewed himself first and foremost as a reporter (Randall, 2005: 179–200). His experience as a news and features journalist has always informed his sportswriting, suggesting that the best sportswriters are their core simply great journalists who happen to write about sports.

Sports journalism, with its mixture of good and bad practice, of the mundane and the magnificent, is in many ways an exemplar of much of modern journalism. As sport, with all its cultural, political and economic implications continues to occupy a very public space in our contemporary culture, both those journalists who help make sense of its narratives, and their associated trade are overdue a reassessment of their position within modern journalism. Perhaps it is time to consign the 'toy department' analogy to the pages of journalism history.

NOTES

1 From a US perspective, two books that give a compelling account of the issues involved in being a sports journalist are Leonard Koppett's *The Rise and Fall of the Press Box* (Sport Media, Toronto, 2003) and Gerald Eskenazi's *A Sportswriter's Life: From the Desk of a New York Times Reporter* (University of Missouri Press, Columbia and London, 2003). The accounts of being a sportswriter given by Tom Humphries in *Laptop Dancing and the Nanny Goat Mambo: A Sportswriter's Year* (Pocket Books Townhouse, Dublin, 2003) and the *Daily Telegraph's* Andrew Baker in *Where Am I and Who's Winning?* (Yellow Jersey Press, London, 2004) should also be compulsory reading for any person thinking of entering the industry.

2 For an interesting discussion of some of the wider issues for journalism, its image and the growth of university degrees in journalism and journalism studies see S. Frith and P. Meech 'Becoming a journalist: Journalism education and journalism culture, in *Journalism: Theory, Culture and Practice* (Sage, London, forthcoming).

BIBLIOGRAPHY

Aamidor, A. (ed.) (2003) *Real Sports Reporting*. Bloomington: Indiana University Press.

Alabarces, P., Tomlinson, A. and Young, C. (2001) 'Argentina versus England at the France '98 World Cup: Narratives of nation and the mythologizing of the popular', *Media, Culture and Society*, 23: 547–66.

Allan, S. (ed.) (2005) *Journalism: Critical Issues*. Maidenhead: Open University Press.

Andrews, D.L. and Jackson, S.J. (eds) (2001) *Sports Stars: The Cultural Politics of Sporting Celebrity*. London and New York: Routledge.

Andrews, E. and Andrews, G. (1990) *For Ever and Ever, Eamonn: The Public and Private Life of Eamonn Andrews*. London: Grafton Books.

Andrews, P. (2005) *Sports Journalism: A Practical Introduction*. London: Sage.

Aura Sports (2005) 'Aura Sports Fan Survey 2004'. Available online: http://www.aurasports.com

Baker, A. (2004) *Where Am I and Who's Winning*. London: Yellow Jersey Press.

Baldock, A. (2003) 'PA Lions Report', accessed at www.icwales.icnetwork.co.uk

Bazalgette, P. (2005) *Billion Dollar Game: How Three Men Risked It All and Changed the Face of Television*. London: Time Warner Books.

BBC (1991) 'The Sportswriter', *Arena*, 27 March.

Bell, E. (2005) 'End of the offline?', *British Journalism Review*, 16(1): 41–5.

Benaud, R. (1998) *Anything But an Autobiography*. London: Hodder and Stoughton.

Berkow, I. (1986) *Red: A Biography of Red Smith*. New York: Times Books.

Bernstein, A. (2002) 'Is it time for a victory lap? Changes in the media coverage of women in sport', *International Review for the Sociology of Sport*, 37: 415–28.

Betts, J.R. (1953) 'Sporting journalism in nineteenth-century America', *American Quarterly*, 5(1): 40.

Blain, N. and O'Donnell, H. (1998) 'European sports journalism and its readers during Euro '96', in M. Roche (ed.), *Sport, Popular Culture and Identity*. Aachen: Meyer and Meyer.

Blain, N., Boyle, R. and O'Donnell, H. (1993) *Sport and National Identity in the European Media.* Leicester: Leicester University Press.

Bower, T. (2003) *Broken Dreams: Vanity, Greed and the Souring of British Football.* London: Simon & Schuster.

Boyle, R. (1992) 'From our Gaelic fields: Radio, sport and nation in post-partition Ireland', *Media, Culture and Society*, 14: 623–36.

Boyle, R. and Haynes, R. (2000) *Power Play: Sport, the Media and Popular Culture.* London: Longman.

Boyle, R. and Haynes, R. (2004) *Football in the New Media Age.* London: Routledge.

Boyle, R. and Monteiro, C. (2005) '"A small country with a big ambition": Representations of Portugal and England in Euro 2004 British and Portuguese newspaper coverage', *European Journal of Communication*, 20: 223–44.

Boyle, R., Morrow, S. and Dinan, W. (2002) '"Doing the business?" The newspaper reporting of the business of football', *Journalism: Theory, Practice and Criticism*, 3(2): 161–81.

Broad, C. and Waddell, D. (1999) *and Welcome to the Highlights: 61 Years of BBC TV Cricket.* London: BBC Worldwide.

Bromley, M. (1998) 'The "tabloidising" of Britain: "Quality" newspapers in the 1990s', in H. Stephenson and M. Bromley (eds), *Sex, Lies and Democracy: The Press and the Public.* London: Longman.

Brookes, R. (2002) *Representing Sport.* London: Arnold.

Buckley, W. (2004) *The Man Who Hated Football.* London: Fourth Estate.

Burns, G. (1986) *Pocket Money: Bad-Boys, Business-Heads and Boom-Time Snooker.* London: Heinemann.

Campbell, A. (2005) 'Alastair Cambell on Clive Woodward', *Esquire*, July.

Campbell, V. (2004) *Information Age Journalism.* London: Arnold.

Chambers, D., Steiner, L. and Fleming, C. (2004) *Women and Journalism.* Routledge: London.

Chandler, J.M. (1996) 'Media', in D. Levinson and K. Christensen (eds), *Encyclopedia of World Sport*, Oxford. ABC–CLIO.

Clifton, P. (2000) 'The future of sports journalism on the Internet', paper given at Play the Game conference, Copenhagen, Denmark.

Coleman, N. and Hornby, N. (eds) (1996) *The Picador Book of Sports Writing.* London: Macmillan.

Collins, P. (2003) 'United we fall', *British Journalism Review*, 14(4): 49–54.

Conboy, M. (2004) *Journalism: A Critical History.* London: Sage.

Conn, D. (2005) *The Beautiful Game? Searching for the Soul of football.* London: Yellow Jersey Press.

Conn, D., Green, C., McIlroy, R. and Mousley, K. (2003) *Football Confidential 2: Scams, Scandals and Screw Ups.* London: BBC Worldwide.

Coogan, T.P. (1976) 'An old lady and her pupils, in L. McRedmond (ed.), *Written on the Wind.* Dublin: RTE/Gill and Macmillan.

Corrigan, J. (2005) 'Isn't it time we took women's sport more seriously, *The Independent*, 6 June.

Creedon, P. (ed.) (1994) *Women, Media and Sport: Challenging Gender Values*. New York: Sage.

Crolley, L. and Hand, D. (2002) *Football, Europe and the Press*. London: Frank Cass.

Curran, J. and Seaton, J. (2003) *Power Without Responsibility: The Press and Broadcasting in Britain*. London: Routledge.

The Daily Telegraph (2003) 2 October.

The Daily Telegraph (2005) 7 June.

Davies, P. (1990) *All Played Out: The Full Story of Italia '90*. London: Heinemann.

Day, E. (2004) 'Why women love journalism', *British Journalism Review*, 15(2): 21–5.

Douglas Lowes, M. (1997) 'Sports page: A case study in the manufacture of sports news for the daily press', *Sociology of Sport Journal*, 14: 143–59.

Duncan, M.C., Messner, M.A. and Willms, N. (2005) *Gender in Televised Sports: News and Highlights Shows, 1989–2004*. Los Angeles: Amateur Athletic Foundation of Los Angeles.

Dunphy, E. (1987) *Only a Game? The Diary of a Professional Footballer*, 2nd edn. London: Penguin Books.

Dyke, G. (2004) *Inside Story*. London: HarperCollins.

Eastman, S.T. and Billings, A.C. (2000) 'Sportscasting and sports reporting', *Journal of Sport and Social Issues*, 24(2), May: 192–213.

Eco, U. (1986) *Travels in Hyperreality*. London: Harcourt.

Eisenstock, A. (2001) *Sports Talk: A Journey Inside the World of Sports Talk Radio*. New York: Pocket Books.

Engel, M. (1996) *Tickle the Public: One Hundred Years of the Popular Press*. London: Orion.

Engel, M. (2002) 'He simply and innocently blew journalism apart', *Guardian*, 7 October.

Eskenazi, G. (2003) *A Sportswriter's Life: From The Desk of a New York Times Reporter*. Columbia and London: University of Missouri Press.

Foer, F. (2004) *How Soccer Explains the World: An Unlikely Theory of Globalisation*. New York: HarperCollins.

Fountain, C. (1993) *Sportswriter: The Life and Times of Grantland Rice*. Oxford: Oxford University Press.

Franklin, B. (1997) *Newszak and News Media*. London: Arnold.

Garland, J. and Rowe, M. (1999) 'War minus the shooting? Jingoism, the English press, and Euro 96', *Journal of Sport and Social Issues*, 23(1): 80–95.

Giamatti, A.B. (1988) *What's Wrong with American Sports Pages? Proceedings of the American Society of Newspaper Editors*. Washington: ASNE, pp. 201–15.

Glanville, B. (1999) *Football Memories*. London: Virgin.

Goldlust, J. (1987) *Playing for Keeps*. London: Longman.

Gorman, L. and McLean, D. (2003) *Media and Society in the Twentieth Century*. Oxford: Blackwell.

Gray, A. (2005) *Gray Matters: Andy Gray the Autobiography*. London: Pan Books.

Green, A. (2000) *The Green Line*. London: Headline.

Greenslade, R. (2003) *Press Gang: How Newspapers Make Profits from Propaganda*. London: Macmillan.

Guardian (1996) 21 June.

Guardian (2001) 30 July.

Guardian (2002) 7 October.

Guardian (2003a) 12 November.

Guardian (2003b) 13 November.

Guardian (2004) 10 September.

Guardian (2005a) 'Nice PR, shame about the rugby', 27 June.

Guardian (2005b) 20 September.

Hagerty, B. (2005) 'It's cricket, but is it journalism?', *British Journalism Review*, 16(3): 79–84.

Hand, D. and Crolley, L. (2005) 'Spanish identities in the European press: The case of football writing', *The International Journal of the History of Sport*, 22(2), March: 298–313.

Harcup, T. (2004) *Journalism: Principles and Practice*. London: Sage.

Hargreaves, I. (2003) *Journalism: Truth or Dare?* Oxford: Oxford University Press.

Hargreaves, J. (1986) *Sport, Power and Culture*. Oxford: Polity Press.

Hargreaves, J. (1994) *Sporting Females: Critical Issues in the History and Sociology of Women's Sport*. London: Routledge.

Haynes, R. (1999) 'There's many a slip "twixt the eye and the lip": An exploratory history of football broadcasts and running commentaries on BBC radio, 1927–1939', *International Review for the Sociology of Sport*, 34(2): 143–56.

Henderson, M. (2004) 'Why I dread a summer of sport', *The Observer Sports Monthly*, SI, May.

The Herald (2004) 24 December.

Holt, R. (1989) *Sport and the British*. Oxford: Oxford University Press.

Holt, R. and Mason, T. (2000) *Sport in Britain 1945–2000*. Oxford: Blackwell.

Horrie, C. (2003) *Tabloid Nation: From the Birth of the* Daily Mirror *to the Death of the Tabloid*. London: Andre Deutsch.

Hughes, S. (2005) *Morning Everyone: A Sportswriter's Life*. London: Orion.

Humphries, T. (2003) *Laptop Dancing and the Nanny Goat Mambo: A Sportswriter's Year*. Dublin: Pocket Books Townhouse.

Humphries, T. (2004) *Booked!* Dublin: Townhouse.

Hutton, W. (2004) 'A big hand for Michael', *The Observer*, 4 April.

Inabinett, M. (1994) *Grantland Rice and His Heroes: The Sportswriter as Mythmaker in the 1920s.* Knoxville: The University of Tennessee Press.

The Independent (2005a) 11 July.

The Independent (2005b) 25 July.

The Independent (2005c) 5 December.

The Independent on Sunday (2004) 27 June.

The Irish Times (2005) 1 October.

Jennings, A. (1997) 'Sport, lies and stasi files – a golden opportunity for the press', paper given at Sport, Media and Civil Society, Play the Game Conference, Copenhagen, Denmark.

Jones, K. (2000) 'Decline and fall of popular sportwriting', *British Journalism Review*, 11(1): 39–43.

Kaszuba, D. (2003) 'They are Women, Hear Them Roar: Female Sportswriters of the Roaring Twenties', unpublished Ph.D., Penn State University.

Keeble, R. (2004) 'The woman's place?', *Press Gazette*, 10 December.

Kelly, S.F. (1988) *Back Page Football: A Century of Newspaper Coverage.* London: Queen Anne Press.

Kettle, M. (2004) 'Journalists' self-righteous arrogance has gone too far, Comment', *Guardian*, 18 May.

Koppett, L. (2003) *The Rise and Fall of the Press Box.* Toronto, Sport Media.

Kram, M. (1989) 'Great men die twice', *Esquire*, November.

Langer, J. (1998) *Tabloid Television: Popular Journalism and the 'Other News'.* London and New York: Routledge.

Lindsey, E. (2001) 'Notes from the sports desk: Reflections on race, class and gender in British sports', in B. Carrington and I. McDonald (eds), *'Race' Sport and British Society.* Routledge: London.

The Listener (1986) 5 June.

Lloyd, J. (2004a) 'The fourth estate's coup d'etat', *The Observer*, 13 June.

Lloyd, J. (2004b) *What the Media Do to Our Politics.* London: Constable.

McLaughlin, G. (2002) *The War Correspondent.* London: Pluto.

McNair, B. (1999) *Journalism and Democracy: An Evaluation of the Political Public Sphere.* London: Routledge.

MacPherson, A. (2004) *Jock Stein: The Definitive Biography.* London: Highdown.

Magee, S. (2004) 'Whipping boys', *British Journalism Review*, 15(1): 43–9.

Magor, M. (2002) 'News terrorism: Misogyny exposed and the easy journalism of conflict', *Feminist Media Studies*, 2(1): 141–4.

Mahtani, M. (2005) 'Gendered news practices: Examining experiences of women journalists in different national contexts', in S. Allan (ed.), *Journalism: Critical Issues.* Maidenhead: Open University Press.

Marr, A. (2004) *My Trade: A Short History of British Journalism.* London: Macmillan.

Maskell, D. (1989) *OH, I say!* Glasgow: Fontana/Collins.

Media Guardian (2005a) 10 January.

Media Guardian (2005b) 1 August.

Messner, M.A. (2002) *Taking the Field: Women, Men and Sports*. Minneapolis: University of Minnesota Press.

Miller, T., Lawrence, G., McKay, J. and Rowe, D. (2001) *Globalisation and Sport*. London: Sage.

Mills, K. (1997) 'What difference do women journalists make?', in P. Morris (ed.), *Women, Media and Politics*. Oxford: Oxford University Press.

Mondaymorning (2002) *Industry or Independence? Survey of the Scandinavian Sports Press*, Mondaymorning Think Tank of News. Available online: http://www.mm.dk

Moore, B. (1999) *The Final Score*. London: Hodder and Stoughton.

Morgan, P. (2005) *The Insider: The Private Diaries of a Scandalous Decade*. London: Edbury Press.

NMA (2003) 'Hitching men's passion for sport to effective ads', Newspaper Marketing Agency. Available online: http://www.nmauk.co.uk

NMA (2004) 'Euro 2004 – the readership results are in …', September, Newspaper Marketing Agency. Available online: http://www.nmauk.co.uk

The Observer (2004) 31 October.

The Observer (2005) 24 April.

The Observer Sports Monthly (2005a) February.

The Observer Sports Monthly (2005b) August.

O'Donnell, H. (1994) 'Mapping the mythical: A geopolitics of national sporting stereotypes', *Discourse and Society*, 5(3): 345–80.

O'Hehir, M. (1996) *Michael O'Hehir: My Life and Times*. Dublin: Blackwater Press/RTE.

Oriard, M. (1993) *Reading Football: How the Popular Press Created an American Spectacle*. Chapel Hill and London: University of North Carolina Press.

Oriard, M. (2001) *King Football: Sport and Spectacle in the Golden Age of Radio and Newsreels, Movies and Magazines, the Weekly and Daily Press*. Chapel Hill and London: University of North Carolina Press.

Owen, M. (2004) *Michael Owen: Off the Record*. London: HarperCollins Willow.

Pape, S. and Featherstone, S. (2005) *Newspaper Journalism: A Practical Introduction*. London: Sage.

Platell, A. (1999) 'Institutionalized Sexism', in S. Glover (ed.), *Secrets of the Press: Journalists on Journalism*. London: Allen Lane.

Polley, M. (1998) *Moving the Goalposts: A History of Sport and Society Since 1945*. London: Routledge.

Press Gazette (2005a) 22 April.

Press Gazette (2005b) 10 June.

Purcell, S. (1999) *Des Lynam: The Biography*. London: André Deutsch.

Randall, D. (2005) *The Great Reporters*. London: Pluto Press.

Reid, H. (2005) *The Final Whistle? Scottish Football, the Best of Times, the Worst of Times*. Edinburgh: Birlinn.

Robinson, J. (2004) 'Why Sven is played up front', *The Observer*, 8 August.

Rooney, D. (2000) 'Thirty years of competition in the British tabloid press: The *Mirror* and the *Sun* 1968–1998', in C. Sparks and J. Tulloch (eds), *Tabloid Tales: Global Debates Over Media Standards*. Oxford: Rowman & Littlefield.

Rowe, D. (1992) 'Modes of sports writing', in P. Dahlgren and C. Sparks (eds), *Journalism and Popular Culture*. London: Sage.

Rowe, D. (1995) *Popular Cultures: Rock, Music, Sport and the Politics of Pleasure*. London: Sage.

Rowe, D. (1999) *Sport, Culture and the Media*. Buckingham: Open University Press.

Rowe, D. (2003) 'Sport and the repudiation of the global', *International Review for the Sociology of Sport*, 38(3): 281–94.

Rowe, D. (2004) 'Introduction: Mapping the media sports cultural complex', in D. Rowe (ed.), *Critical Readings: Sport, Culture and the Media*. Maidenhead: Open University Press.

Rowe, D. (2005) 'Fourth estate or fan club? Sports journalism engages the popular', in S. Allan (ed.), *Journalism: Critical Issues*. Maidenhead: Open University Press.

Rudd, A. (1998) *Astroturf Blonde*. London: Headline.

Rudin, R. and Ibbotson, M. (2002) *An Introduction to Journalism*. London: Focal Press.

Rusbridger, A. (2000) Versions of seriousness, *Guardian*, 4 November. Available online: http://www.guardian.co.uk/dumb

Salwen, M.B. and Garrison, B. (1998) 'Finding their place in journalism: Newspaper sports journalists' professional "problems"', *Journal of Sport and Social Issues*, 22(1): 88–102.

Sampson, A. (1996) 'The crisis at the heart of our media', *British Journalism Review*, 7(3): 42–51.

Sebba, A. (1994) *Battling for News: The Rise of the Woman Reporter*. London: Hodder and Stoughton.

Sejer Anderson, J. (2000) 'Victims of passive doping', paper given at Play the Game conference, Copenhagen, Denmark.

Schlesinger, P. (2006) 'The crisis in British journalism?', *Media, Culture and Society*.

Shea, J. (2000) 'The King: How ESPN changes everything', *Columbia Journalism Review*, Jan/Feb: accessed from www.cjr.org

Shennan, B. (2004) 'Kelvin must realise that we live in a competitive world', *Media Weekly, The Independent*, 4 October.

Simons, L.M. (1999) 'The state of the American newspaper: Follow the ball', *American Journalism Review*, November: 12–18.

Smart, B. (2005) *The Sport Star: Modern Sport and the Cultural Economy of Sporting Celebrity*. London: Sage.

Smucker, M.K., Whisenant, W.A. and Pedersen, P.M. (2003) 'An investigation of job satisfaction and female sports journalists', *Sex Roles*, 49(7/8): 401–7.

Snow, J. (2005) *Shooting History*. London: HarperCollins.

Sparks, C. (2000) 'Introduction: The panic over tabloid news', in C. Sparks and J. Tulloch (eds), *Tabloid Tales: Global Debates Over Media Standards*. Oxford: Rowman & Littlefield.

Sparks, C. and Tulloch, J. (eds) (2000) *Tabloid Tales: Global Debates over Media Standards*. Oxford: Rowman and Littlefield.

Steiner, L. (2005) 'The "gender matters" debate in journalism: Lessons from the front', in S. Allan (ed.), *Journalism: Critical Issues*. Maidenhead: Open University Press.

Stewart, G. (2005) *The History of The Times: The Murdoch Years*. London: HarperCollins.

Swanton, E.W. (1996) *Last Over: A Life in Cricket*. London: Richard Cohen Books.

Sun (2005) 'Lennon will be Captain Marvel', 7 July.

Sunday Star Times (2005) 'Try spinning this Alastair', 26 June.

The Sunday Times (2004a) 6 June.

The Sunday Times (2004b) 4 July.

The Sunday Times (2005a) 10 July.

The Sunday Times (2005b) 4 September.

The Times (1988) 17 October.

The Times (2004) 'Dismayed attitude towards team play limits Americans', 20 September.

The Times (2005a) 7 May.

The Times (2005b) 'Woodward's men may learn the hard way that being caught in the spin cycle just won't wash', 15 June.

The Times (2005c) 'Spin no shield in face of poor form and spear tackles', 30 June.

The Times (2005d) 6 August.

The Times Magazine (2005) 'THE REAL DEAL', 19 February.

Toibin, C. (1995) 'Ireland's war on Eamon Dunphy', in G. Williams (ed.), *The Esquire Book of Sports Writing*. London: Penguin. Originally published in *Esquire* in 1992.

Truss, L. (1999) 'On the terraces', in S. Glover (ed.), *Secrets of the Press: Journalists on Journalism*. London: Allen Lane.

Tulloch, J. (2000) 'The eternal recurrence of new journalism', in C. Sparks and J. Tulloch (eds), *Tabloid Tales: Global Debates Over Media Standards*. Oxford: Rowman & Littlefield.

Turner, B. (2004) *The Pits: The Real World of Formula One*. London: Atlantic Books.

Turner, G. (2004) *Understanding Celebrity*. London: Sage.

Tunstall, J. (1971) *Journalists at Work*. London: Constable.

Tunstall, J. (1996) *Newspaper Power: The New National Press in Britain*. Oxford: Oxford University Press.

Van Zoonen, L. (1998) '"One of the girls": The changing gender of journalism', in C. Carter, G. Branston and S. Allan (eds), *News, Gender and Power*. London: Routledge.

Wagg, S. (1984) *Football World: A Contemporary Social History*. London: Harverster.

Wenner, L.A. (ed.) (1998) *MediaSport*. London: Penguin.

Whannel, G. (1992) *Fields in Vision: Television Sport and Cultural Transformation*. London: Routledge.

Whannel, G. (2002) *Media Sports Stars: Masculinities and Moralities*. London and New York: Routledge.

White, K. (2005) 'Breaking news, breaking boundaries. Available online: http://www.nacwaa.org

Williams, K. (1997) *Get Me a Murder a Day! History of Mass Communications in Britain*. London: Arnold.

Williams, R. (1998) *Racers*. London: Penguin.

Williams, R. (2003) *The View from the High Board: Writings on Sport*. London: Aurum Press.

Wilson, B. (2004) *Bob Wilson: My Autobiography, Behind the Network*. London: Coronet Books.

Women's Sports Foundation (2003) *Britain's Best Kept Secret*. London: Women's Sports Foundation.

Woolnough, B. (2000) *Poisoned Chalice: The Inside Story of Kevin Keegan and England*. London: Ebury Press.

Zelizer, B. (2000) 'Foreword', in C. Sparks and J. Tulloch (eds), *Tabloid Tales: Global Debates over Media Standards*. Oxford: Rowman and Littlefield.

INDEX